P9-DIG-303

Caring for Alzheimer's Patients

A Guide for Family and Healthcare Providers

Caring for Alzheimer's Patients

A Guide for Family and Healthcare Providers

Edited by

Gary D. Miner, Ph.D.
Linda A. Winters-Miner, Ph.D.
John P. Blass, M.D., Ph.D.
Ralph W. Richter, M.D.

and

Jimmie L. Valentine, Ph.D.

INSIGHT BOOKS
PLENUM PRESS • NEW YORK AND LONDON

Library of Congress Cataloging in Publication Data

Caring for Alzheimer's patients: a guide for family and healthcare providers / co-
editors, Gary and Linda Miner . . . [et al.].
    p.   cm.
Bibliography: p.
Includes index.
ISBN 0-306-43199-8
    1. Alzheimer's disease. 2. Alzheimer's disease—Patients—Family relationships. 3.
Alzheimer's disease—Social aspects. I. Miner, Gary.
    [DNLM: 1. Alzheimer's Disease. 2. Family. 3. Self-Help Groups. 4. Social en-
vironment. WM 220 C2773]
RC523.C36   1989
618.97'683—dc19
DNLM/DLC   88-13001
for Library of Congress   CIP

© 1989 Plenum Press, New York
A Division of Plenum Publishing Corporation
233 Spring Street, New York, N.Y. 10013
An *Insight Book*

Printed in the United States of America

To all families who suffer with Alzheimer's disease,
and those who care for them,

and to

Mr. Willard Scott, in appreciation for his support of
the Familial Alzheimer's Disease Research Foundation
as Chairperson of its Honorary Advisory Board, and his
positive spokesmanship for the need of research on
Alzheimer's disease

Preface

This book had its beginning on July 5, 1986, at a seemingly commonplace event that turned out to be a most historic occasion. The event was held in a small community in the Midwest and became known as the "July 5th Oklahoma Alzheimer's Disease Workshop." It was a one-day scientific meeting held in a church (the only available air-conditioned building that was suitable) and attended by noted research scientists from Harvard University; Burke Rehabilitation Center–Cornell Medical School; University of Washington, Seattle–Alzheimer Disease Research Center; University of Kentucky–Alzheimer Disease Research Center; and from other institutions, as well as members of Alzheimer's disease families, some of whom also spoke. Scientific papers were presented, and important research samples were shared by researchers from the institutions named and by scientists from the Duke University–Alzheimer Disease Research Center and the University of California, San Diego–Institute for Research on Aging. That evening, after the formal scientific presentations, the scientists and family members, including caregivers, gathered together for a "brainstorming session" to recap the day's events and to discuss the future. Out of this meeting came the idea for this book.

Since that July day, many scientists have joined with the Familial Alzheimer's Disease Research Foundation (FADRF) in its mission to facilitate cooperative research around the world and to arrive at a speedy answer to the problem of Alzheimer's disease (AD). The First International Symposium on Familial Alzheimer's Disease was held in Tulsa, Oklahoma, on October 22–23, 1987. Over 165 of the world's finest scientists were in attendance. This was the first time so many scientists of this quality had convened to discuss familial Alzheimer's disease (FAD). The Second International Meeting was held in Seattle in May, 1989, with over 200 in attendance. The third meeting is being planned for 1991 in Heidelburg, West Germany.

These events and this book had their beginning in an idea and a vision: doing something about the problem of FAD. This vision was gradually presented to us over the years 1973 to 1982, as we became acquainted with FAD families. These families asked us to help. During the summers of 1981 to 1985, we did help: a "neuropsychological risk factor study" was conducted by us, financed primarily out of our own pockets, with the help of some of the families. We traveled and tested at the homes of these families, lived with them during these times, attended their family reunions, and in reality became adopted by the families. During this time, most of the medical research was not paying any attention to their needs, so our help was greatly appreciated. We laughed with those families and cried with them, and although we do not have any history of AD in our blood relatives, we feel as if we are part of the "Alzheimer Family."

The content of this book is divided into five sections: (1) the Introduction, which gives an overview of the problem of AD; (2) "The Biology of Alzheimer's Disease," which includes scientific studies that deal with selected areas of current research, including an excellent review of the genetics of AD by a researcher who is also a member of an FAD family, as well as other areas, such as the clinical diagnosis of AD; (3) "Dealing with Alzheimer's Disease" looks at social and legal issues, and at dilemmas facing the helping professionals and caregivers, such as nursing-home management, day care, support groups, and the cost of care; the legal chapter in this section is one of the most thorough presentations currently available; (4) "Personal Perspectives," which provides a touching description of the agony of coping with AD, in which the caregiver and the family are the sufferers; and (5) the Appendixes, which supply supplemental information. The coeditors decided to delete all specific citations from the scientific chapters of this book; the sources used appear in Appendix C.

The book's unique importance lies in its pulling together of family and professional interests in order to provide a realistic appraisal of "where we are" and "what needs to be done" in facing this problem. The book is aimed at family physicians and helping professionals, who often do not fully comprehend the problems facing AD families, and at the families themselves, who must cope with this dreadful disease.

Gary D. Miner
and
Linda A. Winters-Miner

Tulsa, Oklahoma

Contents

Chapter 5. Clinical Diagnosis of Dementia of the Alzheimer Type **57**

PART III. DEALING WITH ALZHEIMER'S DISEASE

Chapter 6. Principles in Caring for Alzheimer's Patients **79**

Chapter 8. Alzheimer's Disease and Public Policy .. 199

PART IV. PERSONAL PERSPECTIVES

Chapter 9. Family Reactions: Plight of Alzheimer's Victims and Caregivers 217

APPENDIXES

Part I

Introduction

Chapter 1

Introduction

Gary D. Miner, Ralph W. Richter, and John P. Blass

JUSTIFICATION

During the last ten years, Alzheimer's disease has gone from being an understudied problem to being a fashionable one. Ten years ago, one might have questioned why a book on Alzheimer's dementia should be written. Today, the question is "Why another one?" The answer, of course, is to provide information and to express a viewpoint not yet readily accessible to a portion of the public; this book is directed to caregivers and other health-care providers struggling with the problems presented by patients with Alzheimer's disease. It is written for the educated American who has some background in biology and wants rigorous information at the price of some jargon and duplication. This book also attempts to present a particular viewpoint.

AIMS

St. Thomas Aquinas divided the human soul into three parts: vegetative, efficient, and higher. This tripartite division goes back at least to Plotinus, a second-century romanized Egyptian philosopher. It may derive in part from the Sanskrit division of life into Tamas, Rajas, and Sattra. The analogous Hebraic terminology for the soul is *nefesh, ruach,* and *neshamah.* Neurobiology deals primarily with the vegetative aspects of the nervous system; it describes the wiring system, down to the level of the molecules that make up the wiring. Psychology deals with the efficient aspects—with the learned behavior that leads us to do the things we do. Psychology is a broad subject, ranging from types of physiological psychology and neuropsychology, which are really parts of neurobiology, to psychoanalytic scholarship, which has a spiritual and even religious element (as in Jung). What Aquinas regarded as the "higher soul" is in the realm of nonbiological disciplines: philosophy and theology. To draw an analogy with computers, the "vegetative" functions can be associated with the hardware of the brain, the "efficient" functions with the software. For a religious dualist, the higher functions are associated with the programmer. Mixing these areas of discourse is called, in the jargon of artificial intelligence, a *format problem.* Certain aspects of the care of Alzheimer's patients, including the search for a way to cure or even prevent the disease, are clearly within the realm of neurobiology. On the other hand, the spiritual pain of the patients and of those who love and care for them is, like death itself, an inexplicable, deeply personal, existential experience. It is, in the theological sense, a "mystery." There are schools, notably Epicurean philosophy and its modern descendants, that reduce such suffering to atomistic, molecular, or other material terms. The editors of this book find such reductionism a trivialization. This book aims to deal with each of these three realms of the experience of Alzheimer's disease in its own terms.

Chapters 2, 3, 4, and 5 deal with the "vegetative" level. Chapter 2 reviews the biology of Alzheimer's disease. Chapter 3 deal with the genetic aspects, of particular interest at the present time. Chapter 4 presents some proposed definitions of what is and is not familial dementia of the Alzheimer's type (DAT). Chapter 5 discusses how to make the diagnosis; it is written with health professionals in mind and requires some grasp of medical terminology.

The behavioral ("efficient") aspects are discussed in part in Chapter 5, which includes information on the neuropsychology of Alzheimer's disease. Chapters 6, 7, and 8 deal with related problems. Chapter 6 presents some principles for dealing in practice with Alzheimer's patients. Chapter 7 discusses legal and financial problems and the mechanisms used to deal with them. It is relatively extensive, as this information is not widely and compactly available in any other nonprofessional sources of which we are aware. Chapter 8 clarifies the public policy issues that underlie the relevant laws as they are now written.

The spiritual problems and emotional anguish, as seen from the personal perspective of several family caregivers, are presented in Chapter 9, which included a frankly inspirational article by Mrs. Bea Gorman, describing the role of her faith in her struggle.

The editors chose to provide a selective reading list (Appendix A), rather than the extensive references included with the original manuscripts. Appendix B is a glossary of terms often used in the discussion of Alzheimer's disease; it is included to assist the reader less familiar with biomedical terminology. Appendix C is a bibliography for selected chapters. Appendix D is a list of resources for AD victims and their families. Appendix E outlines a model of a bus–wheelchair service for AD patients as well as other geriatric patients.

The editors maintained some redundancy among the chapters, for several reasons: to allow each chapter to stand alone in its discussions of its particular topic; to provide a transition from one chapter to the next; and to emphasize certain critical points by reiteration. The detailed table of contents is meant to aid the reader in locating information on particular topics.

We hope this volume will prove useful to the caretakers and patients and families whom we aim to serve. *Curans ipse curator.* ("He who serves is himself served.")

Part II

The Biology of Alzheimer's Disease

Chapter 2

Overview of Alzheimer's Disease

Jimmie L. Valentine and
Carrie R. Valentine

INTRODUCTION

Family Experience

If Alzheimer's disease were as prevalent as cancer, it would replace cancer as the most dread disease. Cancer patients often face a long, painful death with little hope of recovery; however, they do normally retain their mental capacities and personalities, albeit under stress, until the last few weeks or even moments of life. The period of bedridden debilitation is usually several weeks or months. Alzheimer's patients, however, experience gradual mental deterioration that affects their ability to perform routine physical tasks and to relate to their closest family members; the period that they live beyond the loss of these capacities is often years. The stage at which they retain strong will and physical capability but have lost their rational processes is a particularly difficult one for family members to manage. A list of suggestions to families at the end of Chapter 6 indicates some of the problems of this stage. The final stage, in which the patients are devoid of former memories of their family and yet live for years, is an enormous financial and emotional burden to their spouses and/or children. Full-time professional care is eventually needed, and the decision to have someone else provide the care is difficult and often requires support from other family members. Although this is not a physically painful disease, the patients themselves are aware initially that they are losing their mental capacities and may react fearfully or belligerently. Eventually, they apparently lose that awareness, and increasingly, the true victim becomes the family member responsible for the care of the affected person. The length of time that a family has to deal physically, emotionally, and financially with the physical needs of the patient without a responsive emotional bond is what makes the disease so dreadful.

History Leading to This Book

Changes in the brain of a fifty-five-year-old woman who had died following progressive dementia were first described in the scientific literature in 1907 by a German physician. That disease, which bears his name, Alzheimer, can be characterized through a microscopic examination of one of the regions of the brain: the cerebral cortex. Following death, a finding in the brain of abnormal nerve cells containing tangles of fibers (neurofibrillary tangles) and clusters of degenerating nerve endings (neuritic plaques) confirms and is required for the diagnosis. *Dementia* is a general term used to designate a mental deterioration. Today, it is recognized that most dementias fall into two different and broad categories: (1) those with characteristic Alzheimer's changes in the brain and (2) those produced by strokes or other blood vessel diseases.

This book is an outgrowth of a symposium held July 5, 1986, in a small town on the plains of the western United States (the exact identity of this town will remain anonymous to protect the family members), which is the original home-town of a family with numerous members affected with Alzheimer's dementia. Present at this symposium were many leaders in Alzheimer's research in the United States. As two of the medical scientists at the symposium, we were impressed, for the first time, with the human side of Alzheimer's disease. This disease, we found, affects both the victims and their families. We had the distinct pleasure of meeting members of two families that are afflicted with an inherited form of the disease. (Later, we discuss this form of the disease.) In addition, we met members of families whose loved ones had another form of the disease that is often referred to as *sporadic*. Other chapters in this book give the personal stories of several persons whose loved ones were afflicted with Alzheimer's disease. Dealing with these people personally and hearing their interactions with a group of scientists allowed us to be blessed with a new insight into this mentally debilitating disease. As we were driving home from this town, we passed a historic roadside sign that read "No Man's Land" in reference to the early pioneers who had crossed these plains in search of new homes. The sign reminded us that these family members are modern-day pioneers, encouraging the scientific community to search out new information and to find better treatment methods and ultimately a cure for this disease.

Some months later, we ran a booth on Alzheimer's disease in a local shopping center during a county medical society fair. The questions asked by the public during this event confirmed to us the need to write this chapter in order to give an overview of Alzheimer's disease that will help families understand some of the scientific terms associated with this disease and to answer some questions that arise about the disease itself. In this chapter, we attempt to interpret for a nonscientifically educated individual the facts about Alzheimer's disease. Also, whenever we include a scientific term that is commonly used in describing a certain aspect of the disease, we define it. References to some of the original scientific literature are found in Appendixes A and C, so that the reader may go to those sources for additional information. In addition, the reader may obtain other information concerning most of these areas in the later scientific chapters of this book.

CHARACTERISTICS OF ALZHEIMER'S DISEASE

Memory Loss

Early signs of Alzheimer's disease are characterized by memory loss, confusion, and an inability to reason, to understand, and to conduct simple thought processes. All these mind-controlled patterns get progressively worse in the afflicted individual. In some cases, the patient may exhibit aphasia, which is a defect in or a loss of speech. Some scientific evidence has been reported correlating the degree of aphasia with an earlier onset of the disease. Often, the patients themselves become aware of the foregoing symptoms. However, the family often notices mostly behavioral changes, for example, changes in mood or personality. The following description of the stages of Alzheimer's disease has been adapted from a number of scientific sources. Different authorities use different stages to classify the disease. (A more complete scientific description can be found in Chapter 5.) A simpler three-stage model has been chosen to aid family members in identifying and anticipating future changes. In the personal stories told by several family members in this book, each of these stages is well documented.

First Stage

In the first stage, there is an inability to remember recent events. Often, this is accompanied by disorientation with respect to the time and place at which the event occurred. The family may note an impairment in the concentration span and episodes of fatigue. Depression may occur that is variable and fleeting. Close family members may note changes in personality that are totally uncharacteristic of the loved one. For example, outbursts of anger may occur in a normally placid individual; conversely, periods of silence may occur in a normally talkative individual. Fastidious individuals may become even harder to please, or persons who were once neat and tidy may become sloppy. Difficulty in making decisions and plans becomes apparent. Many victims have transitory delusions that they are being persecuted. Mild errors in calculations and judgments are often noted. The patients perceive some of the changes in themselves, and a tendency develops to prefer familiar surroundings and to shun the unfamiliar.

Second Stage

All the normal aspects of memory begin to fail progressively. Dysphasia (impairment of speech and failure to arrange words in a proper order) becomes more pronounced, and often, dyspraxia (loss of the ability to perform coordinated movements) and agnosia (loss of the ability to perceive normal stimuli of the five senses) become very apparent to the family members. In 5%–10% of the victims, seizures may occur. Alexia (difficulty in reading) and agraphia (difficulty in writing) may also be very apparent. Other symptoms that may be noticed are an increased inability to comprehend and carry on a conversation, restlessness at night, persistence in pursuing one idea or thought, getting lost in what should be familiar territory, trouble in finding the bathroom, and the need of constant reminding of things routinely performed in everyday living, for example, brushing the teeth or combing the hair. In addition, family members may note a change in the walking ability of their loved one, such as staggering or the dragging of a leg resulting in a shuffling walk. Some of these changes may be due to hypertonia, that is, increased muscle tension.

Third Stage

In this final stage of the disease, there are large disturbances in all mental functions. Most patients need constant supervision and attention. They become unable to carry on the simplest of conversations, and often, there is no recognition of relatives or there is misidentification of persons or objects. Emotional disinhibitions occur, and the former personality gradually disappears. Both fecal and urinary incontinence (the inability to control natural discharges) occur, and the patient may even become bedridden. Seizures may occur. The patient may have trouble swallowing food, and frequent choking spells may occur during eating. There is a progressive weight loss, although the patient may be eating high-calorie diets. In the latter part of this stage, the patient becomes totally helpless and needs assistance in all activities of daily living. Eventually, the patient may lapse into a coma prior to death.

Age of Onset and Duration

Two different types of Alzheimer's disease can be distinguished with regard to the age of onset. The so-called Type I form of the disease is most apparent in the aged population, whereas the Type II form of the disease occurs at a much earlier age. These two types may represent an artificial categorization and may not reflect the true differences, but at the present time, these categories help one to communicate the observed differences in the development of the disease. Many scientific studies have amply shown that the risk of developing Alzheimer's disease increases steeply with advancing age: it is very rare below age fifty and may affect 5%–15% of the population over eighty.

At present, it appears that the earlier onset form (Type II) of the disease is most likely inherited and occurs between forty-five and fifty-five years of age, whereas the later form (Type 1) occurs after age sixty-five. A study by Selzer and Sherwin compared the clinical features of early-onset and late-onset Alzheimer's disease. They found a higher prevalence of speech disorders and walking-pattern disturbances in the early-onset form of the disease. There were no differences in the ability to use objects correctly (apraxia), in epileptic seizures, or in most primitive reflexes. This study also presented evidence that early-onset Alzheimer's disease shortens life expectancy.

The total course of Alzheimer's disease is quite variable. As was pointed out above, the early-onset form of the disease is usually associated with a shortened life. In this form of the disease, the patient usually lives six to eight years after noticeable physical and personality changes have occurred. Also, the earlier-onset form of the disease appears to be more aggressive, a condition that explains the shorter life expectancy. When the illness progresses at a slower rate, the life expectancy may be twenty years or more following the first detectable signs of the disease.

Inheritance Patterns

Some families have been observed in which numerous members have developed Alzheimer's disease in their forties or fifties. The age of onset may be specific within a few years for a given family. An analysis of all the known family members has suggested strongly that this type of disease is inherited in a strictly dominant, autosomal fashion. Dominant means that only one copy of the disease-producing gene—from either parent—is sufficient to produce the disease. Autosomal means that it is inherited on one of the chromosomes that is not a sex chromosome; therefore, it is inherited by both sons and daughters from either parent. In an inheritance pattern of this nature, the offspring of an affected individual have a 50% chance of developing the disease. (Such patterns of inheritance are discussed in more detail in Chapter 3.) These people, before they develop the disease, are referred to as being "at risk" for the disease. They are in the same situation as those people who are "at risk" for Huntington's chorea, a gradually debilitating and, ultimately, fatal disease that is neurological (affecting the brain and nerves). Recently, a genetic marker has been identified for Huntington's chorea that will determine with fair accuracy whether a person "at risk" does have the disease-producing gene. Some of these people want to know if they have the disease gene and others do not; the ethics of providing this information are being debated. If recent reports of a gene marker for familial Alzheimer's disease hold up, the personal and spiritual problems it raises will be similar.

Most cases of Alzheimer's disease are what is called *sporadic;* that is, they appear randomly in different families. However, the normal age of onset, which is about seventy-five years, is old enough so that other family members who might have developed the disease may have died of other causes. Some scientists argue that even these sporadic cases may be inherited but don't appear clustered in families because of the death of the at-risk relatives from other causes before Alzheimer's onset. Dementia that includes amnesia with aphasia (loss of speech) or agraphia (loss of writing ability) are thought to be of the sporadic type. Knowing whether these sporadic cases are genetic (inherited) is probably not of concern to most families, as the actual manifestation of the disease is only occasional. However, to scientists trying to determine the cause of the disease in hope of devising effective prevention or treatment, this issue is a significant one. First, an identification of the genes involved in dementia may lead us to an understanding of the function of those genes and ultimately to a treatment. Current recombinant-DNA technology and molecular biology do allow the isolation of specific human genes (cloning), the identification of their protein products, and the localization of those products in cells. If other methods fail to identify the cause of the disease, the identification of a gene linked to dementia by inheritance would provide another route of investigation. Further, it may be that some therapy in the years preceding onset would be beneficial in delaying or preventing dementia. In this case, it would be necessary to know which individuals have a genetic makeup that predicts their susceptibility to the disease. However, as with Huntington's chorea, such genetic markers do not offer immediate hope of treatment or prevention. Nevertheless, the absence of such markers could assure an individual potentially at risk that he or she will not develop the disease or pass it on to subsequent generations.

Although late-onset as well as early-onset Alzheimer's dementia may be inherited, it is not known if they are basically the same disease, in which the age of onset and the clinical symptoms are influenced by other familial characteristics, or whether each is a different genetic disease. The availability of tissue samples from large families with inherited disease will aid scientists in identifying the genetic components of Alzheimer's dementia. Collecting these samples was one of the purposes of holding the July 5, 1986, meeting in a town where a number of the members of one of these Alzheimer's families had gathered for a family reunion; the other purpose was to honor the families bearing the burden of this disease.

Biochemical Changes in the Brain

Within the brain are many nerve pathways; these pathways have junctures or connections at which certain chemicals must be present to allow the conduction of a nervous impulse. A simplistic analogy would be the electrical circuits in a house or an automobile. Circuit breakers or fuses are placed in the electrical lines to prevent a "short circuit" from occurring and causing a fire. In the same manner, the circuit breaker in the neuron (the fiber in the nervous system), termed the *synapse*, uses various chemicals either to transmit the electrical impulse along the neuron or to retard the impulse. Constant transmission of these electrical impulses is required to carry on functions such as memory recall, muscle movement, and speech patterns. In Alzheimer's disease, changes occur in the structure of the brain tissue that affect the release of the chemicals that transmit or retard electrical impulses. Analyses of the brain tissue of Alzheimer's disease patients after death have shown a decrease in acetylcholine, norepinephrine, and serotonin. These three chemicals are known transmitters in the nervous system. In addition, some peptides (these are chains of amino acids, the building blocks of proteins) that are believed to be transmitters in the nervous system have also been shown to be reduced in Alzheimer's disease. Examples of these peptides are beta-endorphin, somatostatin, methionine-enkephalin, and substance P.

Several studies have shown that choline acetyltransferase (an enzyme responsible for the formation of acetylcholine, one of the transmitters in the brain) is decreased in the brains of Alzheimer's disease patients. A number of studies have been conducted in which choline and lecithin, which can form acetylcholine in the body, were administered to Alzheimer's patients. These substances have failed to result in any improvement in memory or psychological function. Another approach has been to administer a drug (physostigmine) that blocks the breakdown of acetylcholine in the body. Although the administration of this drug resulted in some modest improvement on memory tests, it has proved to be of limited value. Physostigmine has a short lifetime in the body, which may explain its lack of effective activity. Another explanation is that the gradual destruction of the brain tissue most likely includes the nerve pathways, which lose their ability to form acetylcholine; if acetylcholine cannot be produced, a drug that blocks its destruction will have little effect. Such a drug might be of some use in the very early stages of

Alzheimer's disease but would be anticipated to be of no value in the later stages.

Diagnosis and Treatment

As has been pointed out in previous sections, Alzheimer's disease has a slow, insidious onset. Therefore, an important criterion in diagnosing the disease is determining whether the memory loss was abrupt in its onset or has progressed slowly. The latter effect would be more characteristic of Alzheimer's disease, and the former, of a stroke. An important factor in establishing a diagnosis is a complete history of the patient and some knowledge of blood relatives who have had similar symptoms or who have been confirmed to be victims of Alzheimer's disease by autopsy and microscopic examination of the brain following death.

Most victims of the disease or their families seek medical help when the intellectual deterioration becomes severe enough to affect occupational or social functions. Various mental-function tests often aid in evaluating the patient in the earlier stages of the disease. Dementia can be caused by more than sixty different types of disorders; therefore, it is important to rule out other causes of dementia prior to diagnosing Alzheimer's disease. Of the different types of dementia, it has been estimated that 50%–60% are due to Alzheimer's disease and the remainder to other causes, such as vascular disease or tumors. A careful history, often provided by the family, as well as a clinical examination can produce a diagnostic accuracy of about 80% in Alzheimer's disease. To increase the accuracy to about 90% requires additional laboratory tests, such as mental testing, computerized axial tomography scans (the so-called "CAT" scan), blood tests, and an electroencephalogram (a recording of the brain waves). At present, there is no blood marker that can unequivocally determine that a person has Alzheimer's disease. Thus, it becomes important for family members to authorize an autopsy on their loved one at death to confirm the diagnosis of Alzheimer's disease.

Diagnosis and treatment are discussed in more detail in Chapters 5 and 6.

Chapter 3

Genetics and Alzheimer's Disease

Paul A. Bell

INTRODUCTION

"No," said the neurologist, "it's not hereditary." That was in 1979 when my mother, aged sixty-five at the time, was diagnosed as having a "dementia, presumably of organic origin." Mom, my brother, and I talked or corresponded often but each of us lived a thousand miles from the others. We had noticed a gradual decline in Mom's cognitive abilities for about three years. Since we did not live close enough to her to observe her daily, and since she was nearing retirement, we were not overly concerned at first. When her short-term memory became alarmingly impaired, however, we forced her to have a thorough neurological workup. Just before her diagnosis, we became aware that her younger sister by four years and her older sister by ten years were also experiencing significant memory and cognitive deficits. It seemed very reasonable to my brother and me, both being scientists, to ask the neurologist who had diagnosed our mother about a potential genetic link for the dementia. That neurologist and others told us it was not hereditary. Unfortunately, they were wrong. Another neurologist, who had been a close friend earlier in my life, subsequently told me that dementia certainly could run in families. He was right. Several years later, we traced our family history, uncovering more detail than we had ever learned as children. We learned that our great-grandfather on our mother's side had had a severe dementia. Three of his seven children had also had a dementia. A fourth child, our grandfather, had died in the post–World War I flu epidemic, too young to have developed a dementia. He had fathered six children before his death, however; three of those, including our mother, developed dementia. The youngest of those children has been autopsy-verified as having Alzheimer's disease (AD or DAT: dementia of the Alzheimer's type). Today, the evidence is growing, though the question is still controversial, that Alzheimer's is indeed hereditary, at least in part, in at least some cases. However, despite my family history and even more convincing history in other families, some of my closest medical and scientific friends still insist that the evidence of a genetic link in Alzheimer's is weak and inconclusive.

Why all the controversy? Why are some scientific authorities so reluctant to acknowledge the genetic etiology of Alzheimer's, when others are so eager to acknowledge it? In this chapter, I review what scientists know about the issue to date, with an eye to explaining the controversy to professionals and families of Alzheimer's patients alike. It should be clear from the above personal information that I can hardly be considered an impartial observer of the debate. I do believe that the evidence supports a probable strong genetic component in the majority of cases. However, I also believe that the evidence shows that the situation is not as dire for relatives as a strictly genetic etiology would imply: the odds that a given sibling or child of an Alzheimer's victim will come down with the disease are less than the 50/50 that a simple autosomal dominant model would predict. Ironically, the evidence also indicates that individuals without a family history of Alzheimer's have more to worry about than such a simple model would predict. To understand this reasoning (and it is reasoning—the author is not demented yet), it is necessary to examine some background information about Alzheimer's and the special difficulties it poses for studying genetic links. I then present some early lines of research that show evidence for and against the hereditary hypothesis, as well as some more recent research that helps clarify the situation. In the process I hope to show Alzheimer families our current best guess about their own odds of getting DAT, and then show what the future holds for adjusting the guess.

EARLY HISTORY

Alzheimer's disease was first described clinically and neuropathologically in 1906 by the German neurologist Alois Alzheimer. Although it most certainly had existed before that time, and other forms of dementia had been described in the literature before then, Alzheimer's description was sufficiently spelled out so that the disease was named after him. Because he described it in a woman in her early fifties, it was thought to be a disease of the relatively young, or presenile. Senile dementia, on the other hand, was thought to be a dementia of the relatively old. It was not until the late 1970s, after two decades of mounting research, that medical authorities concluded that the presenile (onset before age sixty-five) and senile (onset after age sixty-five) forms were the same disease. The reason it is worth reviewing this classification history is that seeing the disease, not as a continuum, but as two diseases instead, helped hide clues to the involvement of genetics.

Two types of evidence would suggest genetic transmission of a disease. First, *pedigree* studies trace a given family tree and look for relatives with the same disease. A little more than two decades after Alzheimer published his description, evidence that dementia ran in families began to appear in the medical literature. That evidence, though, still was presented with the assumption that DAT was a disease of the relatively young, and most dementia patients showed no family history of dementia.

A second type of evidence comes from *epidemiological* or *population* studies, in which a disease is studied in a fairly large sample of a population. If genetics is involved, cases in the sample should be more likely than controls in the sample to have relatives with the disease. Several such studies of dementia cases, conducted four or five decades after Alzheimer published his initial description, showed that cases were somewhat more likely than control subjects to have relatives with dementia. Even so, most of the dementia patients had no family history of DAT or other dementing disorders. Were genetics substantially involved in the etiology, one would expect a much stronger relationship.

In the most common genetic pattern studied, that of autosomal dominance, a person carries two genes for a specific trait. If both of the genes are recessive, the trait represented by the dominant gene does not appear. If one of the two genes is dominant, however, the trait should appear. Moreover, half the offspring in the latter case should inherit the dominant gene and show the trait, and one of the parents should also have the dominant gene (in order to pass the gene along in the first place). Other genetic patterns also exist, and they can be detected by regularities in the data. In early studies, familiar trends could be identified only in some specific families, and studies of dementia in larger populations failed to show ratios of family history consistent with autosomal dominance in the whole population. A reasonable conclusion from such evidence was that Alzheimer's was not autosomal dominant, at least in most cases. If genetics were indeed involved, it appeared, it was in a complex manner not yet identified. Alternative hypotheses seemed to be more tenable. Based on such evidence, it would certainly have been prudent for practitioners to tell families of DAT victims that the disease was not hereditary.

COMPLICATING FACTORS

In epidemiological studies of the type used for Alzheimer's, a number of problems occur that really complicate the picture for anyone trying to test a genetic hypothesis. In essence, these complicating factors cloud the picture so much that even if autosomal dominance is present, it is not apparent. Listed below are the major factors that muddy the waters for those trying to detect genetic trends.

Problems with Diagnosis

1. *Lack of a common diagnostic label.* In studying the prevalence of a disease in a population, it helps if all segments of the population use the same label for the disease. Unfortu-

nately, such is not the case with Alzheimer's. Because DAT was initially thought to be a disease of the relatively young, senior citizens with it were labeled with a variety of interesting terms, including, but not limited to, *senility, senile dementia* (SD), *senile psychosis, hardening of the arteries to the brain* (or *cerebral atherosclerosis* or other variations of the same thing), and *organic brain syndrome.* Other terms in use today (and a large nursing home is likely to have patients with each of these diagnoses on the charts) include *primary degenerative dementia, dementia of the Alzheimer's type* (DAT), and *senile dementia of the Alzheimer's type* (SDAT). Although the latter labels are almost synonymous with Alzheimer's disease, most of the former labels can be used for dementias other than Alzheimer's. In looking for relatives of a DAT case who also have (had) DAT, which labels should be considered confirmatory and which nonconfirmatory? Incorrect confirmations or rejections easily give an inaccurate picture of genetic links.

2. *Accuracy of diagnosis.* Even when the labels are agreed upon, what if the labels are wrong? Diagnosis of DAT occurs through the clinical elimination of alternative explanations for the dementia. Clinical diagnosis today of Alzheimer's disease is a little more than 80% accurate, although it is improving. Confirmation of the diagnosis through biopsy and autopsy is often not possible, certainly not when one is tracing diseases in ancestors. Before autopsy verification, then, perhaps 10% to as many as 50% of DAT diagnoses have been incorrect. Depending on the situation, such inaccuracies can underestimate or overestimate the degree of genetic link in pedigree and epidemiological studies of DAT. In a broader sense, even autopsy verification can be inaccurate. Neuropathologists look for neurofibrillary tangles and senile plaques, among other things, to verify the diagnosis. However, these pathological indicators are present in other disorders as well, such as dementia pugilistica, Creutzfeldt-Jakob disease, and

Down's syndrome. Although other indicators may be specific to these alternative diagnoses, the diagnosis is sometimes a judgment call. Moreover, tangles and plaques are common in the aging brain, whether DAT is present or not. What is presumed to distinguish DAT from "benign" tangles and plaques is the concentration. In DAT, the concentration is higher and in specific locations. Lower concentrations may not be indicative of the disease but could mean that the brain pathology has not progressed very far at the time of autopsy: that is, an alternative diagnosis may be appropriate, but the Alzheimer process may also be present in a less advanced stage. This point will become important later, in the discussion of potential subtypes. For the moment, it is important to say that inaccurate clinical or neuropathological diagnosis can distort the degree to which genetics appears to be involved in the etiology.

3. *Exclusion of DAT cases.* In order to deal as much as possible only with known cases of DAT, epidemiological studies may be overly conservative and may omit cases from consideration that actually do represent DAT, but that are omitted from study because there are enough questions present to warrant a potential alternative diagnosis. For example, autopsies of dementia cases show that a little over 50% are strictly DAT, 15%–20% are strictly multi-infarct dementia (MID), perhaps 25% are a combination of DAT and MID, and 10% or so are attributable to other dementias, such as Parkinson's. In order to make sure that the observed risk-factor relationships are attributable only to DAT, only those cases that are strictly DAT should be considered in statistical analyses. However, such a conservative statistical approach could omit from consideration at least 25% of the cases of DAT that might otherwise be included in the sample. That is, if DAT is present but there is reason to believe a vascular or other etiology is also involved, the case is omitted from the sample,

even though it is a legitimate DAT case. Although appropriate for epidemiological risk-factor analysis, this exclusionary policy probably underestimates hereditary components in the disease.

Inadequate Family Records

Pedigree and epidemiological studies rely heavily on relatives' recollections about the presence of dementia in the family. Very few families have access to written or even oral records of ancestors' either having or not having a dementing illness. Moreover, because of problems of labeling, family members may not volunteer information about potential DAT. If either families or researchers consider DAT a disease of only the relatively young, they may overlook cases of the very elderly. When asked if there is a history of "Alzheimer's disease," families may well respond in the negative, but if asked about "hardening of the arteries to the brain," respondents may offer numerous examples in the family. The case-control study conducted in Denver in 1985 illustrates this point. One section of the questionnaire for families asked for a list of diseases in the family (without specifying diseases to the respondent), along with age at death and cause of death of first-degree relatives. Out of 68 cases and 68 controls in the final analysis, only 22 had a family history of dementia identified from this line of questioning. However, when specifically asked about any "family history of dementia, senility, organic brain syndrome or OBS, hardening of the arteries or other memory problems," 49 of the 136 respondents identified a family history of dementia. Of these affirmative family histories, some were undoubtedly DAT and others were not, and it would be almost impossible for researchers to find out which was which. The result is that inadequate family records distort the degree of genetic linkage in specific studies and in the population as a whole.

Age-Dependent Penetrance

Genetic characteristics such as eye color and hair color are apparent at birth or shortly after birth. Other hereditary characteristics such as baldness are not apparent until later in life. Such characteristics are said to be age-dependent for expression or to represent "age-dependent penetrance." If a person is destined to be bald at age fifty-two but dies in an automobile accident at age forty-five, there will be no evidence that the person had a genetic endowment for baldness. Most dementias, whether hereditary or environmental in etiology, do not develop until later in life. Far less than 1% of the population is demented before age sixty-five, but at least 5% of the population over age sixty-five is demented, and the percentage rises to perhaps 20% or more by age eighty-five. Age alone is the greatest risk factor for dementia, whether DAT or another type. One dementia known to be hereditary, in a simple autosomal dominant fashion, is Huntington's disease. The gene is present in half the offspring of an affected parent but is generally expressed only in the fourth or fifth decade of life. If the offspring dies in a war at age twenty-two, there is no way of knowing whether the offspring carried the gene or not (although a genetic test is now available). The situation with Alzheimer's is especially complicated by the probability of late onset. If a family carries a DAT gene that is destined to be expressed at age seventy-eight, but the relatives tend to die of strokes or heart attacks by age seventy-five, there will be little or no family history of DAT. As life expectancy expands, however, more and more of these family members will live into their eighties and beyond, so that the gene will be expressed. It will appear that a family that has no history of DAT is developing a number of cases of unexplained dementia. Such a pattern does not, of course, prove that a gene is involved, as another etiology (a toxin or a virus) could explain the occurrence. The absence of a family history, however, does not eliminate a genetic component when penetrance is age-dependent. The main point for the moment is that studying pedigrees or epidemiological samples for genetic trends becomes very complex when penetrance is late-onset age-dependent.

Summary

Given the confusion of labels, the potential for inaccurate diagnosis, the exclusion of "legitimate" cases from study, inadequate records of family history, and age-dependent penetrance, it is little wonder that early studies found only weak evidence of a genetic etiology in DAT. The potential for contamination would so muddy the water that no observer could detect a distinct genetic pattern. The existence of only a few suspect pedigrees would carry little weight in the face of "clean" pedigrees for most cases of DAT. The presence of a few cases with some family history of dementia is not impressive if most cases report no family history and if some controls also report a family history. Conservatively, most authorities would conclude from such results that there is little support for a simple genetic hypothesis, and some would even conclude that there is indeed little or no genetic risk.

Those who still adhere to a genetic hypothesis, however, could say that the water is too muddy to allow a rejection of heredity. Just because the water is translucent, though, does not mean that genetics must be involved. With these caveats, it is worthwhile to examine both pedigree and epidemiological studies to learn about both the limitations and the statistical possibilities of the role of genetics in DAT.

PEDIGREE STUDIES

Within three decades of Alois Alzheimer's original description, the medical literature was reporting a number of instances in which DAT seemed to occur in several members of the same family. Feldman, Chandler, Levy, and Glaser listed twenty-one reports published between 1929 and 1959 that showed DAT in several family members. Only one of these reports showed DAT in as many as three generations of the same family, however. Exposure to an infectious agent or to an environmental toxin is a tenable hypothesis for these occurrences. To make a more convincing case for genetic transmission, two things are needed. First, several generations need to be affected, not just siblings in the same generation or parents and children in the same house. Second, a regular pattern should appear in which some offspring show the trait and others do not. Furthermore, those who do not show the trait should have children who do not show the trait, and those with the trait should, on the average, show the trait in half the offspring (for autosomal dominance) or in some other predictable pattern (for other modes of transmission).

It was not long before several investigators reported increasing numbers of families who fit this pattern, and by 1980, a phenomenon of strong familial tendencies was apparent. For example, Lauter reported thirteen cases in five generations of one family; Feldman and colleagues reported thirteen cases in four generations; Heston and White reported the pedigrees of thirty different families with DAT; Cook and colleagues reported DAT in three families, one of which extended for four generations; and Powell and Folstein reported pedigrees of twenty-one DAT families, finding evidence of genetic transmission for three generations in seven of the families. Goudsmit and colleagues reported probable DAT in four generations of one family and three in another. Nee and Polinsky and colleagues have traced a Canadian family for eight generations, finding DAT in fifty-one members across five of those generations thus far. At least in the more recent generations, it has been possible to confirm the DAT diagnosis histologically for some of these cases. The same research group is studying other similar extended families. The patterns reported thus far are consistent with autosomal dominant transmission: on the average, half of the offspring of affected adults show the disease. Incidentally, the pedigrees reported thus far as positive for DAT represent a broad spectrum of racial and ethnic ancestry. However, some reports indicate that Alzheimer's disease is relatively rare in some groups, for instance, the Chinese and the Japanese.

Based on the patterns identified to date, it is highly likely that continued monitoring in the future will confirm an autosomal dominant component in the etiology of dementia for the families studied and others. Clearly, DAT is genetically transmitted in some families—even diehard antagonists of the genetic hypothesis would be hard pressed to deny the pedigree evidence for these identified families. A more important question is the extent to which DAT is hereditary or is caused by other factors in families where the pedigree is not as convincing and, if not entirely genetic, the extent to which DAT is genetic or of other etiology in the population as a whole.

Pedigree evidence *against* the genetic hypothesis is of two forms: some cases do not show a family history, and some cases of monozygotic (identical) twins do not show concordance (i.e., one twin gets DAT, and the other does not). As for the absence of family history in some cases, it is instructive to note that, in most cases where the pedigree is positive for DAT, the age of onset in the family is relatively young. Quite possibly, it is in those families where penetrance occurs at a fairly young age that the confirming pedigree is very complete. In other families, penetrance may be delayed into the ninth or tenth decade, so that penetrance, on the average, is beyond life expectancy. In such a situation, the pedigree would not appear very positive for DAT, even though the gene might be present. As indicated above, inadequate family records would further complicate the picture, but increasing life expectancies would eventually turn up familial cases of DAT that appeared to be sporadic instead. This line of reasoning is far from strong support for the genetic hypothesis, but it is a means of saying that the absence of DAT in the pedigree of a confirmed case does not rule out a genetic etiology. This reasoning will be elaborated upon in more detail later.

As for twin studies, there are, indeed, reports in the literature of one monozygotic twin with DAT and another without. However, such evidence does not rule out genetics in these or other cases. The concordance rate is positive in some studies and is stronger in monozygotic than in dizygotic (fraternal) twins, suggesting a genetic component. Kallmann, for example, found 42.8% concordance in monozygotic twins and only an 8.9% concordance in dizygotic pairs. It is conceivable that, in some cases of nonconcordance, the dementia present is something other than DAT, especially given the difficulty of diagnosis noted above. Histological confirmation is not always available in the twin studies. Alternatively, penetrance may not be entirely dependent on genetics. That is, a virus, toxin, or other factor may be necessary for gene expression to occur, and that factor may be present in one twin but not in the other. Possibly, a series of environmental events is necessary before the clinical pattern of DAT will appear, and the surviving twin of a case may not have had enough such exposure. Moreover, if the surviving twin were to live long enough, the probability of penetrance would approach unity (1.0). In essence, an imperfect concordance rate in identical twins does not rule out the genetic hypothesis. It does, however, suggest that, if a DAT gene exists, it is not necessarily a simple gene timed from birth to show penetrance at a specific age regardless of environmental or other factors. More on this notion follows a discussion of epidemiological studies.

In sum, pedigree and twin studies offer very suggestive support for a genetic component in DAT. However, the same studies raise questions about the ability of genetics to explain all cases of DAT, as well as the age of onset in presumed hereditary cases. Even so, pedigree and twin studies do not rule out a very substantial role for genetics in the etiology of DAT.

EPIDEMIOLOGICAL STUDIES

Epidemiological studies are designed to uncover trends in the incidence of DAT in the population and/or to detect risk factors associated with the likelihood of getting the disease. A number of such studies are available, and they show considerable variation in results. Kay summarized several of the more well-known studies, and others are available. The principal means of assessing genetic risk in these studies is first to delineate the risk in the general population or in control subjects, then to test to see if relatives of DAT cases are at higher risk than the general population or controls. Alternatively, in a case-control study, one can compare the frequency of a case's having relatives with DAT to the frequency of a control's having relatives with DAT.

In the former situation, it is instructive to note that risk of DAT increases with age, so it is important to look at risk in various age groups. Unfortunately, different studies suggest different levels of risk for the same age groups. For example, Kay noted that a Swedish study estimated the risk in the general population for someone at age eighty to be 2.5%, whereas data from at least two other studies suggest that the general population risk at age eighty is closer to 20%. One way to get around the problem of these disparate estimates is to draw a sample of cases and controls from the same population, and to compare the incidence rates of DAT in the relatives of cases and controls. Heston and colleagues reported a valuable study of this nature, based on 125 autopsy-verified cases drawn from Minnesota state hospitals. The age interval of eighty to eighty-four is illustrative of their findings. Controls had a cumulative probability of .055 of developing DAT if they survived into the eighty to eighty-four age interval. Siblings of cases had a .151 probability for the same age interval, and parents of cases had a .17 probability. For second-degree relatives (e.g., aunts, and uncles), the probability was only .070. For the sixty-five to sixty-nine age interval, the cumulative probabilities were .004 (controls), .038 (siblings), .063 (parents), and .022 (second-degree relatives). In summarizing a number of studies, Kay calculated the cumulative risk in first-degree relatives at 2%–5% by age seventy, 5%–

10% by age seventy-five, 10%–17% by age eighty, and 15%–21% by age eighty-five; all of these risks were elevated when compared to those of controls. Thus, it is clear that risk increases substantially with age, and that the closer the genetic relationship with a case, the greater the risk. However, if a simple genetic model were to hold, one would expect the risk to parents and siblings to be closer to .500 by age eighty-five or so. Although the Heston data strongly suggest a genetic component, they also suggest that something beyond simple genetics is involved.

A second approach to assessing genetic etiology in epidemiological studies is to note the percentage of cases with a family history of DAT and to compare the figure with the percentage of controls with a family history. The data of Heston and colleagues are enlightening in this regard because they had autopsy verification for cases and many relatives. None of the autopsied relatives of controls had DAT. For cases, 51 of the 125 families had a total of 87 additional instances of DAT. Some of the families were too small or too young to have additional members at risk, so the incidence of family history in cases is likely to be somewhat greater than reported. However, there were some large families of cases without family histories, indicating that a simple autosomal dominant pattern could not account for all occurrences.

Other studies comparing the DAT incidence in family history for cases and controls have yielded mixed results. Both Heyman and Amaducci reported significantly higher frequencies of dementia in families of cases than in families of controls. For example, Heyman found dementia in 55.3% of case families and 14.5% of control families. It should be noted that the diagnoses were not histologically verified, and that dementia in a family history could include far more than just DAT. Chandra *et al.* (1987) found that when the family history was known, 41% of the case families and 31% of the control families had a history of dementia, but the difference was not statistically significant. Thus, two case-control studies found a positive association with family history, and one did not. Interestingly, the Chandra *et al.* (1987) study sample showed that no familial association was considerably older than the others. For example, 95% of the Denver cases had an onset of DAT after age seventy, whereas Heyman used only cases with onset before age 70. Although the differences in these studies could be attributable to sampling errors, it is also possible, as is discussed later, that DAT is much more widespread in the elderly than was previously thought, so that, in the very elderly, both cases and controls would be expected to have considerable chance of familial involvement.

In sum, epidemiological studies, whether examining the cumulative risk in cases and controls or the incidence of DAT in families of cases versus controls, offer mixed support for a genetic hypothesis. Only two of three case-control studies found a positive association. Numerous examples were found of cases without a family history. Nevertheless, a family history of DAT does increase risk. In essence, epidemiological studies generally support a genetic component in the etiology of DAT, but they also suggest that a simple autosomal dominant model is inadequate to explain the data.

ADDITIONAL GENETIC CONNECTIONS

In addition to examining pedigrees and population studies, there are other ways of testing for a genetic tendency in DAT. For example, if certain disorders known to be genetic are more common in DAT families than in control families, a genetic connection is suggested. One such connection that has been studied involves Down's syndrome, also known as *trisomy-21* because an extra twenty-first chromosome is present. Heston observed an increased incidence of Down's in families of DAT cases relative to the population in general, although others found no connections in DAT families. Hematological malignancies (e.g., leukemia) may occur with excess frequency in relatives of Down's cases, but studies of DAT cases have not shown increased frequency of such malignancies in the families. Heston did report an elevation of lymphomas (e.g., Hodgkin's disease) in DAT families, but other investigators have found no such association.

The Down's connection is interesting for other reasons. Down's victims who live long enough universally develop tangles, plaques, and other brain pathologies characteristic of DAT. So convincing is the relationship, in fact, that at one point it was believed that all Down's cases developed DAT. However, the clinical progression of dementia does not accompany all these Down's cases, so DAT may not always be present in Down's. In addition, the fact that Down's is characterized by an extra twenty-first chromosome suggests that chromosome frequency may be involved in the neuropathology of DAT. Aneuploidy, meaning too few (hypoploidy) or too many (hyperploidy) chromosomes in some cells, has been observed in some histological studies of DAT cases. These anomalies involve more than just the twenty-first chromosome and on further study, may become very important. In addition, the mother's age at the birth of a child is known to be related to Down's: older mothers, especially over age thirty-five, are at higher risk of having a Down's child. On the average, children with a lower birth order (e.g., sixth-born vs. first-born) are more likely to have older mothers at birth. Three studies have thus found some association between the age of the mother at birth and the risk of DAT in the child, but other comparisons have found no such relationship.

Other chromosomes besides the twenty-first have been

implicated in one form or another in DAT. For example, Chromosomes 6 and 14 have been studied for genetic links with familial cases, and Chromosome 22 and others may be implicated. There may also be cellular, biochemical, and other differences between familial and sporadic cases of DAT. These and other promising connections are discussed in detail elsewhere.

One intriguing connection is the study of fingerprints, or dermatoglyphics. Weinreb reported that an increased frequency of ulnar loops and other patterns may distinguish those with DAT from others. At present, the test is far from being error-free, but it does offer fascinating possibilities.

Recent but controversial data imply a parallel change in the DNA, the genetic material in familial Alzheimer's disease and in Down's syndrome. If proven, these data will provide a clear and mechanistic link between these two diseases.

In sum, there are numerous possibilities for finding genetic links in DAT besides pedigree and epidemiological studies. To date, these additional bits of evidence suggest that genetics is indeed involved in DAT to some extent. Although they have not as yet clarified the nature of the genetic model involved, they offer great promise for future research and insight.

FAMILY RISK

In spite of the lack of a clear genetic model, families are still curious about what the genetic connection means for them. Even without a solid model, it is possible to estimate the risk for family members based on estimations from relatively large samples. That is, if the sample is sufficiently large, one should be able to examine the incidence of DAT among family members in that sample and to estimate the probability that relatives of other DAT cases will eventually develop DAT. Such a sample is available through the work of Heston and colleagues cited above. Although this sample does consist of autopsy-verified cases, its size (125 cases) and source (state hospital records) mean that using it to generalize to the total population may lead to undetected errors. Nevertheless, it is worthwhile to examine the probabilities in the sample.

Heston and colleagues pointed out that, as only 51 of the 125 families were found to have relatives with DAT, it is worthwhile to look for factors that would further distinguish these families from the others. Two such factors appear in their data: age of onset and having an affected parent. In a further refinement, Heston and co-workers noted that onset before or after age seventy and the number of relatives affected seem to be the most useful factors in assessing probability of risk. As indicated in Table 1, these two factors separate the sample data into four groups: (1) those without affected relatives; (2) those with one DAT relative whose age of onset was over seventy; (3) those with one DAT relative whose age of onset was under seventy; and (4) two or more relatives affected, with the age of onset in at least one being under seventy. For those with no relatives, risk starts at age seventy and increases 4% every five years, reaching 16% by age ninety. For those with one relative and onset after age seventy, risk starts at age sixty-five and increases by 4% every five years, reaching 20% by age ninety. For those with only one relative and onset under age seventy, risk begins at age sixty, increases 4% every five years, and reaches 25% by age ninety. Finally, for those with two or more relatives and age of onset in at least one of them under seventy, risk begins at age forty-five, also increases 4% every five years, and reaches 36% by age ninety.

Several things are apparent from these figures. First, age alone is the most important risk factor. Second, familial risk is also important, but it is most important for those with several relatives and onset in the relatives at a fairly early age. Third, risk is present even for those without affected relatives. Fourth, and most important for DAT families to note, the odds of not getting the disease are greater than the odds of getting it, even if an autosomal dominant pattern is present. Penetrance approaching 50%, as would be expected in an autosomal dominant pattern, is not achieved in high-risk families until almost age 100. Although life expectancy is increasing, the odds still favor that a person carrying a DAT gene will die of other causes before the gene has a chance to become expressed. If the family history involves several DAT cases and the onset in relatives is fairly early, the risk of expression is apparently increased. In all other circumstances, the odds actually favor the person's not getting DAT. Those odds are of little comfort to those who do not beat them, of course. However, the very fact that the age of onset in the case influences the risk for the relative gives some important clues to the complexity of the underlying genetic model. The following section provides some speculation on what that model might be.

FURTHER CONSIDERATIONS, HYPOTHESES, AND GENETIC MODELS

The Role of Age at Onset

Several interesting findings noted thus far merit further consideration because they imply that other avenues of inquiry might be very fruitful. The fact that diagnosis is somewhat tentative and that some DAT cases show familial risk and others do not suggests that there may well be subtypes of DAT. There are numerous references in the literature to potential subtypes, one distinction being familial versus sporadic and another being early versus late onset. Recall that initially, only early onset was regarded as characterizing DAT; late-onset cases were thought to have "senile dementia" instead. Some diagnosticians hypothesized that the two might be distinguished by factors other than age. Larsson and colleagues, for example, reported in 1963 that early-onset cases tended to progress more rapidly than late-onset cases. A more recent report by Sayetta, however, suggests that chronological age at the time of death, and not age at onset or duration of the disease, is the best predictor of death rates, that is, the older you are, the more likely you are to die.

Complete pedigrees showing an autosomal dominant pattern would be more likely to exist if onset were early than if onset were late, because with late-onset patterns most family members would not survive long enough to show penetrance. As a result, there might be an illusory correlation between family history of DAT and early onset. The possibility exists that early onset is indeed more likely to be familial than late onset. For example, Heston and colleagues found that the earlier the onset in a case, the greater the risk to relatives (see Table 1). On the other hand, Chui and colleagues found no average-age-of-onset difference for familial and sporadic cases. Kay observed that a plot of age of onset for random cases (containing both familial and sporadic cases) showed only one peak. If age of onset were related to subtypes, one would expect two or more peaks in such a plot. Thus, there is not much support for the hypothesis that age of onset distinguishes familial from nonfamilial cases. However, Heston and Kay have observed that age of onset is

Table 1. Risk of DAT for Four Types of Family History

	Type of family history (%)				
Age (years)	No relative with DAT	One relative with DAT (onset after age 70)	One relative with DAT (onset before age 70)	Two or more relatives with DAT (onset in at least one before age 70)	Age (years)
45	—	—	—	a	45
50	—	—	—	4	50
55	—	—	—	8	55
60	—	—	a	12	60
65	—	—	4	16	65
70	a	4	8	20	70
75	4	8	12	24	75
80	8	12	16	28	80
85	12	16	20	32	85
90	16	20	24	36	90

[a]Risk begins at this point and increases .8% each year.

correlated within families, so that the younger a case is at onset, the younger relatives are likely to be at onset, and the older a case at onset, the older the relatives would be when the onset occurs. Thus, not only can DAT run in families, but age of onset can aggregate in families as well. If common environmental factors were solely responsible for the aggregation of DAT in families, age of onset should vary within the family because the number of years between exposure and onset would be significant, and the ages at exposure would vary widely. Thus, the correlation of the age of onset within families supports a genetic hypothesis, but it implies that something modifies the time of penetrance across families.

The *aaa* Syndrome

In a study of fifty-four rather advanced cases of DAT in nursing homes, Folstein and Breitner observed that their sample could be divided on the basis of aphasia and apraxia. *Aphasia* refers to loss of the capacity to understand and use language; *apraxia* refers to the loss of skilled motor movements. *Agraphia* refers to loss of the ability to write, and is a way of measuring apraxia. Aphasia and agraphia are closely related in DAT. The apraxic cannot carry out an intended action, such as moving a book from a table to a chair on request. These researchers were able to pick out the subsamples of DAT cases with aphasia, agraphia, and apraxia simply by asking them to write a sentence. Some 78% could not do so and were labeled as being or having *aaa* (aphasia and apraxia in combination with amnesia). Other research has also suggested that aphasia may indicate a specific subgroup of DAT. The average age of the nursing-home sample was eighty-two years, considerably older than in most other studies but comparable to that in the Chandra *et al.* (1987) study. Thus, it was easier to assess risk in relatives who were older than those who had previously been studied. The results were startling. For non-*aaa* cases and for controls, the risk in relatives up to age ninety was under 10%. For *aaa* cases, however, the risk among relatives increased dramatically with age and slightly exceeded 50% by age ninety. Such findings are truly remarkable, for they demonstrate the 50% risk that would be expected in a fully penetrated autosomal dominant trait. There is a caution: The sample size for evaluating the risks was fairly small, and in fact, the familial association with agraphia was not replicated in one study. Breitner, however, noted that the nonreplication occurred in a less advanced sample, which would not be expected to show as much agraphia because that characteristic normally does not appear in the progression of DAT until the middle stages.

With the above caveats in mind, it is instructive to examine the further development of the Breitner and Folstein data. Indeed, these authors presented a statistical model that seems to account for many of the complex findings discussed thus far. They proposed that there is a familial form of DAT, characterized by *aaa*, and a nonfamilial form that has some other origin but that represents one or more phenocopies (i.e., diseases that look like DAT). The familial form is proposed to be autosomal dominant with age-dependent penetrance, with nearly complete penetrance being achieved by age ninety. Because penetrance would be late for some cases with the *aaa* subtype, the known family history would be negative for DAT even though the gene would be present in the family. Thus, many of the apparent nonfamilial cases could actually be *aaa* familial. The means of telling if the type is familial is simply discovering whether *aaa* characterizes the case, not whether there is a family history. With these assumptions (and it must be emphasized that these are assumptions), it is possible to demonstrate that perhaps 90% of all DAT is familial, with the remaining 10% or so consisting of one or more phenocopies. The model proposed by Breitner, Folstein, and Murphy relies on a gamma probability distribution to account for age-dependent penetrance. Essentially, the gene is expressed only after enough "hits" or insults from the environment have been received. Perhaps these hits are successive exposures to toxins, viruses, or autoimmune reactions. As the hits build up with age, the likelihood of penetrance increases. The model actually does a very respectable job of predicting the incidence of DAT, and it can be set to agree with Heston's probabilities presented in Table 1. It is, however, currently dependent on a small sample and a lot of assumptions that have not been replicated. In contrast to the Breitner, Folstein, and Murphy model, which postulates autosomal dominance reaching nearly 100% penetrance by age ninety, Larsson and associates, using a larger sample but with less well-refined diagnostic criteria, suggested only 40% penetrance at age ninety. At least part of the discrepancy may rest with the difficulty of determining how much of the overall population carries the gene. Larsson and colleagues estimate it at 12%, but Breitner and colleagues suggest that it could be much higher. The validity of any of these assumptions will be empirically testable in the long run as the population ages. Following more individuals longitudinally as they reach their ninth decade and beyond will permit better analyses of prevalence and potential penetrance.

Extension of Autosomal Dominance

Following a large sample of individuals longitudinally as they move into and past their nineties may yield some surprises. Current estimates of the prevalence of DAT are based on limited samples, most of which include few individuals over age 90. The population is aging rapidly, however, so that 20% of the population will be over age 65 by the year 2025, up from 11.3% in 1985. The very elderly population will increase even faster, with those over 85 increasing from 2 million to 16 million. By the year 2050, there will be over 8.5 million DAT victims, 5 million of them over age 85. Well before that time, it will be possible to have very accurate estimates of the cumulative probability of anyone's getting DAT by age 100. *If*, and that is an *if* with extra emphasis, one uses projections from the small samples of individuals under age 90 available today, it is possible to estimate that the incidence of DAT would approach 75% in those over 100. If an autosomal dominant trait is fully distributed throughout a population, it should eventually be expressed in 75% of the population. That is a highly speculative idea. However, recent data from Sayetta on a sample of 519 individuals born before 1919 suggest that, after age 95, the risk of DAT in the population may exceed 50%. Unlike the Breitner and Folstein data, which began specifically with DAT cases having *aaa* and then found risk in first-degree relatives at age 90 to slightly exceed 50%, the Sayetta data are based on a sample of individuals who were not cognitively impaired when first selected. They were simply studied to show what percentages would get DAT at various age levels. Thus, if they were a truly random sample (which they probably were not), they would represent risks for the whole population, not just for relatives of DAT cases. If the projections are accurate, they imply that over half the population will have DAT if they live to age 95. Although highly speculative, this line of reasoning implies that DAT may be autosomal dominant with age-dependent penetrance throughout the entire population. Before the U.S. population of individuals over age 85 reaches 16 million in 2050, it will be possible to determine from population statistics whether this broader model has validity.

Along these lines, it is interesting to note that at least components of the neuropathology of DAT are present in just about all individuals as they age: the tangles and plaques are there; they are just lower in number in those without DAT. Perhaps the pathology is building in early stages in individuals without DAT, and if given time for enough environmental "hits," the pathology would exceed the DAT threshold in anyone. An autosomal dominant pattern for DAT might appear in families who have genes predisposing them to susceptibility to the "hits," whereas those without the DAT gene(s) simply become vulnerable at a later age. In essence, DAT may simply represent part of the normal aging process, which is simply accelerated in those diagnosed as having DAT. In this case by the year 2050 all persons over, perhaps, 110 years old would have DAT. This idea, again, is *speculative*, but there is debate on it already, and it should be testable in the long run.

Other Mechanisms for Observed Genetic Patterns

It has been noted several times above that an autosomal dominant model requires age-dependent penetrance. It is possible that the variation in penetrance depends on numerous environmental factors, such as exposure to toxins or viruses. The fact that the age of expression is correlated within families suggests that another gene may be involved. A polygenic model might involve an autosomal dominant gene that determines whether a person is susceptible to DAT, as well as one or more other genes that determine when this DAT gene will be expressed. Additional research will be necessary, but this type of model certainly has possibilities.

Another variation on the autosomal dominant model is that the gene involved is not one that "causes" DAT directly; rather, as hinted above, it may be a gene that is missing and that would normally protect against DAT. What may be inherited is the state of missing the gene that would otherwise protect one from a DAT virus or toxin. Still another possibility follows from what is sometimes called an *ecological model*, in which almost all genes have a useful function. That is, if a gene is really detrimental to a person, those possessing it should die out in the long run and take it out of the gene pool. For the most part, genes that get into the gene pool have survival value; that is, those who possess it are in some way superior in dealing with their environment, so they survive long enough to keep the gene in the pool. For example, it is now thought that the gene for sickle-cell anemia (which is autosomal recessive), though certainly detrimental when it makes the individual anemic, also protects against malaria. Those who possess it are likely to survive malaria and to keep the gene in the pool. Perhaps Alzheimer's works the same way: even though the gene for it is devastating when expressed, possessing it may protect one from some other ailment. If that is the case, people with DAT should have a lower than normal incidence of some other disorder. The limited research to date has found no such relationship, but it is a possibility for the future.

CONCLUDING REMARKS

It is quite clear from the available data that a genetic component almost certainly exists for DAT. It is also quite clear that a simple autosomal dominant model is inadequate to explain the data. At the very least, an age-dependent mechanism for expression must be added to the model. Whether that mechanism is environmental or represents a polygenic system is unknown. It is also unknown just how much DAT really is familial, and how much it may be non-familial or sporadic. When a clear familial tendency runs in a pedigree, there is increased risk to relatives. However, given current life expectancies, the odds favor even a DAT gene carrier's succumbing to some other fatal ailment before the gene is expressed. The risk of penetrance may be somewhat greater if there is a family history of early onset, or if life expectancy increases.

What does the future hold? Certainly, more cases of DAT will appear, and more unknowns will be encountered. However, with long-term prospective studies, refinements in diagnostic techniques, a better understanding of neuropathology, and the discovery of genetic markers, more of these unknowns will become knowns. The pace of discovery in DAT is accelerating rapidly, and the volume of knowns to come holds great promise.

Chapter 4

Proposed Definitions

Robert Mullan Cook-Deegan

For decades, lack of rigorous definitions has hampered the interpretation of studies of familial Alzheimer's disease. Failure to specify the criteria by which one calls a case of Alzheimer's disease familial makes a comparison of different studies impossible. More important, and much more often overlooked, is the carelessness associated with use of the term *sporadic*. Many studies attach the term *sporadic* to all cases that are not clearly familial. This label biases interpretation in a way that has not been widely recognized. Using *sporadic* as a synonym for *not necessarily familial* has obscured the fundamental lack of definitive information in published pedigrees.

For the purpose of titling papers for publication or engaging in informal discussion or delivering health-care services, attention to a rigorous definition of *familial Alzheimer's disease* is not generally necessary. In the body of papers on Alzheimer's disease, however—particularly in epidemiological investigations and papers on the genetics of Alzheimer's disease—great care must be taken not only to identify familial cases, but also to limit the designation *sporadic* only to those cases that are clearly not genetic (or at least not inherited; it would be impossible to differentiate new mutations from sporadic cases in the absence of a direct genetic test).

Most cases of Alzheimer's disease are neither clearly familial nor clearly sporadic. This large group of uncertain origin should be analyzed separately from the better defined groups. Previous studies have lumped this very large number of cases with the smaller number of familial and truly sporadic ones, to the detriment of clear-headed analysis.

A provisional classification of Alzheimer's disease is proposed here. It is intended as a basis for further discussion and is far from definitive. The suggested classification builds on other definitions of Alzheimer's disease, such as the NIA or the criteria set forth by the National Institute for Neurological and Communicative Disorders and Stroke, and the Alzheimer's Disease and Related Disorders Association (NINCDS–ADRDA).

Familial Alzheimer's disease (FAD) requires:

- At least three affected members, in
- at least two generations, with
- autopsy or biopsy confirmation in at least two cases from at least two generations, and
- an inheritance pattern compatible with autosomal dominant transmission.

Probable FAD requires:

- At least two cases, in
- at least two generations, with

- autopsy verification in at least one case, and
- an inheritance pattern compatible with autosomal dominant transmission.

Sporadic Alzheimer's disease requires:

- One case with no others among primary relatives, with
- complete information about dementia available for all primary relatives who should have developed Alzheimer's disease if the patient were at risk.

Complete information about dementia in primary relatives means either that both parents lived to age eighty-five with no evidence of dementia, or that there is sufficient information about the parents' siblings and parents to verify that they—and consequently the proband—were not at risk of inheriting it. The focus here is on establishing that the case could not have been directly inherited.

Alzheimer's disease, unqualified, would refer to cases not fitting into any of the above categories.

A category of probable sporadic Alzheimer's disease might be useful, with relaxed conditions about the survival of the parents, but it is not clear that this category would aid analysis, as most of the uncertainty derives from the very late age of onset in most cases of Alzheimer's disease. (The rise in incidence is most rapid in the decade from seventy-five to eighty-five, trailing off after that.)

The proportion of cases in the different categories is revealing, and it underscores the degree of ignorance about the true prevalence of familial and, especially, sporadic Alzheimer's disease. In pursuing research on familial Alzheimer's disease in the late 1970s, the author had the opportunity of reviewing all records of the neurology services at the University of Colorado affiliated hospitals (University Hospital, Denver General Hospital, and the Denver Veterans Administration Hospital). By means of principal and secondary diagnoses, several hundred cases of possible dementia were screened from the several thousand records reviewed. The diagnosis of Alzheimer's disease or another dementia could be verified in thirty to fifty of the several hundred cases, and of these cases, ten to twenty fell into possible family clusters. Two years of work in following up initial leads, contacting families, constructing pedigrees, and gathering medical records resulted in three families that would be called FAD, another nine families with probable FAD, and the vast majority of cases with Alzheimer's disease. This was a highly biased sample, as those cases likely to be familial were most intensively investigated. In particular, genetic information about the possible sporadic cases was not specifically sought.

Those who do genetic clinical investigation will recognize that the criteria for sporadic Alzheimer's disease would lead to extremely few cases so labeled. This is an important practical consideration, and yet it seems prudent to insist on just such a stringent category. In the absence of such criteria, investigators are left with standard tools of actuarial practice, such as life tables and other probabilistic assessments. This is not necessarily bad, or even less rigorous, but those using life table analysis in the past have been criticized for doing so. Ironically, some have criticized life table studies for the uncertainty of their conclusions, while ignoring a much larger source of error: incomplete information about individual cases.

Chapter 5

Clinical Diagnosis of Dementia of the Alzheimer Type

Jeffrey L. Cummings

INTRODUCTION

Dementia of the Alzheimer type (DAT) was recognized in 1907 by Alois Alzheimer to be a distinct clinical entity unlike other forms of "senility." In his description of the index case, he noted the patient's aphasia, amnesia, apraxia, paranoid delusions, and relative preservation of motor function, and at autopsy he demonstrated that she suffered from "a unique illness involving the cerebral cortex" characterized by neurofibrillary changes and "miliary foci." His initial report ended by voicing the hope that more clinical cases would be confirmed pathologically and would be isolated from the larger classifications. Thus, Alzheimer provided a clinical as well as a pathological description of the disease that came to bear his name. Since then, the clinical diagnosis of DAT has been a problematic and controversial topic. When applied too loosely, many important non-DAT disorders are encompassed within the term; when excessively constrained or limited exclusively to a pathological diagnosis, the term loses clinical relevance. Contemporary approaches to clinical diagnosis attempt to be sufficiently rigorous to exclude other causes of intellectual deterioration in the elderly and to predict the pathological diagnosis with reasonable certainty. This chapter reviews current criteria for the clinical diagnosis of dementia and DAT, discusses the clinical variants of DAT, and describes the changing clinical appearance of the disorder as it progresses.

DIAGNOSTIC CRITERIA FOR DEMENTIA

Definition of Dementia

The first step in the recognition of DAT is identification of a dementia syndrome. The third edition of the American Psychiatric Association's *Diagnostic and Statistical Manual of Mental Disorders* (DSM-III) provides the most widely used criteria for dementia. As shown in Table 2, the definition requires that the patient be socially or occupationally disabled by intellectual losses, exhibit memory impairment, have at least one other neuropsychological deficit (loss of abstracting abilities, impaired judgment, aphasia, apraxia, agnosia, constructional disturbance, or personality change), have no delirium, and have either physical or laboratory evidence of a cause of the syndrome or evidence to warrant the conclusion that the disorder is an idiopathic condition. The definition emphasizes the etiologically nonspecific nature of the demen-

Table 2. DSM-III Criteria for Recognition of Dementia and Primary Degenerative Dementia

Dementia
1. Social or occupational disability secondary to loss of intellectual function
2. Memory impairment
3. At least one of the following:
   a. Loss of abstracting ability
   b. Impaired judgment
   c. Aphasia, apraxia, agnosia, constructional impairment, or personality change
4. No delirium
5. Either:
   a. Laboratory or physical examination evidence demonstrating a cause of the brain dysfunction, or
   b. Assurance that other potential explanations for the behavioral change have been excluded

Primary degenerative dementia
1. Dementia (as outlined above)
2. Insidious onset and uniformly progressive course
3. Exclusion of all other specific types of dementia

tia syndrome and the need for a careful evaluation to determine its cause.

Another widely used definition was constructed by Cummings and Benson. They defined dementia as an acquired persistent compromise in intellectual function with impairments in at least three of the following spheres of mental activity: language, memory, visuospatial skills, personality, and cognition (e.g., abstraction and mathematics). Like the DSM-III criteria, this definition emphasizes that dementia is a nonspecific clinical syndrome produced by a wide variety of disorders, affecting brain function. It differs from the DSM-III approach in allowing any combination of three neuropsychological deficits to qualify for the identification of a dementia syndrome and in applying the definition regardless of the severity of the intellectual losses (i.e., social or occupational disability is not required).

Non-Alzheimer Dementias

There are several reasons that every patient with the dementia syndrome requires full medical-neurological appraisal. The clinical diagnosis of Alzheimer's disease in a living patient depends on identifying a characteristic clinical syndrome and by excluding other causes of dementia. Therefore, the diagnosis of Alzheimer's disease requires a careful search for other potential causes(s). More important, a number of potentially treatable disorders can produce the dementia syndrome. These are listed in Tables 3 and 4. Often enough, when excess sensitivity to a medication or another metabolic or other insult "tips" a patient into dementia, the brain reserve is already compromised by an underlying dementing process. That process can, for instance, include "subclinical" Alzheimer's disease or unrecognized strokes. Such patients may "never quite come back," even if the superimposed reversible illness is treated effectively. Nevertheless, remedying the treatable cause of dementia can still allow them years of better functioning. It is particularly important to recognize depressions as a contributory factor in any phase of the dementing illness. Depression can mimic dementia, exacerbate dementia, or complicate dementia. A variety of effective medicines and other treatments are available for depressive syndromes. Although the wary clinician is unlikely to confuse frank depression with frank dementia, failure to recognize and treat the depressive component in a dementing illness is all too common.

Table 3. Potentially Treatable Causes of Dementia

1. Drugs and alcohol: beta-blockers, methyldopa, clonidine, haloperidol, chlorpromazine, phenytoin, bromides, phenobarbital, cimetidine, steroids, procainamide, disopyramide, atropine.
2. Tumors
   a. Direct CNS invasion
   b. Remote effect: mostly lung, but occasionally ovary, prostate, rectum, or breast
3. Nutritional disorders
   a. B_{12} deficiency (dementia may precede anemia)
   b. Folate, pellagra, Wernicke–Korsakoff's syndrome
4. Infection: syphilis, abscess, encephalitis
5. Metabolic disorders: electrolytes, hepatic, renal, pulmonary
6. Inflammatory disorders: systemic lupus erythematosis
7. Endocrine disorders: thyroid (hypo- or hyper-), adrenal, parathyroid
8. Trauma: subdural hematoma
9. Psychiatric/neurological disorders
   a. Schizophrenia
   b. Seizures
   c. Normal-pressure hydrocephalus (dementia, ataxia, incontinence)
   d. Depression

DIAGNOSTIC CRITERIA FOR DEMENTIA OF THE ALZHEIMER TYPE

The DSM-III criteria for primary degenerative dementia subsume the diagnosis of DAT as well as of other more rare degenerative disorders, such as Pick's disease. The patient must meet the criteria for dementia outlined above; in addition, the disorder must have an insidious onset and a progressive course, and other causes of dementias must be excluded (Table 2). Sulkava and associates demonstrated that such criteria, when carefully applied, are associated with an accurate diagnosis of DAT at autopsy in 82% of cases.

Refinements in the clinical diagnosis of DAT were produced by a task force of the National Institute of Neurologic

Table 4. Evaluation of the Demented Patient

1. History from patient and relative or friend
2. Mental status examination
3. Physical examination with vital signs
4. Neurological examination
5. CT scan, or MRI and EEG
6. Thyroid functions, serum B_{12}, folic acid
7. Chest X ray, EKG
8. CBC, UA, VDRL, and FTA, glucose, BUN, Ca, albumin, electrolytes, alkaline phosphatase, ESR

Others (as indicated)
1. Drug levels
2. Toxic screen
3. Brain scan
4. Lumbar puncture—*not routinely*

and Communicative Diseases and Stroke and the Alzheimer's Disease and Related Disorders Association (NINCDS-ADRDA). Diagnostic certainty of DAT was divided into definite, probable, and possible levels (Table 5). *Definite DAT* requires the occurrence of standard clinical features plus autopsy or biopsy confirmation of the diagnosis. *Probable DAT* represents the most credible clinical diagnosis of DAT based on features characteristic of the disease in patients with no other explanation for their dementia syndrome. *Possible DAT* is diagnosed when a second disorder exists that could produce the dementia but that is thought not to be responsible for the intellectual losses, or when the clinical features deviate from those of probable DAT but no alternative explanation exists.

Within the category of probable DAT, there are necessary, supportive, consistent, and unlikely clinical features. Necessary features are those required for the diagnosis of DAT; supportive characteristics strengthen the diagnosis but

Table 5. NINCDS-ADRDA Criteria for the Diagnosis of Dementia of the Alzheimer Type (DAT)

Probable DAT
1. Necessary features
   a. Dementia established by clinical examination, rating scale, and neuropsychological tests
   b. Deficits in two or more areas of cognition
   c. Progressive worsening of memory and other cognitive functions; no disturbance of consciousness
   d. Onset between 40 and 90, most often after age 65
   e. Absence of systemic or other brain disorders possibly producing the dementia
2. Supportive features
   a. Progressive deterioration of specific cognitive functions, such as aphasia, apraxia, and agnosia
   b. Impaired activities of daily living and altered behavior
   c. Family history of similar disorders, particularly if confirmed neuropathologically
   c. Laboratory results:
      i. Normal lumbar puncture (standard tests)
      ii. Normal or nonspecific EEG changes
      iii. Evidence of cerebral atrophy on CT with progression documented by serial observation
3. Consistent features
   a. Plateau periods
   b. Associated behavioral symptoms, including depression; insomnia; incontinence; delusions; illusions; hallucinations; catastrophic verbal, emotional, or physical outbursts; sexual disorders; and weight loss
   c. Neurological abnormalities, particularly in advanced cases, including increased muscle tone, myoclonus, and gait disorder
Possible DAT
1. Unexplained dementia syndrome with variations in the onset, presentation, or clinical course
2. A second potential cause of the dementia syndrome is present but is thought *not* to be the cause of the disorder
3. Single progressive cognitive deficit without an identifiable cause
Definite DAT
1. Clinical criteria for probable DAT, and
2. Histopathological evidence (neurofibrillary tangles and neuritic plaques) from biopsy or autopsy
Specific DAT subtypes
1. Familial occurrence
2. Onset before age 65
3. Presence of trisomy-21 (Down's syndrome)
4. Coexistence of other relevant conditions such as Parkinson's disease

may not be present in every case; consistent features are not necessary and do not aid in distinguishing DAT from other dementias but are common in the course of DAT; unlikely characteristics are observations or findings that rarely occur in DAT and should cause one to regard the diagnosis with skepticism.

Necessary features for a diagnosis of probable DAT include the presence of a documented dementia syndrome, deficits in two or more areas of cognition, progressive course, no delirium, age of onset between forty and ninety, and absence of systemic or other brain disorders potentially responsible for the intellectual losses. Clinical features considered *supportive* of the diagnosis of probable DAT include progressive deterioration of specific functions such as aphasia and apraxia, behavioral changes and impaired activities of daily living, a family history of similar conditions, and appropriate laboratory or diagnostic findings (e.g., normal spinal fluid, normal or nonspecific EEG slowing, cerebral atrophy on computerized tomographic [CT] scan). Characteristics that are *consistent* with a diagnosis of DAT but are not necessary and have little differential-diagnostic value include plateau periods in the course; behavioral symptoms such as depression, insomnia, incontinence, delusions, illusions, hallucinations, catastrophic outbursts, sexual disorders, and weight loss; and neurological abnormalities, including increased muscle tone, myoclonus, and gait alterations (particularly when the latter occur late in the clinical course). Clinical features that make the diagnosis of DAT *unlikely* include a sudden onset of the disorder, focal neurological findings, and the occurrence of seizures or gait abnormalities early in the course of the disease. The NINCDS-ADRDA criteria have greater precision than previous definitions, enumerate exclusionary features more comprehensively, and improve potential diagnostic validity by stratifying the diagnosis into definite, probable, and possible levels of certainty.

CLINICAL FEATURES OF DEMENTIA OF THE ALZHEIMER TYPE

The definitions above have aided in the clinical recognition of DAT by specifying the clinical features necessary for the diagnosis and by delineating the appropriate evaluation for excluding other potential causes of the dementia syndrome. The definitions, however, are not operationalized and do not describe precisely the nature of the neurobehavioral disturbances occurring in DAT. The clinical features of classic DAT include memory loss, aphasia, visuospatial abnormalities, disturbances of calculation and abstraction, and neuropsychiatric alterations, along with preserved speech articulation, normal gait, preserved posture, normal tone, and absence of extrapyramidal motor system abnormalities (Table 6).

The typical memory abnormality of DAT includes loss of the ability both to learn new information and to recall material learned in the remote past. Tests of memory of personal and politico-social events reveal that there is a tendency for facts from the earliest decades of life to be recalled more accurately than the more recent decades, but memory for all decades is impaired. Failure of learning new information reflects primarily a disturbance of encoding the novel material. In learning lists of words, DAT patients are not aided by acoustic similarity between words or categorization of the words—organizational aids that improve the ability of normal sub-

Table 6. Characteristics of Dementia of the Alzheimer Type in Three Progressive Stages

Clinical function	I	II	III
Language	Anomia	Transcortical sensory aphasia	Echolalia; palilalia
Memory	Amnesia	Recent and remote memory impaired	Untestable
Visuospatial skills	Mild to moderate abnormality	Abnormal	Untestable
Abstraction	Impaired	Impaired	Untestable
Neuropsychiatric alterations	Indifferent; ± delusional	Indifferent; ± delusional	Agitated
Articulation	Normal	Normal	Relatively preserved
Gait	Normal	Wandering	Abnormal
Posture	Normal	Normal	Flexed
Tone	Normal	Normal	Increased
Movement abnormality	None	None	Myoclonus
EEG	Normal	Theta-range slowing	Theta- and delta-range slowing
CT scan	Normal	Atrophy	Atrophy

jects to memorize lists. In addition, the recall of DAT patients is not aided by cuing. Thus, the memory disturbance in DAT involves primarily the encoding or storage of new information. This pattern contrasts with the memory disturbance of dementias such as Huntington's disease and Parkinson's disease, where the recollection of adequately stored information is impaired and recall is aided by cues.

Aphasia has been underemphasized as an important and consistent clinical feature of DAT. Difficulty producing lists of words (e.g., the number of animals named in one minute or the number of words beginning with a specific letter generated in one minute) and an anomia are early signs of linguistic impairment in DAT. Throughout most of the course of the disorder, DAT patients manifest fluent but empty spontaneous speech, impaired auditory comprehension, relative preservation of repetition, anomia, and aphasic agraphia. Reading comprehension is impaired, but reading aloud is resistant to the disease process and is preserved until late in the clinical course. The pattern of verbal output resembles transcortical sensory aphasia and may also be seen in Pick's disease and vascular dementias but is rare in other non-DAT etiologies of dementia.

Visuospatial disturbances are an early and regular characteristic of DAT. Patients have difficulty reading maps, finding their way in familiar environments, copying designs, and spontaneously drawing. The copying difficulty can be demonstrated by having the patient copy elementary figures (e.g., a cross or a cube) or Bender–Gestalt figures. More subtle constructional impairments may be revealed by asking the patient to copy the Rey–Osterrieth Complex Figure. Comparative studies suggest that DAT patients have greater difficulty with constructional tasks, whereas patients with Huntington's disease are more impaired on tasks of map reading. Thus, visuospatial abnormalities are a consistent part of the DAT clinical syndrome, and the deficits may exhibit features specific to DAT.

Cognitive abnormalities in DAT also include poor ability to abstract idioms and proverbs, acalculia, and impaired judgment. Experimental studies of DAT patients show that they are impaired on tests of delayed alternation and delayed response, similar to patients with frontal lobe lesions, and frontal lobe dysfunction may contribute to many of the cognitive abnormalities observed in DAT.

A variety of neuropsychiatric alterations occur in DAT. Personality alterations are among the earliest changes noted. Patients become more indifferent, exhibit less independence, and are childish. They are more listless, changeable, unreasonable, and irritable. Depressive symptoms may be observed in the early stages of DAT, but major depressive episodes are rare. Psychosis is not uncommon in DAT: patients exhibit persecutory delusions involving false beliefs about infidelity, theft, or harm.

In contrast to the marked impairment of intellectual functions in DAT, there is preservation of motor, somatosensory, and visual function until late in the clinical course. There is no dysarthria, and the precision of speech articulation is intact. Likewise, gait, posture, and tone remain unaltered throughout most of the disease course. Abnormal involuntary movements such as tremor, chorea, or athetosis are not a part of the DAT clinical syndrome, although myoclonic jerks may occur.

Using the ten behavioral and motoric features discussed here and listed in Table 6, Cummings and Benson constructed a DAT Inventory and, in a retrospective review of fifty patients with clinically diagnosed dementias, were able to correctly identify 100% of DAT patients and 94% of non-DAT patients.

The clinical manifestations correlate with the distribution of histopathological, metabolic, and neurochemical alterations described in DAT. Brun and colleagues have demonstrated that the medial and lateral temporal lobes and the temporo-parieto-occipital junction regions have the greatest abundance of neuritic plaques and neurons with neurofibrillary degeneration, whereas the primary motor, somatosensory, and primary visual cortices are relatively spared. Likewise, levels of choline acetyltransferase and acetylcholinesterase, enzyme markers of the cholinergic system, are significantly reduced in hippocampus, parietal cortex, and convexity and orbitofrontal cortex, whereas normal enzyme levels are found in pre- and postcentral gyrus and occipital cortex. In DAT patients, positron emission tomography (PET) scans demonstrate a similar topography of metabolic alterations. Normal metabolic levels are found in motor and sensory cortices and subcortical structures, whereas diminished metabolism is demonstrated in the regions of the frontal convexity and the temporo-parieto-occipital junction. Thus, the pattern of cerebral cortical abnormalities is reflected in the memory loss, the visuospatial abnormalities, the fluent aphasia, and the preserved motor and sensory function characteristic of DAT.

CLINICAL VARIANTS OF DEMENTIA OF THE ALZHEIMER TYPE

DAT may present with variant syndromes that deviate from the classical clinical symptom complex discussed above. Patients may manifest predominantly memory, visuospatial, or linguistic abnormalities. PET studies demonstrate that those with disproportionate visuoconstructive disturbances have greater loss of metabolic activity in the right cerebral hemisphere, whereas the left hemisphere is more hypo-metabolic in those with predominant language disturbances. The asymmetries have been shown to persist for many months and may characterize individual subjects throughout most of the disease course. Patients with disproportionate involvement of one faculty nevertheless manifest abnormalities in other areas of neuropsychological function: the diagnosis of DAT cannot be made if deficits are limited to a single area of mental activity.

Age of onset may also distinguish two variants of DAT. Early-onset patients (variously defined as showing the onset of symptoms before age sixty-five or before age eighty) tend to manifest more pronounced language disturbances and to exhibit a more aggressive course with shorter periods of survival after onset. Neuropathologically, patients with early-onset disease exhibit more involvement of nucleus basalis of Meynert and locus coeruleus and have more severe and more widespread neurochemical deficits.

A mild parkinsonian-type extrapyramidal syndrome with modest akinesia and rigidity may also identify a subtype of DAT. Chui and associates reported that 33.8% of their patients who had not received neuroleptic agents manifested such symptoms. Other have reported extrapyramidal symptoms in from 30% to 92% of DAT patients. Mayeux and colleagues observed an extrapyramidal syndrome in 34% of their patients and found that this subgroup had greater intellectual impairment and more psychosis than DAT patients without extrapyramidal dysfunction.

The early appearance of myoclonus may mark a DAT subgroup with a more severe form of the disease. Mayeux and co-workers observed myoclonus in 10% of DAT patients when they were first assessed and noted that it developed in an additional 16% over a four-year period. Patients with myoclonus were more intellectually impaired than those without. Bird and associates found that DAT patients with myoclonus had significantly lower levels of cholinergic-system enzymes. In most cases, myoclonus occurs late in the course of DAT.

DAT occurs prematurely in many individuals with Down's syndrome and may occur with increased frequency in individuals with Parkinson's disease.

STAGES OF DEMENTIA OF THE ALZHEIMER TYPE

DAT is an insidiously progressive disorder, usually progressing from onset to death in six to twelve years. Patients change markedly as the disorder advances. Several staging systems have been proposed; one convenient model divides the illness into early, middle, and late stages (Table 6).

In the first stage of the illness, language alterations include emptyness of spontaneous speech, mild anomia, and poor word-list generation. Learning of new information is partially impaired, particularly for complex memory tasks, and copying of complicated constructions is disturbed. Abstracting skills and judgment are also abnormal, and indifference begins to dominate the personality style. Motor functions, sensation, and vision are unaltered. Laboratory investigations such as the EEG and CT scans of the head are normal in this stage of the illness.

A more diagnostic group of symptoms emerges in the second stage of the illness. Language comprehension is impaired, and the verbal output assumes the pattern of transcortical sensory aphasia. Recall of remote information and of recently acquired material is impaired. Visuospatial abilities continue to decline and the patient may get lost in familiar neighborhoods or even within his or her own house. Drawings also deteriorate further. Abstract thought is impaired and judgment is lost. Indifference continues to characterize the overall demeanor, but delusions and intermittent agitation and uncooperativeness may occur. The motor examination remains normal, but the patients often engage in restless wandering and pacing. At this stage, the EEG may reveal theta-range slowing, and the CT scan may demonstrate mild to moderate cerebral atrophy.

In the third and final stage of the illness, the specific

clinical findings of DAT are obliterated by the advancing disease, and global impairment supervenes. Verbal output may include echolalic repetition of the examiner's words but is dominated by palilalic repetition of words or syllables spontaneously produced by the patient. Uncontrolled repetitious shouting or singing may occur; there may be terminal mutism. Memory, visuospatial abilities, and abstraction are so severely impaired as to be untestable. Behaviorally, the patient may remain indifferent when left alone but may be agitated and combative when attempts are made to engage or redirect her or him. Motor abilities are also compromised in this stage of DAT. Muscle tone is increased, limb flexion slowly progresses, and ambulation is eventually lost. Myoclonus is not unusual, and primitive reflexes such as grasping and sucking can be elicited. The patient becomes bed-bound and incontinent of urine and stool. In this phase, the EEG demonstrates mixed theta- and delta-range slowing; the CT scan may reveal moderate to severe cerebral atrophy with ventricular dilation and sulcal widening. Death from aspiration pneumonia or urinary tract infection terminates the third stage.

DIAGNOSTIC EVALUATION

There are currently no laboratory tests with results pathognomonic for DAT. The function of the laboratory assessment is (1) to exclude disorders that may mimic DAT, (2) to identify conditions such as pneumonia, urinary tract infections, electrolyte imbalance, or anemia that may be exacerbating the DAT patient's deficits.

In uncomplicated DAT, urine and serum studies are unremarkable. As noted above, the EEG demonstrates progressive slowing of the electrocortical rhythms as the disease progresses. EEG tracings are normal in the early phase of the illness, and slow progressively with theta and delta activity as the disease advances.

A variety of more advanced electrophysiological techniques have been used to attempt to strengthen the clinical diagnosis of DAT. Frequency analysis of the EEG demonstrates that, even in the early stages, there is a loss of alpha and beta activity, an increase in theta-range slowing, and decreased mean frequency. Topographic electrical activity mapping (TEAM) reveals abnormalities in the right parietal and left temporal regions in early-onset DAT and in the frontal lobes in late-onset DAT, but the sensitivity and specificity of the findings remain to be determined. Application of evoked-potential techniques to DAT demonstrate that P300 long-latency potentials are delayed in approximately 80% of cases. Abnormal P300 latency occurs in several types of dementia, however, and provides limited differential-diagnostic information.

CT scans are the most widely available brain images used in the evaluation of DAT. The principal value of the CT scan is to exclude other causes of dementia, such as strokes, hydrocephalus, neoplasms, subdural hematomas, abscesses, and demyelinating disorders. Although atrophy is present on most scans of DAT patients and increases with advancing disease, atrophic changes may also occur in the course of normal aging and cannot be used to substantiate a diagnosis of DAT. The correlation between the severity of atrophy and the magnitude of intellectual abnormalities is weak.

Magnetic resonance imaging (MRI) provides an anatomically more revealing brain image than CT scanning. MRI is more sensitive to vascular ischemic lesions and aids substantially in the differential diagnosis of DAT and multi-infarct dementia. MRI findings specific to DAT have not been identified.

Cerebral blood flow (CBF) studies and PET scanning provide avenues for investigating brain metabolism in DAT. CBF is diminished in DAT: the magnitude of the reduction correlates with the severity of the intellectual compromise, and the CBF is maximally reduced in the brain regions most affected by the disease. CBF studies may distinguish DAT from stroke-related dementia. PET scanning provides a metabolic image of brain activity in DAT. There is bilateral reduction of metabolism in the temporal, the temporo-parieto-occipital, and the frontal regions. The motor, sensory, and somatosensory areas are normal. This pattern may be unique to DAT, but the specificity of the metabolic pattern is still under study.

Neuropsychological testing provides a formal means of quantifying the deficits of DAT, of determining the involved faculties, and of establishing a baseline for following the progress of the disorder. As indicated above, testing of patients with DAT should include specific assessments of language, memory, visuospatial skills, and abstraction. Currently, a pathognomonic neuropsychological profile of DAT has not been established, and the neuropsychological assessment must be buttressed with clinical, historical, and laboratory information.

SUMMARY

The clinical diagnosis of DAT has considerable credibility when approached through the application of specific inclusionary criteria as well as a diagnostic evaluation that excludes other causes of dementia. The typical behavioral profile includes memory loss, fluent aphasia, visuospatial abnormalities, disturbances of abstraction and judgment, an indifferent personality, and preserved motor function. The EEG shows progressive slowing, and CT scanning reveals cerebral atrophy in most cases. More specific laboratory tests are being developed, but careful clinical observation remains the most valid diagnostic approach to DAT.

Part III

Dealing with Alzheimer's Disease

Chapter 6

Principles in Caring for Alzheimer's Patients

Ralph W. Richter, John P. Blass, and Jimmie L. Valentine

INTRODUCTION

A number of excellent and detailed recent monographs on the care of patients with Alzheimer's disease and other dementias have appeared and are listed in Appendix A. Rather than duplicate them, this chapter lists a number of principles which have proved useful to many caregivers.

COURSE

Alzheimer's disease is typically a progressive disease, with the manifestations proceeding from subtle to overwhelming.

Earlier Stages

Harold Wolf pointed out years ago that the first sign of dementing illness that is noticed by family and friends is "loss of sparkle." Modern terminology might be "loss of edge." At this stage, the dementing illness can be hard to distinguish from depression, boredom, grief, fatigue, or anxiety. Indeed, all of these may accompany it. This stage is often recognized only in retrospect. It can be particularly difficult and trying for the patient. The frustration and anger of the patient is often equalled by the frustration and anger of the family or other close contacts. The more responsible the position of the patient (and the more money involved), the greater the chance of damage.

As the disease progresses, it becomes clearer that something serious is going on. The banker whose judgment may or may not have been deteriorating now cannot balance her check book; the carpenter whose work may or may not have been up to his previous standard now cannot organize his tools; the post deliverer who has had the same route for twenty years may get lost. This is a stage at which professional help is often sought. It is also the stage at which the amelioration of *treatable* components may allow the patient to return to near-normal functioning. It is incumbent on family physicians and other health professionals who see patients at this stage to evaluate them fully, to obtain whatever consultations are necessary, and to establish a relationship of trust and mutual respect with the caregivers to prepare for the long and demanding course of this illness.

In the earlier stages, the neuropsychobiological impairments may be relatively selective. Chronic diseases of the brain tend to be asymmetric in onset; that is, they tend first to affect some areas of the brain more severely than others. If the Alzheimer's disease process affects the dominant (left) side of the brain first, then problems with language tend to be most evident early. These may mimic the linguistic difficulties that accompany certain strokes ("aphasias" or "verbal apraxias"). In other patients, the nondominant right hemisphere is involved more markedly in the earlier stages. These patients tend to have problems organizing activities in space and a kind of flattening of expressed feelings. One of our patients confused a supermarket with a courtroom, when her projected *verbal* IQ was 140. In some patients, the disease process first prominently affects areas of the brain subsuming emotion and organization of thought (limbic and/or frontal areas). In these patients, personality changes and psychoses may be particularly prominent.

Later Stages

As the disease progresses, more and more of the brain becomes involved, until all these functions become increasingly impaired. The patient then clearly has "global" cognitive impairments. As discussed in previous chapters, in the last phases the patient depends on care providers for the simplest functions of feeding, toileting, and even mobility.

Rate of Progression

The rate of progression can be surprisingly variable. Patients can go from health to the terminal stages in a couple of years; others survive longer than a quarter century. The 50% survival was eight years in a series studied at the Burke Rehabilitation Center; in general, these patients had few social or economic restraints on access to excellent general medical care. True remissions do not occur in Alzheimer's disease, although there may be fluctuations, particularly if a superimposed insult (like an inappropriate medication) is withdrawn. Mayeux has pointed out that there are several typical patterns. A relatively accelerated course is associated with Alzheimer's disease that involves the motor systems (perhaps because the disorder then involves more of the brain). Another uncommon form is associated with true plateaus in function, which can last for years. In our experience, the most common pattern is a more-or-less continuous progression. After the illness is recognized, there can be an apparent relative plateau *behaviorally*, in which changes are relatively slow and mild. These can be good years for an adaptable patient and family. Eventually, the patient "falls off the edge." This phase of rapid deterioration probably indicates the end of significant cerebral reserves. At this point, the patient may seem to lose the capacity to struggle.

REHABILITATION

Because the illness reduces the patient's ability to adapt to circumstances, the environment will have to be adapted to the patient.

The principle is typical of the "rehabilitation" strategies for any chronic disability. Because Alzheimer's disease is a progressive dementia, the modifications of the environment must also be progressive. Techniques for dealing with dementing patients are described in detail in a number of monographs (see Appendix A); Tables 7 and 8 summarize several key techniques. Many of these methods are informed common sense; many were originally developed by relatives and other caretakers who taught them to the professional community.

Patients should be allowed their dignity to the last possible moment. Some patients can still enjoy music or dance

Table 7. Tips for the Caregiver

Stairs	To keep a family member from going up or down the stairs, place a wrought-iron gate or baby gate at the top or bottom of the stairs.
Bathing	Make baths and showers easier by using a detachable shower head on a hose.
Doorknobs	Baby safety latches for doors and cupboards can be very helpful in keeping doors and cupboards closed.
Deadbolts	If there is a dead-bolt lock without a turn latch, keep the key in a nearby location for an emergency.
Mirrors	These can frighten the patient; turn mirrors around or remove them completely.
Playthings	If the patient likes to "fiddle" with things, give him or her a string of large plastic baby beads, baby toys, or a stuffed animal.
Recreation	Simple arts and crafts, like watercolors or large playing cards.
Breakables	All breakable objects should be put away because patients can cut themselves.
Eating	Offer only one food item at a time; a choice may be confusing. Allow ample time for eating and chewing.
Utensils	The utensils may have to be put in the patient's hand to get him or her started eating. Try using a baby plate with a suction bottom to keep the plate in one spot, as well as baby cups with covers to minimize spills.
Dressing	If a man cannot tie his tie, use a clip-on tie or a turtle neck or open-collar shirt.
Changes	Make changes very slowly. The patient must be well prepared for any physical, emotional, drug, nutritional, geographic, or caregiver change.
Exercise	Have a daily exercise routine such as a walk. It is important to keep the patient ambulatory as long as possible.
Crowds	Avoid large crowds or large spaces without boundaries.
Hygiene	Help the patient remember to brush her or his teeth regularly. Have a regular routine for bowel and bladder

(continued)

Table 7. (*Continued*)

	consistency. As the patient's disease progresses, use clothing with simple fasteners or elastic waistbands for pants.
Environment	Ensure that information is available to the patient about the time and place of landmarks that provide reality, for example, calendars with huge figures, clocks with all numbers for the hours, and reminders of special events such as birthdays, anniversaries, and holidays.

when they can no longer use words, and they should be encouraged to do so. One of our patients, a very intellectual lawyer, took pride in helping with housecleaning in the earlier stages of his illness when he still could. As with any other disease of the brain, one supports the "islands of normality." These will clearly differ, depending on the patient's premor-

Table 8. Tips for Effective Communication with the Patient

1. Touch and establish eye contact.
2. Beckon; use gestures to augment words; hold hands out; smile
3. Be attentive to messages communicated by the patient's body position and movement.
4. Find a quiet setting; reduce environmental confusion.
5. Speak in concise, clear sentences.
6. Take advantage of calm moments to express warmth and caring with a gentle touch.
7. Aberrant behavior is less likely to be motivated by unconscious conflicts than by needs or fears.
8. Listen to the patient even though his or her words do not make sense.
9. Construct sentences using words the patient uses.
10. Keep voice calm, low, and reasonably modulated.
11. If unable to attract the patient's attention, leave and try again in 1–2 minutes.
12. The patient may respond to verbalization very slowly; allow sufficient time.

bid skills and on what parts of the brain happen to be most involved.

Modification of the environment can be carried to excess, if it destroys the environment for the caretaker. If a couple have devoted their life to living graciously, neither the patient nor the spouse is likely to enjoy having the home converted into a one-person nursing home. Individuality must be respected, in the caretakers as well as in the patients.

MEDICATIONS

The psychotropic medications used for Alzheimer's patients are "chemical splints" for function.

Specific Remedies

Specific remedies of demonstrable benefit for the cognitive defects and the biological abnormalities of Alzheimer's disease are not yet available. Research is accelerating, and the authors profoundly hope that that statement will soon be outdated. Increasing numbers of clinical trials involving increasing numbers of medications and of patients are under way or are projected at the time this paragraph is being written.

In the present state of knowledge, medications are used to counteract disabilities that would otherwise severely impair function in the patient. Classic indications include sleeplessness, anxiety, depression, psychosis, uncontrolled and aggressive behavior, and wandering. Table 9 provides a list of

Table 9. List of Medications Currently in Use to Help Alleviate Secondary Symptoms Associated with Alzheimer's Disease

A. List of generic and trade names of some drugs that may be used for depression in Alzheimer's disease:

Antidepressants

Amitriptyline (Elavil, Endep)	Amoxapine (Asendin)
Imipiramine (Janimine, Sk-Pramine, Tofranil)	Doxepin (Adapin, Sinequan)
	Maprotiline (Ludiomil)
Nortriptyline (Aventyl, Pamelor)	Protriptyline (Vivactil)
Desipramine (Norpramin, Pertofrane)	Trazodone (Desyrel)
	Trimipramine (Surmontil)

Monoamine oxidase inhibitors

Phenelzine (Nardil)	Tranylcypromine (Parnate)
Isocarboxazid (Marplan)	

B. Generic and trade names of antipsychotic drugs sometimes used in Alzheimer's disease:

Haloperidol (Haldol)	Fluphenazine (Permitil, Prolixin)
Thiothixene (Navane)	Molindone (Moban)
Chlorpromazine (Thorazine)	Loxapine (Loxitane)
Trifluoperazine (Stelazine)	Thioridazine (Mellaril)

C. Generic and trade names of antianxiety drugs that may be used in Alzheimer's disease:

Diazepam (Valium)	Lorazepam (Ativan)
Chlordiazepoxide (Librium)	Clorazepate (Tranxene)
Triazolam (Halcion)	Oxazepam (Serax)
Alprazolam (Xanax)	Fluazepam (Dalmane)[a]

[a]Used as a sleeping aid.

the medications frequently used and a discussion of other drugs follows.

Memory-Enhancing Drugs

The principle of the use of one these drugs, physostigmine, was covered in Chapter 2. Physostigmine has been used, but the results are not astounding, as pointed out above. A mixture containing ergot alkaloids and papaverine (Hydergine and Deapril-ST are the commercial trade names) has also been tried in the early stages of Alzheimer's disease. This material acts as a vasodilator (that is, it causes an expansion or enlargement of the blood vessels in the brain) and appears to be most helpful in the depression associated with the early stages. If this preparation is to be used, it is usually tried for a six-month period, and if no results are noted, it is often discontinued. A number of other memory enhancers are in clinical trials. Preliminary data have shown modest memory improvement in some cases.

Antidepressants

The intellectual deterioration that occurs in the Alzheimer's disease victim often leads to depression, but depression is not observed in all patients. This depression can be rationalized if we understand that people who once had keen intellects now find themselves losing their mental faculties without apparent recourse. Quite probably, the depression also has a biochemical basis, as the gradual destruction of the nerve pathways in the brain results in diminished amounts of the neurotransmitters necessary to maintain normal mental health. If depression is a problem in the care of the patient, two different classes of drugs may be tried: tricyclic antidepressants and monoamine oxidase inhibitors. Some of these drugs, along with their trade names, are given in Table 9. The use of these drugs may produce some side effects, such as dry mouth and palpitations of the heart. In men, there may be a decreased ability to achieve an erection. Also, if the monoamine oxidase inhibitors are used, the patient has to avoid foods that may contain tyramine (a chemical that can cause an increase in blood pressure and changes in heart rate, but that is normally destroyed in the body by monoamine oxidase), such as cheeses, bananas, and some types of wines. If these agents are prescribed for the patient, the family should be certain to get clear advice on the drug from the physician and/or the pharmacist.

Antipsychotics

Some Alzheimer's patients suffer behavioral disorders requiring medication that will permit the caregiver to more easily manage the patient at home. Table 9 lists some of the more commonly used drugs in this category. The more common side effects experienced with these drugs include dry mouth and lethargy. Long-term use of these drugs can lead to a condition called *tardive dyskinesia,* which is characterized by uncontrolled movements consisting of sucking and smacking of the lips, lateral jaw twitches, and sticking the tongue in and out of the mouth repeatedly. In addition, there may be some uncontrolled jerking of the arms and twisting of the head from side to side.

Antianxiety Drugs

The fear of an impending event often makes a healthy person anxious about its outcome. This same fear is often present in the early stages of Alzheimer's disease when the patient is aware of the gradual loss of memory and other capacities. Also in these stages the sleep patterns are disturbed so that the person sleeps for only short periods. These conditions are often treated with antianxiety drugs. Table 9 lists some of the more common drugs in this class. In general, these drugs are relatively free of side effects, although no alcoholic beverages may be consumed while a patient is on these drugs. A mixture of the drugs in Table 9 and alcohol can lead to stopped breathing and death.

Antimanic Drugs

Another drug that is often used to aid in the care of the patient at home is lithium carbonate (Eskalith, Lithane, and Lithobid). The common side effects of this drug are nausea and vomiting, diarrhea, and in some cases, mild shaking of the hands (tremors).

Chelating Agents

The Chamorros of Guam have a remarkably high incidence of degenerative disorders of the nervous system such as amyotrophic lateral sclerosis, a parkinsonian-dementia-amyotrophic-lateral sclerosis complex, and have high levels of aluminum in their brains. This finding, as well as several reports of finding aluminum or aluminum complexes in either the brain or the plaques of Alzheimer's disease victims, has led to the speculation that aluminum concentration in the body has some causal relationship to the disease. To date, a direct relationship between aluminum and aluminum deposits in the brain and Alzheimer's disease has not been established. Therefore, the use of any chelating drugs, such as EDTA (ethylenediaminetetraacetic acid), that remove metals such as aluminum from the body is not recommended. Such agents also remove calcium, which may make the elderly person even more susceptible to bone breaking during a fall.

Sleep Disorders

Sleep disorders are characteristic of Alzheimer's disease. The disorder involves portions of the brain required to maintain the normal sleep–wakefulness cycle (notably the serotonergic nuclei of the dorsal raphe). Giving enough of a hypnotic (sleep medication) to ensure that the patient will sleep all night is likely to cause oversedation during the day. Manifestations are likely to include irritability, impaired function, and increased daytime dozing. Flurazepam (Dalmane) is a benzodiazapine of relatively long biological half-life and is a recognized offender. A gram of tryptophan at bedtime has been reported to be effective in about a third of geriatric patients. It is a normal dietary constituent and is without significant reported side effects. Often a small dose of a nonprescription antihistamine, such as diphenhydramine (Benadryl), *when the patient awakes* proves useful. Other nonprescription antihistamines, such as chlorpheniramine (Chlortrimeton, 4 mg), Teldrin, and histaspan, can be useful (despite their recognized anticholinergic properties). Chloral hydrate is often effective when other medications are not. It should not be mixed with alcohol. (A Mickey Finn is whiskey or gin with chloral hydrate in it.)

Anxiety

Anxiety to a point that is debilitating occurs in some Alzheimer's patients, although others seem blessedly free of it. Anxiety is classically treated with drugs of the benzodiazepine family, the typical example being diazepam (Valium). The rate at which these drugs are inactivated or removed from the body varies and increases with age. Drugs such as oxazepam (Serax) are removed relatively rapidly and therefore are relatively safe. Drugs such as chlordiazepoxide (Librium) have a long biological half-life (over a day for Librium), which facilitates the maintenance of stable blood levels at the cost of an increased risk of accumulation in the body. Sometimes, anxiety requires the use of other "tranquilizers," inducing the "antipsychotics" discussed below.

Depression

Depression of clinical significance occurs at some point in the course of the disease in a significant proportion of Alzheimer's patients—about 30% in the Burke series. It is normally associated with early Alzheimer's disease, but that may reflect the difficulty of recognizing a disorder of affect in patients who have lost the ability to use language and to organize their actions. We recall one of our patients whose major communication was a sad reiteration of the word *why*. Sir Martin Roth pointed out years ago that depression classically responds to treatment even in the presence of dementia. The medications are the same as for other depressive illnesses (Table 9).

Hallucinations, Delusions, and Psychotic Thinking

Hallucinations, delusions, and other manifestations of psychotic thinking are not rare in Alzheimer's disease. They may be part of depressive psychoses. These target symptoms are typically treated with major tranquilizers such as haloperidol (Haldol), thioridazine (Mellaril, which also has antidepressant properties), chlorpromazine (Thorazine), and trifluoperazine (Stelazine). It is important to question who is bothered by the hallucinations or delusions. If they don't bother the patient, they need not bother the caretaker, and medication may not be indicated. These major tranquilizers all have the risk of including a movement disorder characterized by restlessness, unusual lip-smacking movements, and eventual parkinsonian signs (dyskinesia tardive). Like all other medications, they should not be given unless the patient needs them; however, they should not be withheld in this life-threatening illness if the patient does need them.

Purposefully Aggressive Behavior

Purposefully aggressive behavior normally requires a degree of mental organization that is often beyond a patient with moderate or severe Alzheimer's disease. On the other hand, outbursts—perhaps of frustration—are all too common. Frequently, one can jolly a patient out of such outbursts. On the other hand, a physically healthy man with Alzheimer's disease can terrify a wife or other caretaker. Providing some kind of chemical restraint may be necessary to keep the care system intact. If so, major tranquilizers are normally used, most often haloperidol. Because haloperidol is available as an oral elixir, very small doses are possible. In truly recalcitrant patients, parenteral injections are possible.

Wandering

Wandering has defied medication control except in doses that nearly immobilize the patient. Major tranquilizers are often used, but with little success. Behavioral techniques are better. Allowing the patient to wander in a fenced-in garden or to take long walks with a caretaker sometimes helps. Alarms that alert caretakers to the patient's wandering and tricky locks that prevent wandering outside can be important. One of our patients tragically figured out such a lock and wandered out in a blizzard to her death.

Dosage

In general, patients with damaged brains are sensitive to chemicals that act on the brain. Furthermore, our brains differ from each other's as much as our faces do, and we tend to get more different from each other as we grow older. In the Alzheimer's patient, the variable effects of the disease are added to the other sources of variation. Not surprisingly, individualization of dosage is the rule. Often, surprisingly small doses are effective; too often, standard doses from the *Physician's Desk Reference* (PDR) turn out to be toxic.

It cannot be overemphasized that medications must be under a physician's control. The understandable tendency of caretakers to experiment with medications from different physicians can, frankly, be dangerous. Inappropriate reactions of patients to drugs and interactions among drugs are common and can have devastating sequelae, even including death. The physician should work with the family, but the family *must* work with a physician.

GENERAL MEDICAL CARE AND NUTRITION

Medical Care

An understandable reluctance to harass patients with Alzheimer's disease can unfortunately turn into inadequate nutritional and other medical support. Frequency and urgency from a urinary tract infection are particularly stressful for a patient struggling to remember where the bathroom is. A patient who is confused to begin with does not need the added stress of intermittent heart block with transient impairment of the blood supply to the brain. In such cases, a pacemaker may be helpful. On the other hand, surgery and specifically general anesthesia can precipitate marked declines in function in these vulnerable patients. Good medical judgment is necessary in deciding how and with what to treat them.

Nutrition

Nutrition in Alzheimer patients is a complex issue. One of the learned skills that the patients lose with time is the ability to manipulate utensils such as a knife and fork. At some stages of their illness, they may be better nourished given a roll and a hard-boiled egg than given an elegant omelet. At a later stage, they require assistance in eating. Patients in the earlier stages of Alzheimer's disease may develop a "ravenous appetite." Sometimes it appears to caretakers that the patients forget that they have eaten. Patients in the later stages of Alzheimer's disease typically lose weight despite apparently adequate intake. This phenomenon has been documented in detail in a recent study from Sweden. In the last stages, the patients may appear starved even though they have been carefully fed by devoted caretakers. In theory, if a patient with Alzheimer's disease ingests an ideal balanced diet, vitamin supplements are not needed. In practice, it seems sensible to give a multivitamin supplement daily.

SUPPORT OF CAREGIVERS

When the major caregiver gives out, the care system gives out. (This principle is known as *Eisdorfer's rule*.) Seeing someone you love suffer from Alzheimer's disease is a major stress; caring for that person is even more stressful. No matter how saintly a person wants to be, and no matter how much one loves the victim of Alzheimer's disease, human beings are made of flesh and blood and not of spring steel. The caretaker's duty to care for himself or herself is part of a responsibility *to the patient*. If the caretaker suffers from a physical illness (such as a heart attack) or from psychic exhaustion (such as a debilitating depression), the care of the patient will, predictably, deteriorate. Gwyther and George and their co-workers have found that all the strong predictors of nursing-home placement reside in the family; the characteristics of the patients are relatively unimportant (including sleeplessness, incontinence, and wandering). These observations have several implications.

Family members need support from each other. Family dynamics are classically complex. Old wounds and half-ground axes are apt to reemerge under the stress of caring for an Alzheimer's patient. The child who has moved so far away that assuming responsibility is difficult is at risk of feeling guilty; the child on whom the primary responsibility falls is likely to feel at least some anger and isolation. They are at risk for tearing at each other and at the healthy parent rather than helping each other. Sometimes the stresses destroy what is left of family life. The stresses can, however, also strengthen more fortunate families.

Social supports, including nursing-home placement, should be used in a timely manner.

If the care system collapses, emergency placement is likely. Under those circumstances, the placement is less likely to be optimal than if there is time to consider the details carefully. If the care system—which really means the prime caregiver—appears close to being overwhelmed, social supports should be introduced. If necessary, placement of the patient should be undertaken.

In our view, another indication for placement is a patient who no longer recognizes who is giving him or her care. At that point, care might as well be given in eight-hour shifts by people less emotionally involved.

SOCIAL SUPPORTS

The mix of social support systems should be individualized for the patient, with the help of a trained social worker or other specialist.

Services for patients with Alzheimer's disease in the United States compare with those available in most other developed countries. These are, by definition, inadequate to deal with the overwhelming burden that a loved one with this disease presents to a family. On the other hand, the fiscal and other public-policy constraints discussed in Chapter 8 by Cook-Deegan suggest that an ideal system will not be readily developed.

Home Services

Home services can be very useful for Alzheimer's patients even if not originally designed for them. "Meals on Wheels" programs are widely available for patients who can no longer be depended on to prepare their own food safely. Homemaker services are available in most localities, for individuals who require assistance with daily activities other than health care. Home health aides provide more health-oriented care. They are professionals with a level of training somewhat less than licensed practical nurses, but frequently with impressive empathic and other personal skills. Visiting nurses can ensure management and supervision of medication and other health care. Many of these services may be covered, at least in part, by government or other third-party payers, but the rules of eligibility differ among jurisdictions.

Day Care

Day care typically amounts to intermittent respite. It gives the caretaker time to shop, to read, to be alone, and to take care of other personal necessities. The patient is provided with the opportunity to mix socially with others in the same predicament. In our experience, a major asset of day-care programs is the advice the day-care staff can give to families. (In return, the ideas about management that the families develop are a major source of improved techniques for the day-care staff.) Day care is the most rapidly growing form of health care in the United States.

Inpatient Respite Care

Inpatient respite care, where studied, has turned out to be a path into more permanent nursing-home residence. The temporary placement of a patient in a respite setting requires preparing the patient, who often does not understand or believe that the placement is temporary. It can arouse as much fear and guilt in the caretaker and other family members as a more permanent transfer. On the other hand, the ease with which the patient adapts to the respite setting and the relief of the temporarily unburdened caretaker may be so dramatic as to make permanent placement a more acceptable alternative. Whether residential respite care, either in the patient's own home or in custodial facilities, will become a more important part of the health-care delivery system for Alzheimer's patients in the United States remains to be seen.

Custodial Care

Custodial care often, although not invariably, becomes appropriate for patients by the last, preterminal stages of Alzheimer's disease. This care is often given in a nursing home, either a health-related facility or a more medically oriented skilled-nursing facility. The characteristics of these two different kinds of nursing homes are governed by individual state regulations. About half the patients in nursing homes in the United States are believed to be victims of dementia, most often Alzheimer's disease. Other custodial institutions include the Veterans Administration hospitals and domiciliaries and private-sector organizations, including church-sponsored facilities and those funded by unions and other fraternal organizations. Patients with major components of psychiatric disability may be cared for in state mental hospitals.

The details of caring for these patients in custodial facilities are an area of active study and are beyond the scope of this presentation. One of the newer programs of the National Institute on Aging is "teaching nursing homes," academic analogues of the academic university teaching hospitals. These not only conduct research but train medical students, resident physicians, and specialized fellows in the care of elderly patients, including particularly those with Alzheimer's disease.

Finding Social Services

The network of the services available is so complicated that a trained guide is needed to utilize it effectively.

By design, in our large, diverse, avowedly pluralistic society, services vary in different jurisdictions. Indeed, as Cook-Deegan points out in Chapter 8 on public policy, the Medicare laws were designed to allow such flexibility. An inevitable result is that generalizations either are too vague to be useful in specific cases or are inaccurate for many localities. One valid generalization is that families need a guide to the available services. That guide can be a skilled social worker or a gerontologist or some other individual in the local Office of Aging. Some voluntary organizations also provide substantive advice and assistance (see below).

VOLUNTARY ORGANIZATIONS

The voluntary sector now includes a number of organizations that aid individual families afflicted with Alzheimer's disease. They provide education, including tips about the management of patients. They often facilitate access to the available services. They provide for social life with other caretakers suffering under the same burdens. They provide a forum for positive actions in raising money and political support for research and for improved care. These organizations typically act as private-sector lobbying organizations, providing active feedback to elected representatives at local, state, and federal levels. Examples of prominent voluntary organizations are included in the following subsections.

Alzheimer's Disease and Related Disorders Association (Alzheimer's Association)

The first chapter of this organization was started in the late 1970s by Bobby Glaze of Bloomington, Minnesota. From this single chapter, a national organization with headquarters in Chicago and chapters in almost every state has developed. The association is devoted to facilitating support groups and public awareness of AD. It has been active in pushing federal legislation to aid in research and caregiving.*

Familial Alzheimer's Disease Research Foundation (Alzheimer's Foundation)

With Scientific Advisory Board members from over 10 nations, this organization is international in scope and includes many of the major AD research laboratories in the world. While the foundation sponsors scientific symposia to facilitate the exchange of ideas in the hope of finding faster answers to AD, its main function is research. The foundation is a leading private organization dedicated solely to the promotion of basic scientific research on AD.†

The John Douglas French Foundation for Alzheimer's Disease

This foundation was named for the prominent surgeon and medical investigator who fell victim to AD, and was

---

*National telephone number for information on closest active chapter: (312) 853–3060.
†Mailing address: 8177 South Harvard, Tulsa, OK 74137. Telephone: (918) 631–3665.

founded by his wife, Dorothy. The French Foundation develops model care systems (complete hospitals, the first of which opened in California in November, 1987) devoted specifically to AD. *

ETHICAL ISSUES

How much care and how long to give it are ethical questions that involve a spiritual dimension and that challenge faith.

In the United States, questions of how much care to give and when to allow death are, by definition, ethical. This terminology recognizes the pluralism of our society and the need to reach agreement among different groups. The consensus view, now incorporated into case law, is that an individual who is mentally competent can decide for himself or herself how much care to accept. The need to appoint a surrogate for a person who is no longer *compos mentis* is recognized, but no consensus has yet emerged on how to choose that surrogate. Probably several different mechanisms will eventually be available. Where legal challenges are likely— for instance, where significant property is involved—attention to legal remedies is particularly important. These are discussed by Sandoe in Chapter 7.

The questions of life and death are profoundly spiritual and, therefore, religious. The spiritual support that can come from religion can be critical. The religious dimension provides a framework for the ultimate preservation of human dignity. For the individual, it can provide the support that

*Mailing address: 11620 Wilshire Boulevard, Los Angeles, CA 90025. Telephone: (213) 470–5462

makes an inherently intolerable situation bearable without bitterness. Why the righteous suffer is an old, fundamental, painful philosophical question. That suffering can lead to personal and spiritual growth and to deeper understanding of the needs of others is, however, unquestioned. Chapter 9 documents the role that Christianity has played in the lives of several individuals who have cared for loved ones with Alzheimer's disease. Analogous passages could be found for other diseases and other religions. In real life, the victims of Alzheimer's disease and those who love and care for them are faced with spiritual questions.

Chapter 7

Alzheimer's and the Law
Clinical Perspectives
Anthony B. Sandoe

INTRODUCTION

Early in the course of dementia of the Alzheimer's type (DAT), a patient begins to experience a gradually diminished capacity to manage his or her personal and business affairs. It becomes increasingly apparent that assistance will be required in this regard. Accordingly, the patient's family must identify the patient's assets and sources of income that will require management. The family must, therefore, address the form of ownership in which these assets are held, the forms of management that may eventually be employed, and the issue of who will have the authority to make such decisions in recognition of the patient's diminishing personal capacity.

As the disease progresses, further and more difficult issues begin to emerge as the patient begins to lose the capacity to care for himself or herself physically and financially. Considerations must now transcend the mere management of assets, and accordingly, the family must determine the nature and type of care that will be required at each successive stage of the deterioration as well as the issue of who will have the authority to make such decisions.

At some point in this progressively degenerative process, a medical diagnosis will be made. At such time, the family becomes well aware that the normal life expectancy of the patient is going to be tragically shortened, and the family's attention must turn from issues of asset and personal management to the inevitability of the patient's mental and physical decline, her or his death, and beyond. The family must confront such traditional estate-planning issues as whether there is a will, whether there are other testamentary substitutes such as an *inter vivos* trust or joint accounts established for the transfer of the patient's assets, whether these devices in the aggregate are adequate from a variety of perspectives, and if not, whether there are other, more suitable measures available. Moreover, the family must confront some other, rather unique estate-planning issues such as whether there are sufficient financial resources available to pay for the extended custodial care that will eventually be required, whether there will be sufficient financial resources remaining to care for the patient's spouse and other dependents, and whether, indeed, there will be any assets at all to transfer upon the patient's death.

For purposes of analysis, therefore, it might be suggested that the principal areas of legal concern to the Alzheimer's patient and the family fall into four categories: (1) the care and management of the patient's assets during his or her lifetime; (2) the care and management of the patient himself or herself; (3) the preservation and conservation of the patient's assets during this time for the benefit of the patient's dependents—the *inter vivos* estate plan; and (4) the passage of the patient's assets upon death—the postmortem estate plan. This chapter outlines some of the more important considerations of these areas.

INTER VIVOS ASSET MANAGEMENT

The Nature of the Problem

During the early stages of Alzheimer's, frequently before diagnosis, DAT seems to manifest itself through small lapses of memory and capacity too minute to notice. As the disease progresses, however, and memory problems increase, it becomes gradually more difficult for patients to perform once-routine daily tasks. Although patients may become more forgetful, especially of recent events, they can, nevertheless, still cope with daily management matters with slight behavioral modifications and can still live effectively with such modifications for extended periods. Forgetfulness, in the absence of other symptoms, may be interpreted as inattentiveness, and it has been suggested that a unique characteristic of Alzheimer's is that a patient's ability to think logically is far superior to his or her recent-memory capacity, although this, too, diminishes over time. These characteristics, coupled with the probability that DAT is not yet suspected, often enable loss of memory and other cognitive functions to remain undetected by family and friends for a long period, during which there may be no particularly serious consequences regarding property.

Critical problems and issues, however, may begin when

the memory loss and diminished intellectual capacity begin to intrude more seriously on the daily management of an individual's business and personal financial affairs. It is at this later stage of the disease that the undiagnosed patient may begin to forget appointments or may fail to meet important deadlines. Symptomatically, for example, significant amounts of cash may be misplaced, deposits and withdrawals forgotten, and a checking account inadvertently overdrawn. Insurance policies may be allowed to lapse, investments may be allowed to mature untended, and recurring bills and other obligations may be neglected. Clearly, such lapses of memory are now becoming more than the occasional, inadvertent oversights that everyone experiences, to his or her embarrassment, at one time or another. Rather, these lapses are becoming chronic and, therefore, much more serious. Because of continual mistakes such as these, undiagnosed patients have lost both valuable and sentimental personal possessions, significant amounts of cash and other property, their credit standing, and even worse—in the absence of other apparent symptoms to their employers—their jobs. Creating a conscious or even unconscious confidence crisis in the patient, such continued, seemingly unexplainable lapses, together with the frustration they cause, provoke defensiveness, irrational outbursts, and other wholly uncharacteristic, bizarre behavior. When confronted by understandably mystified family and friends, it is not unusual for a patient, in exasperation and denial, to discount the problem. In an apparent effort to compensate for such lapses, individuals may modify lifelong behavior patterns. Cash may be hidden away in unusual locations, household items may disappear and reappear without explanation, and reminder notes may proliferate.

As the frequency of these mental lapses and the seriousness of their consequences increase, it eventually becomes apparent to family and friends that there is indeed a problem. This awareness may be gradual or sudden; yet once the problem is recognized and understood, the fact that the patient's deteriorating mental condition has placed her or his personal financial affairs at considerable risk must be acknowledged, and appropriate measures must immediately be taken to remedy the situation and to reduce, insofar as possible, the vulnerability of the patient and his or her property.

Depending on the extent of the patient's mental deterioration at this time, it may be sufficient, initially, for someone merely to assist the patient in the daily management of personal affairs. Eventually, however, it will become necessary for someone to assume complete control. Whatever the situation, at this stage the principal concern of the family is usually asset management. Although there will be other, far more difficult problems later, for now, there are assets to manage, income to collect, and recurring liabilities to discharge—the constant financial-management responsibilities that the patient is barely able to discharge, if at all.

General Considerations

The initial issues confronting the family will be the location and identification of the various assets, sources of income, and liabilities that will require proper attention on behalf of the patient. Although no two individuals or family situations are identical, the patient will, in all probability, have an interest in a variety of assets. These may include:

1. *Real estate*—the family home, condominium, or apartment, perhaps even investment properties—a multifamily dwelling, commercial buildings, or undeveloped land.

2. *Securities*—Stocks, bonds, and notes of publicly traded companies and of governmental units, held individually or in common in mutual-fund form.
3. *Cash and equivalents*—Demand and term deposit accounts and fund investments in a variety of financial institutions.
4. *Life insurance*—Policies issued on the life of the patient and perhaps on the life of others. These policies, depending on the owner's objectives, may simply provide for insurance (term) or may, in addition, contain a savings or investment component (whole life).
5. *Business interests*—A family or other closely held business entity held in corporate, partnership, or sole proprietorship form.
6. *Tangible personal property*—Art, antiques, precious metals, or a stamp or coin collection held for investment or for their heuristic value, as well as automobiles, furniture, furnishings, and other household possessions held principally for use and consumption.

As noted, individual circumstances clearly differ; a person's holdings may certainly be more extensive and perhaps far more sophisticated and complex. Yet, many individuals have an aggregate of ownership interests not unlike the foregoing. Moreover, the nature of these interests is affected by the manner in which the individuals hold title to them: individually or together with others (either as joint tenants or as tenants in common).

Complementing these assets may be sources of income requiring similar attention. These may include:

1. *Entitlements*—Social security, Veterans Administration, or other forms of entitlement income, depending on age, service, and physical condition.
2. *Retirement*—Pension, profit-sharing, deferred-compensation, or salary-reduction plans, IRAs or Keoghs,

depending on current or former status of employment.

3. *Beneficial*—Various forms of insurance, annuity, or trust income that may be coupled with a power to appoint underlying assets during lifetime or at death by will, depending on the existence and generosity of a relative or friend.

As a result of a person's lifelong financial habits or of the behavior modifications incidental to DAT, simply locating these assets and sources of income may prove to be a formidable challenge.

As the family focus on these issues of asset, income, and liability identification, they must concurrently focus on the related considerations of the identity of the manager, the legal form of the management, and the objectives of the administration: Who will assume the necessary control? What form will that control take? What are to be the immediate and long-term objectives of management once control is established? Of necessity, these decisions and the answers to these questions are interdependent and, accordingly, somewhat involved.

From the family's perspective, certainly, the significant issue in this complex of considerations should be the immediate and long-term objectives of the asset management: What, optimally, should be accomplished by the placement of the patient's assets under the management of another? There are several objectives—some immediate, others of more long-term impact.

Of most immediate concern, clearly, is the physical security of the patient's property—perhaps the principal motivating factor in the first instance. The initial objective, then, should be to remove the property from harm's way. Accordingly, the manager should take possession and assume control of all of the patient's property to preserve and protect its integrity. Unique and valuable tangible personal property (such as jewelry), valuable intangible personal property (such as cash, stocks, bonds, and notes), and important documents of ownership (such as deeds and insurance policies) should be placed in safekeeping to prevent their loss or imprudent sale. Attention may then be turned to matters of daily management: the maintenance of real property; the collection of rents, dividends, interest, social security, and other retirement income (which may be directly deposited to the patient's bank account); and the payment of recurring bills, including mortgages and insurance premiums. Because of the patient's recent mental lapses, these matters may be in a state of disarray.

Once the assets and sources of income are secure and their proper daily management is restored, consideration may be given to other, more long-range matters, such as investment management. The propriety of the patient's present investments requires review both in the context of the patient's present investment objectives and in relation to the constantly changing market conditions. The investment objectives of a younger patient with children still in school, for instance, will be significantly different from those of one nearing retirement whose children have completed their education. The objectives of both will differ from those of one who has previously retired. Such differences in objectives should be carefully considered in determining investment strategies.

In this context, investment portfolios require review, and decisions must be made with respect to continued ownership of certain stocks and bonds. Interest rates require review both daily and as term certificates mature, and decisions must be made to "roll over" the investment or to seek alternatives. The objectives of an insurance plan likewise require review, and decisions must be made about the continued propriety of particular forms of insurance (term versus whole life) as well as about the extent of present coverage.

Business and employment issues must also be addressed. Decisions must be made regarding the continued participation of the patient in a closely held business. There may be an agreement among those who own the business regarding the purchase of the patient's interest in the event of disability or death. If the patient is an employee, decisions must likewise be made about the terms of the termination of employment and the payment of any retirement income or benefits. In either case, decisions must be made regarding application for entitlement income.

The degenerative nature of Alzheimer's disease, however, necessitates more than a mere review of the patient's current investments in light of present investment objectives. The increasing prospects of ultimate confinement in a long-term health-care facility, perhaps for a significant period, and of the extraordinary attendant costs may well cause a complete reassessment of the investment objectives of the patient as well as those of the entire family. Custodial expenses are potentially devastating to the family with inadequate financial resources to meet them. The family must, therefore, anticipate whether the present investments will adequately meet such expenses and in addition will care adequately for the continuing needs of the patient's spouse and others who are economically dependent on the patient. This latter consideration requires an analysis of the entire family as an economic unit—their circumstances and objectives—as well as those of the patient. Such an analysis anticipates a number of issues of *inter vivos* estate planning (asset preservation).

Within the framework of these objectives, both immediate and long-term, and of the particular circumstances of the patient and of the patient's family, each of the types of assets, its current form of ownership, and the various sources of income previously mentioned will present its own set of issues and problems, which must be satisfactorily resolved by the manager. What, for example, should be done with the shares of stock now registered in the patient's name and over which the patient has sole legal control? What should be done with the social security checks now paid by the U.S. Treasury to the patient alone?

A variety of legal management forms is available to the patient with the Alzheimer's disease and to the patient's family. Principally, these include guardianship, conservatorship, power of attorney, *inter vivos* trusts, joint ownership, and transfers with or without retained interests. Each of these management forms possesses unique advantages as well as limitations. They vary considerably in terms of flexibility and sophistication. Although not all of these forms are appropriate for every patient, each of them or perhaps some combination may be used for the care, maintenance, and preservation of assets and income during the remainder of the patient's life. Accordingly, each patient's particular financial circumstances and objectives require careful analysis and the selection of the appropriate form, or combination of forms, by a skilled professional.

Although a person's circumstances, objectives, assets, and income are clearly important factors in the selection of the appropriate form, they are by no means the only considerations. The mental capacity of the patient may well be the most significant factor involved. The law recognizes different degrees of mental capacity. An individual may, for example, be perfectly competent to execute a simple will and yet may lack the necessary capacity to enter into a complex contract. The standards for determining degrees of capacity vary somewhat among the states, but because some degree of capacity is a necessary prerequisite to the application of many of these forms of management, the relative mental capacity of the patient at the time of the analysis is critical and sometimes determines their selection. Moreover, although the objectives of the management, the nature of the assets, and the capacity of the patient may help to determine and in certain circumstances to dictate the choice of management form, the form or forms themselves may in some respects help to determine the identity of the manager. Although a clear and probably desirable choice of manager is often one or more family members, the management form, together with the relative sophistication of the assets and of the management objectives, may prompt a search outside the family for a professional or corporate manager. In certain circumstances, a bank, a trust company, a lawyer, an accountant, or a financial adviser, serving alone or together with a family member, may be a desirable alternative.

Management Forms

Guardianship and Conservatorship

A guardian or a conservator, referred to as a *committee* in some states, is a person or institution that is appointed by the court having jurisdiction over such matters (a probate or surrogate's court), and that is judicially charged with the duty of caring for the property and/or the person of one who is adjudged incapable. These forms of management are traditionally used when a person lacks the required capacity, and they are imposed on the incompetent person by judicial decree, a characteristic that distinguishes them from the other forms considered below, which may be options available to the patient, provided the patient has the requisite competence to select them. Although the terminology and the precise form vary somewhat among the various states, a formal court proceeding is generally required, and the appointment is based on a factual finding by the court that the requisite degree of capacity is absent. Such findings must be supported by the testimony of the person's family, friends, and, usually, a physician or other professional skilled in the diagnosis of mental deterioration. There is normally a requirement that either guardians or conservators render an account of their activities to the court on some periodic basis, customarily annually. Although a close family member, such as a spouse or an adult child of the patient, is normally appointed by the court, few state legislatures actually establish a statutory preference, leaving such choices to the courts in the exercise of judicial discretion, with the expectation that such appointments will be made in the best interests of the patient.

As previously mentioned, most states distinguish among degrees of mental capacity. Such distinctions may determine the degree or extent of care authorized or directed by a court. Many states, for example, draw a distinction between the capacity to care for one's assets and the capacity to care for oneself. Therefore, it is possible for a court to appoint an individual or an institution to manage the financial affairs of the person, while the person retains the capacity and freedom to make decisions with respect to his or her physical needs. In some states, therefore, a conservator is vested with limited authority over the care of the incompetent and has the custody of the assets only, and not the person. A guardian, on the other hand, has custody of both the assets and the person and is charged with the complete responsibility of making decisions with respect to that person, much as a parent acts on behalf of a minor child. Accordingly, this form may be used exclusively for asset management and, under appropriate circumstances, may also be used for the management of the patient's person. As an asset manager, the conservator or guardian may be authorized by the court to conduct, subject to varying degrees of judicial supervision, all of the patient's business affairs for the rest of the patient's life. The death of the patient serves to terminate the office as well as the management responsibilities of the conservator or the guardian. At that point, the remaining duty is to transfer the patient's assets to the duly appointed representative of the patient's estate, that is, the executor or administrator.

Power of Attorney

A power of attorney is merely an agency agreement (principal–agent) in which the patient appoints another individual as her or his agent, for the purpose of transacting a variety of matters on her or his behalf. Depending on the nature of these matters, the patient may, in addition, give the agent possession of certain property, for whatever purposes are desired. Although the creation of such a relationship requires no formal transfer of title and no court authority, it does require a degree of mental capacity. Although in practice a family member is often appointed, there are usually few restrictions with respect to such an appointment. With a few exceptions limited to specific situations, anyone who is of full age and capacity may be granted a power of attorney, regardless of his or her relationship to the patient. A professional adviser, a close friend, or a corporate entity such as a bank could therefore be designated as an agent.

The design of these agency agreements may be expansive or limited. The principal (the patient) could, for example, grant authority to the agent to accomplish only one specific act, such as the sale of a particular security or the rental of an apartment. Alternatively, the principal could confer on the agent a general power granting broad and extensive authority to transact any and all matters on the principal's behalf. The creation and use of these powers may, indeed, become quite sophisticated, particularly when combined with other devices. Yet, as an asset management vehicle, the power of attorney permits the appointed agent to conduct, within designated limits, all of the patient's business and personal affairs for the rest of the patient's life, or until the earlier revocation of this authority by the patient.

Just as this authority may be granted, so may it be revoked. In its traditional form, the death of the principal (the patient) or his or her earlier mental incapacity automatically revokes the power of attorney, rendering it useless in incompetency situations. Recently, however, many states have authorized a new form of power, a so-called durable power of attorney, which survives the incompetence of the principal. Unlike in the traditional form, however, there is a requirement in some states that the holder of a "durable" power bear a particular family relationship to the one granting the power. As an asset management vehicle for the Alzheimer's patient, the durable form of power presents clear advantages over the traditional form, providing such authority is accepted. It should be noted, however, that, as a practical matter, a power of attorney is effective only if third parties are willing to accept it. Because the agreement is between the principal and the agent, third parties are not required to accept or honor them.

While a power of attorney, traditional or durable, is usually intended to take effect immediately in order to accomplish whatever current purposes are desired, the durable power of attorney may be made to become effective only in the event of a disability. By the use of such words as "This power of attorney shall become effective upon the disability or incapacity of the principal," the power may spring into existence on the occurrence of disability, hence the frequently used designation *springing power*. Because a determination of incapacity must be made before a springing power takes effect, it may be more difficult to use this form of power without challenge from some source, probably the third party who is requested to accept its validity and authority. Although this form is unfortunately not yet available in all states, particularly the "springing attribute," it is available in an increasing number of jurisdictions. Either form of power of attorney, however, is terminated by the patient's death, and all of the patient's assets previously managed by the agent then revert to the duly appointed representative of the patient's estate: the executor or administrator.

Inter Vivos Trusts

A trust created during the lifetime of the patient (*inter vivos*) is an agreement in which the patient formally transfers assets or property to a trustee, who agrees to hold and manage the property on behalf of the patient (and sometimes for members of the patient's family as well, that is, the beneficiaries) for some particular period of time. In the case of the Alzheimer's patient, this management would most probably extend for the rest of the patient's life.

Simply defined, a trust is a fiduciary relationship in which the trustee holds the legal title to the property subject to an obligation to use the property so transferred for the benefit of the beneficiary. As in agency agreements, the creation of an *inter vivos* trust relationship requires no court authority. It does, however, require a particular degree of mental capacity. Although a close family member is often selected for the office, there are few restrictions in this regard. Usually, anyone of full age and capacity who is capable of managing the transferred assets may be appointed as trustee regardless of relationship to the patient. As with powers of attorney, the trustee may be a professional adviser, a close friend, or a corporate entity such as a bank or a trust company. When assets are extensive or complex and objectives are sophisticated, a professional or corporate entity could, indeed, be a desirable choice, serving alone or together with a family member.

In its simplest form, the trust may be compared in some ways to the power of attorney. As a legal concept, however, it is more complex and is capable of far greater sophistication. In its more complex form, in the hands of a skilled and imaginative legal practitioner, a trust is capable of accomplishing an almost limitless array of objectives far beyond the capacity of a power of attorney, durable or otherwise. Trust agreements may therefore be as expansive or as limited as the person creating them designs them to be.

As an asset management instrument, the trust may permit the trustee to manage all of the patient's assets transferred to the trust for the rest of the patient's life or until the earlier termination of that trust. Although the patient may revoke the trust under certain circumstances, the patient's death will not necessarily serve to automatically revoke the arrangement. Unlike conservatorships, guardianships, and powers of attorney, the trust may be designed to extend beyond the death of the patient and may provide an instrument through which the trustee may continue to manage the deceased patient's assets for the benefit of those who survive. The fact that a trust may survive the patient and provide continuity of management presents significant asset-transfer and estate-planning advantages.

Joint Tenancies

Joint tenancies are merely forms of joint ownership, established, for example, when one individual places funds in a deposit account or purchases other types of assets, such as securities or real property, in his or her own name and that of another person. This form of transfer or transaction technically requires a particular degree of mental capacity. Joint-tenancy relationships may continue for the lifetime of the depositor or purchaser, or they may be terminated at an earlier time through the complete withdrawal of the account or the sale of the security or real property. Depending on the creator's intent, such joint tenancies may have survivorship attributes, entitling the surviving joint tenant to the entire balance or asset on the death of the cotenant, or they may not, in which case the patient's executor or administrator is entitled to the entire balance or asset upon the creator's death. The survivorship attribute presents obvious asset-transfer and estate-planning benefits to the patient and the family.

Usually, a close family member is "placed on the account" or is added to the security certificate or deed together with the patient. Generally, however, there are no particular requirements in this regard. As an asset management instrument—although an extremely simple one—the joint arrangement permits the joint tenant to manage these assets while the patient retains mental capacity and to continue to manage them after the patient loses capacity. Although this legal form is easily created, it does, by its nature, necessitate management on an asset-by-asset basis, and management in this mode is cumbersome when there is a significant aggregation of assets to be managed. In addition, certain limitations on this form of management are imposed by the nature of the assets themselves or by the requirements of their transfer. These limitations further serve to render joint tenancies somewhat less useful as management vehicles for some assets, particularly after the patient loses mental capacity. Dividends and interest generated by stocks and bonds, for instance, may be readily endorsed and deposited to a bank account by one joint tenant. The sale or other transfer of such a security, however, generally requires the signature of both joint tenants, a requirement that presumes the competency of both signers. Similarly, although rents may be collected and expenses paid by one of the two joint owners of real estate, a sale or other transfer would require the signature and the presumed competence of both. Funds on deposit in a bank account, on the other hand, may be freely withdrawn on a single signature if the agreement with the bank so provides.

Because of their simplicity and ease of creation, forms of joint ownership, with or without rights of survivorship, are a frequently sought and commonly used form of management for the assets of one beginning to lose his or her competence because they require neither court action nor the services of an attorney. Accordingly, the families often resort to their use before seeking formal legal advice and counsel. They are a first line of defense, so to speak. But because of their inherent limitations and cumbersome nature, their use is often limited to the type of asset most readily managed by one of two cotenants, that is, the joint bank account.

Transfers with Retained Interest

A transfer with a retained interest involves the legal transfer of an asset by the patient to another while reserving to the transferor (the patient) certain legal rights to enjoy that property for some period of time—most commonly, for the rest of the patient's life. The transfer is accomplished simply by the execution of a deed of transfer from the transferor to the transferee and by the concurrent execution of a contract between them, which presumes a requisite degree of capacity. An individual would, for example, transfer the family home to a spouse or a child, while legally reserving the right to live there for life. During that period of time, the responsibilities of management, or the burdens of ownership may be shifted to the transferee by contractual agreement, while the transferor (the patient) enjoys residence, or the benefits of ownership. This transaction may involve nearly complete loss of legal control of the asset by the patient except for the privilege of residing at the property. As a management vehicle, however, the transfer with a retained interest does successfully shift the responsibility of management to another. Death terminates the rights and interests of the transferor, at which time title vests completely in the transferee, a result that presents certain advantages with respect to asset transfer and estate planning. Because this form is inherently cumbersome (certain legal difficulties may arise during the period when no one person possesses the entire title), it is infrequently used these days and is often passed over as a management vehicle in favor of the far more flexible trust instrument, which may accomplish the same results.

Outright and Complete Transfer

As its name implies, an outright and complete transfer involves the legal transfer of an asset by the patient to someone else. Unlike the transfer with retained interest described above, this transfer involves no retained legal rights. The transfer is accomplished simply by the execution of a deed of transfer from the transferor to the transferee, which presumes a requisite degree of capacity.

Usually, assets such as real estate, securities, and cash are transferred to a close family member, with the expectation that the transferred property will be managed and used for the transferor's benefit as the need arises. Although legal title formally resides in the family member, there is an understanding that the transferor will have access to the assets for life or until earlier relinquishment. However, it should be understood that, in this form, ownership as a legal matter, and accordingly, management is irrevocably transferred. The right to any continued use by the patient, such as living in the house or receiving dividends or interest, would depend on the largesse of the transferee–family-member. Thus, although a moral obligation may exist, there is no legal one. Accordingly, this transaction involves a complete loss of legal control by the patient, a loss that may produce a certain amount of anxiety. Yet, as a management vehicle, this transfer does successfully shift management responsibilities to someone else and can be effective, provided the family member honors the moral obligation. Death, although terminating the moral obligation of the transferee, is legally irrelevant to the interest and the title, a situation that presents certain advantages in asset transfer and estate planning.

In addition to these principal management vehicles, a relatively simple form of income management of social security benefits is provided by the Social Security Administration: a family member or friend may become a "representative payee" of the benefits on behalf of the patient.

Finally, although these forms have been analyzed and discussed separately, it should be emphasized that they are not mutually exclusive. They are, indeed, frequently used together as circumstances require. In fact, some combination of these forms often overcomes the inherent limitations of one particular form.

Before any of these asset management forms is used, proper consideration should be given to the integrity of the assets once they are transferred: Contrary to the intent and wishes of the patient, could the manager intentionally use the transferred assets for his or her personal benefit? Moreover, could these assets be legally attached and taken to satisfy the personal debts and obligations of the manager?

As a practical matter, it would be possible for the manager to voluntarily convert the assets and income to his or her personal use with any of these forms. In the case of guardians, conservators, agents, and trustees, however, such a possibility is considerably reduced because the manager has no personal interest in the assets; rather, as a legal matter, the manager holds them for the benefit of another or in another's right. Although the manager may have title to or mere possession of th assets, the title or possession is not personal to the manager. Instead, it is held in a representative capacity. The probability of this conversion, therefore, is not great. Even if a manager were successful in converting the assets to personal use, adequate legal remedies exist, provided someone other than the incompetent patient is available to enforce the duties of the manager. Nor is the probability of conversion particularly great in the case of the retained interest, even where the manager possesses a personal title, because of the legal nature of the retained life interest. The possibility of such a conversion is significantly increased, however, in the case of joint ownership, where the manager may have a personal interest in the jointly held property, in the form of a personal title together with the patient. This is particularly true of jointly held bank accounts, where the funds on deposit may be freely withdrawn by either joint tenant on a single signature if the agreement with the bank so provides. In such an arrangement, the chances for recovery are reduced somewhat. In the case of an outright transfer, the possibility of conversion is substantially increased because the manager has sole legal title to the assets transferred and the patient has no legal interests whatsoever and, effectively, no legal remedy. Personal trust, a necessary prerequisite to the establishment of any of these relationships, is particularly important in joint tenancies and outright transfers.

As a legal matter, the assets held by a guardian, a conservator, an agent, or a trustee cannot be attached and applied to the personal obligations of the manager because the manager does not hold them in a personal capacity. The same is not true, however, of joint ownership, where the manager may hold title personally, although with another; of retained interests, where the manager holds title personally, subject to retained rights (a life interest); nor of outright transfers, where the manager holds complete title personally. Accordingly, depending on the nature and extent of the creditor's and the spouse's rights within any particular jurisdiction, these assets themselves may be vulnerable to some degree of involuntary conversion. Of these arrangements, the patient's retained life estate would be the most difficult to affect directly and would therefore be the most secure. Nevertheless, the personal circumstances of the manager, both financial and domestic, should be carefully considered before the establishment of any relationship, particularly joint tenancies and outright transfers.

Reflections

Although this section has concentrated on a few of the more important considerations of asset management for the DAT patient and the family, it should be emphasized that asset management decisions made at this stage may also significantly affect later patient care and estate planning. If possible, asset management decisions should be made in the larger context of the requirements that will be felt during the rest of the patient's life and beyond.

HEALTH CARE AND MANAGEMENT OF THE ALZHEIMER'S PATIENT

The Nature of the Problem

As Alzheimer's disease continues to run its course, and the attendant mental deterioration increases, patients gradually begin to experience increasingly serious difficulties in making appropriate decisions and judgments regarding their own personal physical care.

Initially, for example, the patient's selection of clothing may be inappropriate for the season, and personal hygiene may begin to deteriorate. Such personal difficulties, though embarrassing, may be easily remedied with varying degrees of daily assistance from a family member or a visiting professional.

But as the deterioration progresses, the lapses and forgetfulness may become more threatening. Range burners may be left unattended. The distinction between red and green traffic lights may not be as clear as fellow motorists would prefer. Worse, the patient may wander away from home and may become confused and hopelessly lost. It may, indeed, become physically dangerous for the patient to live alone—to function without some supervision. Moreover, the patient's irrational behavior, previously confined to relatively harmless matters, may now begin to manifest itself in a far more serious and potentially dangerous manner—in a refusal, for instance, to relinquish the automobile keys when driving has become a hazard; in a refusal to seek appropriate medical assistance and treatment when they are required; and in a refusal to consider alternate living arrangements when the current living accommodations are no longer appropriate. The patient's potential for self-harm or the harm of others and the potential of legal liability both to the patient and to the patient's family become a source of significant concern to the patient's family. Once this risk has been acknowledged, appropriate measures must be taken immediately to remedy the situation and to reduce the exposure of the patient.

General Considerations

At this point in the course of the disease, as patients begin to lose their capacity to care for themselves physically, the family must think beyond the mere management of assets and income, which may have occupied much of their time and attention thus far, and must focus on personal care, a far more demanding and emotionally draining set of considerations. In view of the increasing incapacity of the patient, what are to be the immediate and long-range objectives of her or his physical care?

Of immediate concern is the physical security of the patient. The initial objective, then, is to provide a safe living environment for the patient. Although full-time custodial care may ultimately prove necessary, the disease will progress through numerous stages before such extensive care is required. Initially, the patient may need the assistance of a companion for unsupervised times of the day, and later perhaps the services of a day-care center. Whatever the level of the disease's advance, the present and future physical needs of the patient will require study and the assurance of a continuing safe environment.

Once the physical security issues are considered, attention must turn to continuing medical treatment throughout the disease's progression. The patient will require medical attention for the normal processes of aging, not to mention the manifestations of DAT. Not all patients are cooperative with and agreeable to treatment.

Ultimately, patients become incapable of functioning at all without continual twenty-four-hour supervision. Completely unable to care for themselves, they become as needy as newborn infants. But unlike those of newborns, their needs are difficult to meet within the normal household environment. It is not unusual for patients to have irregular sleep patterns, to become violent and uncooperative, to be in almost constant motion, and, in general, to disrupt normal daily family routines.

In an ideal world, such people would continue to live within their familiar and comfortable home settings, sur-

rounded by loved ones able to tend to their increasing physical needs. Unfortunately, the realities of the disease, together with the complexities of present-day living, makes it
unlikely that either the family members or the desired environment will be adequate to the full care of the patient.
When, inevitably, the patient requires twenty-four-hour care
within an environment made safe for Alzheimer's patients,
even the most loving and tireless of family members will be
unable to sustain this herculean effort. Moreover, even if
twenty-four-hour private nursing care could be found and
afforded, such care might not be possible nor even desirable
within the family home. Probably, the patient's move to a
health-care facility will become the best solution.

When it is time for such critical decisions to be made
concerning a patient's physical care and management, it
would be preferable if the patient were both willing and able
to make them. Given the progressively degenerative nature
of the disease, however, it is unlikely that he or she will be
mentally competent either to make such decisions personally
or to designate another to make them instead.

Accordingly, someone will have to make those decisions
on behalf of the patient without the patient's advice and consent. The family must then consider who will undertake to
make those personal management decisions and what form,
legal or otherwise, that management will take. In the absence
of personal decision-making, there are generally three
sources of decision-making authority: judicial determination,
personal grant, and *de facto* management.

Management Forms

Judicial Determination: Guardianship

When the patient can no longer make appropriate decisions concerning his or her physical care, it may be necessary

to seek the authority to make those decisions from the courts in the form of a legal guardianship, previously considered in the section on asset management together with the other form of judicial appointment, the conservatorship.

In the case of Alzheimer's disease, the diagnosis may have been made sufficiently early to enable the family to institute a conservatorship, so that someone appointed by the court could manage the patient's assets. Early in the course of the disease, while still possessed of sufficient mental capacity, the patient himself or herself could personally institute such a proceeding. By the time the DAT patient is unable to physically care for himself or herself, however, the conservatorship is no longer an appropriate legal vehicle, and guardianship is generally the only legal alternative available in most states for the care and management of the Alzheimer's disease patient. If such a conservatorship was, indeed, established earlier in the course of the disease as a form of asset management, such a form may readily be "upgraded" to that of a guardianship by judicial decree when the requisite degree of mental deterioration has been reached and custody and control of the patient are at issue.

Accordingly, the guardian will have physical custody of both the assets and the person and will be charged with the complete responsibility of making decisions with respect to that person, much as a parent acts on behalf of a minor child. Originally, guardianships were initiated most frequently on behalf of minors. As our society ages and becomes more mobile, more and more guardianships are being instituted on behalf of elders. Typically, extended families are no longer available to care for aged relatives. Although many elderly people are able to care for themselves throughout their lives, increasing numbers need someone (or some institution) to care for them properly.

Just as the population of elderly people has grown, so

has the incidence of elder abuse, and guardianship is a mechanism designed to prevent the exploitation of a person and her or his property. In a number of jurisdictions, statutes provide public guardianships for those who do not have friends or relatives to assume the watchdog role.

Making a determination that a friend or a relative needs a legal guardian is often difficult emotionally. When an adult patient becomes a ward, she or he is reduced to the legal status of a child. The ward no longer controls her or his own property and can no longer drive a car, manage money, write checks, or consent to or refuse medical treatment. The guardian determines where the ward will live and every other significant aspect of the ward's life.

The decision to apply for guardianship is often emotionally difficult for yet another reason. Currently, Alzheimer's disease is not recognized *per se* as a category under which guardianship is granted. Therefore, those seeking guardianship for the DAT patient must "fit" the patient into another category, typically that of the "mentally ill." It may be extremely difficult for the family or the friends of the Alzheimer's patient to consider their loved one "mentally ill," and to petition the courts on that basis. Currently, however, there is a national movement to establish a neurological category for guardianship determination.

As previously mentioned, the responsibilities of a guardian encompass a broad spectrum, from the care and management of the patient's assets to the care and management of the person of the ward. The law is very specific about these responsibilities as they relate to the ward's assets. The guardian is charged by the court to identify these assets, to take physical possession of them, and to submit an inventory of them to the court. The guardian is then responsible to the court for the management and conservation of these assets as well as for their expenditure. Moreover, the guardian is responsible to the courts for the expenditure of income produced by these assets as well as income received from other sources. First and foremost, the guardian must always act in the best interests of the ward and must not permit personal interests to stand in conflict with this duty.

The court supervises the guardian's activities through such mechanisms as required annual accountings and petitions to the court for extraordinary expenditures or changes in investment strategies. Procedures may vary according to the type of asset held. Some jurisdictions use a special court-appointed official, known as a *guardian ad litem,* to review the guardianship activities on a periodic basis, as well as in extraordinary situations, and to report to the court.

As might well be imagined, it is easier to establish guidelines for the management of fiscal matters than it is to set guidelines for personal care. It is not unusual, therefore, to discover among the states that the law is less specific about the guardian's responsibilities toward the person than it is toward the person's assets. Historically, it was assumed that the guardian had the best interests of the ward in mind, and unless served with a court order, the guardian was under no obligation to report to the court on the physical or personal status of the ward. There has been a recent trend, however, for the courts to appoint a guardian *ad litem* to review significant decisions with respect to the ward's physical status and condition, particularly with regard to the giving or withholding of medical treatment.

Although not usually prescribed by the court, the guardian may expect to be involved, with the caregiver, in day-to-day patient management. The guardian may be responsible for locating and investigating day-care programs, nursing homes, medical doctors, and other facilities. The guardian may also be involved in the coordination of care activities, particularly for those DAT patients who do not require twenty-four-hour institutional care. For example, although day-care programs may be available, the hours may not correspond with the work schedules of the primary caregiver with whom the DAT patient lives. Arrangements for care and transportation may have to be made to cover the "gap" at the beginning and/or the end of the day.

In addition, the guardian may be the person who has to make the decision to place the ward in a nursing home. Although considerations of cost may appear to be a paramount concern, the quality and type of care are also highly significant and extremely sensitive issues. DAT patients often need a physical environment that allows them to wander without harm to themselves or to other patients. Therefore, it may be difficult to find nursing homes equipped to meet the needs of patients who are not yet bedridden or heavily medicated, and the guardian may anticipate spending a great deal of time arranging for the physical care of the DAT patient, whether at home or in a health-care facility.

Although guardians can make routine decisions about medical treatment, sometimes medical-care institutions and the courts require special authorization to administer certain drugs in nonemergencies. In certain stages of the disease, for example, the patient may experience severe agitation, and the doctor may wish to use antipsychotic medication. In addition, guardians will need to seek judicial permission when decisions need to be made about the withholding or giving of extraordinary medical treatment.

Personal Grant of Decision-Making Authority: Power of Attorney

If Alzheimer's is diagnosed while the patient still has the mental capacity to make decisions regarding his or her assets and personal care, the patient may empower another indi-

vidual to make such decisions when he or she becomes incapable, through the use of the special form of agency agreement known as the *durable power of attorney*, previously
considered in the foregoing section on *inter vivos* asset management. Such a power may accordingly become an informal
alternative to the formality of the judicially determined
guardianship.

Customarily, powers of attorney—both traditional and
durable—have been used for asset management and for financial or estate planning (to be discussed below). Such
powers, however, have been used far less frequently for the
management of the principal's person. Though principals
may specifically designate their conservators or guardians in
their powers of attorney, such designations are nonetheless
generally accorded the judicial status of nominations—that
is, mere expressions of intent and preference—which must
be judicially confirmed. Unless there is good and sufficient
reason not to appoint the nominee and thus to honor the
request of the patient (such as, for example, a conflict of
interest), such nominations routinely receive judicial confirmation.

There is, however, an increasing awareness nationwide
of the need for medical powers to be included within the
scope of agency powers. In recognition of this need, several
states have recently legislated a durable power specifically for
health care. Provided the power is executed in accordance
with statutory requirements, the agent is empowered to
make health-care decisions for the principal, including the
power to give or withhold medical treatment, as would a
court-appointed guardian. Unfortunately, this form is not
available in all states. Given the pressing need for such an
alternative, however, it is anticipated that such form may
soon become more widely available.

De Facto Management

Guardianships and durable powers of attorney may not always prove to be absolutely necessary for the personal management of the Alzheimer's patient. Many nursing homes do not require that there be a guardian to authorize the admission of patients or to approve routine care and treatment, although more and more private institutions are, indeed, requiring this kind of authorization. As a purely practical matter, medical practitioners may simply accept the judgment of the immediate family with respect to ordinary care and treatment, particularly where there is agreement among family members, and where the patient is cooperative. Such acceptance would obviously save on the considerable expenditure of time, emotional energy, and financial resources necessary to obtain a judicially appointed guardian.

Sometimes, however, there is no choice but to seek a judicial determination. The DAT patient, for example, may insist on a course of action that would jeopardize her or his safety and the safety of others, the family members may not be in accord on a particular course of action, or the health provider may require authority. Perhaps it would be fair to say that the proliferation of lawsuits in recent years has resulted in a cautionary approach by the medical community with respect to such decisions. Without proper authority, it is unlikely that any medical facility will authorize a treatment program that may be subject to question, criticism, and ultimately to litigation.

It would seem, though, that before taking the formal guardianship approach to patient management, it would make sense to ask the particular health-care facility about its practices and procedures. It may well be that a little foresight and planning among family members and the facility will obviate the necessity of the "legal" alternative and permit the patient and the family to use simple, pragmatic solutions to questions of health care and management.

Reflections

This section has reviewed a few of the more important considerations of health care and management for the DAT patient and the family, as well as a few of the options available to them for addressing these issues. However, it should be emphasized once again that all of the issues and concerns connected with Alzheimer's disease should be considered together, and not in isolation.

INTER VIVOS ESTATE PLANNING

The Nature of the Problem

At some point during the patient's deterioration, the family will eventually seek medical assistance, and in due course, a diagnosis will be made. At that time, the patient's prognosis will become clear. As there is at present no cure for DAT, there will be no recovery. The disease will inexorably run its course—in some more slowly than in others, yet the result will be the same. The patient will not survive. The considerations of the family must now transcend the mere management of assets and issues of physical care, which thus far may have occupied much of their time. Attention must now focus on issues concerning the patient's inevitable death, and the family must now certainly begin to focus on considerations of estate planning, that is, what will happen to the patient's assets and sources of income before and after the patient's death.

General Estate-Planning Objectives

Many individuals tend to view estate planning as inherently death-oriented, that is, as being principally concerned with the distribution of persons' property upon their death. Reinforcing this view are, of course, the myriad of traditional estate-planning objectives normally considered by estate planners, including the orderly transfer of the patient's property to those who will receive it, the subsequent management of assets for those who will receive them, the minimization of taxes, and the avoidance of costly and time-consuming probate entanglements—all essentially death-oriented issues. This widely held view of estate planning is unfortunate. Its scope is too restricted and is therefore inaccurate.

Conceptually, estate planning is a much broader and more comprehensive subject. All families should have a basic plan that essentially organizes family resources. Optimally, such a plan should use the family's resources to achieve their personal and financial objectives, whatever they may be, and to protect the family during times of personal and financial crisis. Clearly, such objectives are not exclusively death-oriented. They also include such lifetime issues as the education of children or the significant reduction of family income due to the disability of a key member. Thus, the decisions to purchase a health and disability insurance policy or to save a certain percentage of disposable income are as much a part of estate planning as the purchase of a life insurance policy or the making of a will. Similarly, the decision to purchase a second home or to send a child to college is a family-estate-planning issue because it requires the marshaling of family resources for particular purposes that will ultimately have an impact on future decisions. From this broader perspective, it should be clear that a family estate plan ought not to be limited simply to a plan for eventual death; rather, it ought to be a lifetime plan that carries through after death.

Ideally, then, estate planning encompasses more than the mere distribution of property. It covers its acquisition, use, and conservation, as well as its distribution, in such a way that it will best provide for the personal and financial needs of the family members. For purposes of analysis, comprehensive estate-planning should have at least two components: (1) a so-called *inter vivos* estate or financial plan, which is the creation of an estate, its maintenance and conservation, and its use to provide support and security for the family, a process that reflects in a number of significant ways the current popular trend in financial planning, and (2) the traditional estate plan, a so-called postmortem estate plan, which provides for the distribution of the estate thus created, used, and preserved.

General *inter Vivos* Estate-Planning Considerations

Unfortunately for the DAT patient and family, by the time Alzheimer's is finally diagnosed there is, in most cases, little opportunity for further estate creation; rather, the concern will be to protect and to manage what there is—the conservation, management, and use of the then-existing patient and family resources for the benefit of the patient and the patient's family during the remainder of the patient's lifetime.

The lifetime, or *inter vivos*, planning aspect of the Alzheimer's estate plan should, therefore, have at least two principal objectives, among others: (1) current asset management for the benefit of the patient, previously considered, and (2) future asset preservation for the needs of the patient, the patient's spouse, and others for whom the patient may be financially responsible, as well as for the benefit of the patient's heirs.

There will, of course, also be the previously mentioned array of traditional postmortem estate-planning objectives that are normally considered by estate planners and that clearly should be considered by the patient, if the patient is still capable, and by the patient's family. These will be considered in detail in the following section.

In the accomplishment of all of these objectives, both *inter vivos* and postmortem, estate planning for the DAT patient is not entirely dissimilar from estate planning for anyone else. There are, however, two potentially troublesome issues that set the DAT estate plan apart: the loss of mental capacity and the possibility of long-term custodial care. It is the continually deteriorating mental condition of the patient, together with the potential for extraordinary long-term health costs, that adds a unique and somewhat difficult perspective to the DAT estate plan in particular. Their presence adds an air of critical urgency to the creation of the plan.

By the time the nature and the extent of the problem are finally appreciated and the family eventually seeks legal advice, the degree of mental capacity required for many components of a well-designed estate plan may be rapidly diminishing or may, tragically, be absent. The estate planner may therefore have severely limited options available with which to cope with the inevitable. This loss of capacity and, therefore, of planning options places a significant premium on early planning.

Moreover, because the expenses of the extended type of custodial care generally required by an advanced Alzheimer's patient are now covered neither by Medicare nor adequately by the few private insurance contracts that provide for long term care, and because Medicaid benefits are available only to those who qualify under severely restrictive financial qualification tests that permit minimally available assets and income, the patient and the patient's family whose personal financial resources are inadequate to cover such costs are confronted with potential impoverishment. In the absence of proper lifetime estate-planning, a healthy spouse could be left with inadequate financial resources for support. Dependent children could be deprived of an anticipated education, and subsequent generations could be unintentionally but unavoidably disinherited. The patient's estate having been depleted by the payment of health-care expenses, there would simply be no estate remaining for transmission on the death of the patient. Accordingly, in anticipation of potentially devastating custodial expenses, the estate plan of the Alzheimer's patient with limited personal financial resources should include a careful consideration of the availability of public resources, that is, the legal qualifications of the patient for public medical assistance within the public welfare laws and regulations.

Thus, although estate planning may traditionally have focused principally on property distribution and occasionally on *inter vivos* matters, the continual mental deterioration of Alzheimer's patients, together with their potential extended confinement to a health-care facility at exorbitant cost, places an extraordinary premium on *inter vivos* estate-planning for the Alzheimer's patient, perhaps even more than in any other estate-planning context.

Mental Capacity Issues

Overshadowing all aspects of a comprehensive patient plan is the mental capacity of the Alzheimer's patient, which is usually in a state of continual deterioration throughout the planning process. Virtually all of the planning objectives of the DAT patient, *inter vivos* or postmortem, involve the present transfer of property or the present provision for a future transfer, regardless of the extent of the estate.

It is widely understood that a certain degree of mental capacity is required for the execution of a valid last will and testament. Without such capacity, the will cannot effectively provide for property transfer at death. What may not be as widely understood is that a particular degree of mental capacity, perhaps even higher, is also required for all *inter vivos* transfers, whether outright, in trust, or with a retained interest. If the required degree of capacity is absent at the time of the transfer, a patient will be deemed legally incompetent to effect a transfer, and any transfers made by such a patient, individually, will lack full legal force and effect. Accordingly, if a patient is to effect immediate property transfers for asset management and preservation purposes, or to provide for a future transfer by will at death, it is critical that such transfers or arrangements be accomplished while sufficient capacity remains.

For a variety of reasons, not all individuals are equally disposed to begin immediate transfers. Nonetheless, for the DAT patient, timing is crucial. If, however, Alzheimer's is diagnosed sufficiently early, while the patient still retains the necessary mental capacity to make decisions regarding her or his assets, another option may be available. As an alternative to effecting immediate transfers, the patient may empower another individual (through the use of the "durable" power of attorney, "springing" or immediately effective) to make such decisions when the patient eventually becomes incapable. Among other practical applications, the "durable" power, whenever effective, can be used as a funding device in conjunction with a specialized form of *inter vivos* trust, popularly known as the *convertible trust*. Designed essentially to be funded and to begin its management functions upon its creator's incapacity, and to "convert" several of its key elements in response to this disability, the so-called convertible trust has the various attributes common to *inter vivos* trusts generally that were discussed in detail in the section on asset management—in particular, the flexibility to respond to a multitude of objectives.

Because the durable power of attorney survives the incompetency of the principal (the patient), it provides a suitable alternative in that situation to nonaction or to court-authorized action, that is, the conservatorship or guardianship. The "durable" power offers a variety of advantages. It is an inherently simple document that requires little time or expense to prepare. Provided its authority is accepted, its use may be simple and uncomplicated. Nevertheless, the use of these powers may, indeed, become quite sophisticated, particularly when combined with other devices such as the *inter vivos* trust. Their flexibility and ease of creation and use permit them to accomplish a variety of objectives for the DAT patient.

These powers are not without their limitations. An agent may not, for example, execute a will for the patient. Yet when compared to the advantages, the deficiencies appear to be slight. Accordingly, regardless of the size or composition of the assets or the ultimate objectives of any particular DAT patient, it would seem prudent to consider the use of a "durable" power while the patient still has the capacity to execute one.

If, however, Alzheimer's is diagnosed late in its course, and in particular after the patient has lost the necessary mental capacity to make decisions regarding her or his assets, the planning options, unfortunately, become severely circumscribed. Lacking the mental capacity to transfer the assets personally or to delegate another to do so, the patient can take virtually no action legally with respect to the transfer of her or his own assets. Moreover, with perhaps the obvious exception of the withdrawal of an entire bank account by the competent cotenant, there is also little that the patient's cotenants, individually, can do legally with respect to the transfer of assets that they own jointly with the patient. Furthermore, depending on the relative level of incapacity, the execution of any kind of estate-planning document, such as a will, may well be beyond the capacity of the patient. The only remaining option in most states may be the establishment of a conservatorship or a guardianship to effect such transfers.

As was previously discussed, the responsibilities of this court-appointed fiduciary may encompass a broad spectrum, from the care and management of the patient's assets to the care and management of the person of the ward (the patient). Usually, the law is very specific about these responsibilities, as they relate to the ward's assets in particular. Among other enumerated duties, the fiduciary is responsible for assuming control of all the patient's assets and for their proper management, conservation, and expenditure. First and foremost, the fiduciary must always act in the best interests of the ward and must not permit personal or other interests to stand in conflict with these duties. The interests of the spouse, the children, and other family members are, at best, secondary considerations.

Once the fiduciary is appointed by the court, any further

financial arrangements, such as asset transfer, must be accomplished under the aegis of the court, that is, with its advice and consent. Although the courts generally permit the use of those assets and income not specifically required for the ward's own personal maintenance to be "used" for the "support" of the ward's spouse and other dependents, any "divestiture" of the ward's property for "preservation" purposes, however small, would be inherently inimical to the express duties and responsibilities of the fiduciary and would probably not be approved by the court.

Some states, however, recognize that such an inflexible approach to the management of an incompetent's assets is both unrealistic and unnecessary. As a result, several states provide statutory authority for the creation of an estate plan for the benefit of an incompetent person by that person's guardian or conservator. Such statutory authority may, in addition, specifically provide for gifts of the ward's property in certain circumstances as part of the estate plan. These gifts may include the *inter vivos* transfer of those assets not required for adequate support of the ward to those persons likely to receive them upon the ward's death. Although it is extremely unlikely that a court would permit the kind of transfers that may be envisioned in this particular planning context (that is, the complete or nearly complete divestiture of assets or any interest in them for purposes of Medicaid eligibility, which is considered next), it is conceivable that the court might permit some assets, those in excess of need, to be removed from harm's way. Such estate-planning authority, however, is not yet available in all states.

The disadvantages of guardianships and conservatorships are numerous and perhaps obvious. Inherently cumbersome and inflexible in administration, they are expensive to maintain because of the substantial amount of professional time necessary to comply with the extensive statutory re-

quirements. Moreover, any action requiring judicial authorization, including the initial appointment, is subject to the
conventional delays inherent in any court proceeding, not to
mention unanticipated delays. Although the use of a guardianship or a conservatorship may be rendered unavoidable
because of the lack of capacity of the patient or intrafamily
disagreement, other alternatives should be investigated initially, and if suitable, they should be used.

Health Cost Issues

There may still be some families who have enough financial resources to absorb the extraordinary costs of extended
health care and still to provide adequately for the financial
requirements of a spouse and others who are economically
dependent on the family unit. Given the sheer magnitude of
the expenses, it is unlikely that there are many such families.
Although the specific costs of extended care obviously vary
from locale to locale, minimal estimates in the range of
$20,000–$25,000 annually are commonplace, and in many locations, the annual costs are considerably higher. No two
family situations, however, are alike. Not all patients will
require a similar degree of care for similar periods of time, nor
are their financial and personal resources similar. But all families, regardless of the nature and extent of their resources,
should develop a financial plan to meet the crisis and to deal
with it as best they can. Accordingly, when confronted with
the probability of extended custodial health care for a family
member, each family should analyze its own requirements
and its available resources.

Generally, any such analysis would seem to have at least
two principal components: an analysis of the present and
future physical management needs of the patient, together
with an estimate of their cost, and an analysis of the family

resources, financial and personal, that can be assembled to meet these needs.

Physical Management Needs. Because of the nature of Alzheimer's disease, a family may well anticipate that a patient will ultimately live in an infantile status for some time, requiring twenty-four-hour custodial care. As the disease progresses, however, the patient will pass through numerous stages of care before reaching this advanced stage. Initially, however, the present physical needs of the patient must be assessed and met. Thereafter, the family should consult with the attending medical practitioner to develop an understanding of the course of the disease—to ascertain what medical and corresponding behavior changes may be expected over the course of the disease and the time frame within which each may be anticipated. Because the disease seems to run its course erratically, in some more slowly than in others, definitive answers and precise projections are not possible. Moreover, even tentative answers to these questions depend on many variables, such as the age and the physical condition of the particular patient at the onset of the disease. But even the most speculative of timetables, together with an understanding of symptomatic conditions, will be extremely useful for planning purposes. Prepared with this information, however indefinite, the family can begin to project the patient's future physical needs and their attendant costs, and of course, a periodic examination and updated prognosis will help to confirm the rate of the disease's advance.

Once an appreciation of the progressive physical needs and requirements of the patient is developed, a corresponding set of caregiver needs may be formulated—the kind of care that will be required at each successive stage of the disease, as well as the physical and personal resources of the family and the community available to meet these projected needs. Many of the issues associated with the physical care of the DAT patient have been considered in greater detail in the section on health care and management. It was suggested there that the capacity of the family alone to provide total home care would probably be exceeded by the ultimate demands of the patient. Even the deepest emotional commitment and determination and even the most herculean physical effort may be unable to surmount the endless succession of "thirty-six-hour days." At the very least, the patient will eventually require skilled twenty-four-hour nursing care within the home or within a long-term care facility. In the short run, however, the patient may simply need homemaker care, later perhaps a companion ("baby-sitter"), and still later the services of a day-care center, if one exists within the community. Accordingly, the availability within the patient's community of each anticipated kind of caregiver should be examined, as well as the attendant costs. Although the available information will probably be restricted to current cost levels, anticipated inflationary increases must be factored into the equation. Medical insurance policies may cover "some" of the costs for a "limited" period of time, and therefore, families should review the extent of their policy coverage with their insurance carriers. In addition, some states and local communities now have special programs to assist families with home nursing and homemaker needs. Older American programs are excellent repositories of information on the availability of such care resources within a particular area.

Having assessed the current and expected needs of the patient, together with their projected costs over the anticipated lifetime of the patient, the family will now perhaps more fully understand and appreciate the magnitude of the financial and personal commitment that faces them. Attention may now be focused on the nature and extent of the resources they have to cope with that commitment.

Resource Availability. A systematic inventory of family assets, together with present and future sources of income, is a necessary prerequisite to any orderly estate-planning process. Accordingly, one should be prepared. Families with substantial financial resources may already have this information readily available through records held by their attorney, accountant, security broker, or financial planner. Families that have previously engaged in this process through the creation of an estate or financial plan may also have ready access to such information. Moreover, the DAT patient's family, in particular, may have previously compiled this information earlier in the course of the disease in response to a need to provide some degree of asset and income managerial assistance to the patient. On the other hand, the patient's family may unfortunately be starting from scratch at this point. As a result of a person's lifelong financial habits or of the behavior modifications incidental to Alzheimer's disease, accessibility of information may become a critical issue. Simply locating the patient's assets and sources of income and other relevant information may prove to be a formidable challenge. If the patient is unable to help in this compilation, however, the patient's income tax returns will generally prove to be an excellent source of information because of the variety of data required on completed returns.

Whatever the starting point and the availability of information, however, the product should optimally be both a comprehensive and a highly detailed inventory of assets and sources of income that embraces every facet of the family's resources (not merely the patient's alone), and that includes not only what they currently have but what they anticipate receiving (or even losing) at some time in the future. Such an inventory will take into consideration such present holdings as real estate, securities, cash, insurance, interests in business ventures, tangible personal property, salary, trust and other income, *and* such future matters as the receipt of anticipated inheritances, pensions, and entitlements, as well as the possible loss of the patient's salary. Moreover, the inventory should include such detailed specific information as the precise type of asset, the account or security number, the acquisition date and value as well as a recent valuation, and the form of ownership (individually or together with others as joint tenants or as tenants in common). It should also include the income, if any, produced by such assets, together with the frequency of income payment—monthly or quarterly, for example.

In addition to the inventory of financial resources, the family should also prepare an inventory of personal—or perhaps more accurately, "personnel"—resources. Within the immediate or extended family, are there persons available to provide varying degrees of care to the patient on a regular basis during any given stage of the degenerative process? Because of age, occupation, inclination, or family status, there may be members of the family who can and are willing to devote valuable time to the care and management of the patient, thereby conserving precious financial resources.

Once the inventory of family resources, financial and otherwise, has been completed, a similarly comprehensive and highly detailed inventory of family liabilities should be prepared that embraces every facet of the family's living expenses. Families of whatever financial means should have this information readily available in the family checkbook. Whatever the source of information, the result should be an inventory that includes not only current expenses and obligations but those that are anticipated at some time in the future. Such an inventory should take into consideration not only mortgage or rent, utilities, food, clothing, transportation, medical, and other current expenditures, but such future commitments and obligations as the education of children and the health-care requirements of the patient's spouse.

When completed and compared, these two inventories

should provide a reasonably clear picture of the family's current net worth and estimated annual gross and net income, as well as those of the patient, individually. Moreover, there should be an equally clear picture of the changes in asset and income levels that may be anticipated as a result of retirements, bequests, and other future events. That picture, then, may be compared with the anticipated financial requirements of the DAT patient. If the family resources fall short, as may well be expected, or even if they marginally exceed projected patient needs, it would seem prudent for the family to give serious consideration to the availability of public financial assistance.

Overview of Public Welfare

Any consideration of the availability of public financial assistance must begin with an understanding of the pattern of Medicaid and Medicare.

Medicare. The federal health insurance program is designed to assist those who are receiving social security retirement benefits as well as those who are receiving social security disability benefits for a requisite period of time. Medicare pays for necessary doctors' services and for necessary inpatient hospital care. Generally, however, coverage is extremely limited for inpatient skilled nursing-home care and for home-health-agency care in a patient's home and, in particular, for the kind of custodial care required by the Alzheimer's patient.

Medicaid. The medical assistance program administered by the various states with federal aid is designed to assist only those with extremely limited financial resources. Although Medicaid pays for a broad range of medical and medically related services, including extended nursing-home care, a person must qualify under a variety of tests and special rules in order to be eligible to receive such assistance.

Generally, to qualify for Medicaid benefits an individual or a couple must be both categorically and financially eligible. To be categorically eligible, an individual must be over the age of sixty-five and blind or disabled as defined by Social Security Administration regulations. To be financially eligible, an individual or couple must qualify under an asset test as well as an income test, both of which establish maximum acceptable levels.

On July 1, 1988, the Medicare Catastrophic Coverage Act of 1988 (MCCA) became law. This Act not only expanded Medicare benefits, but also made significant changes to the Medicaid program, particularly with respect to eligibility. Some provisions of the law do not become effective until September 30, 1989, while other provisions arguably became effective on July 1, 1988. The following review of the statutory and regulatory framework of Medicaid, although necessarily general in scope, must therefore include both the Medicaid eligibility rules as they currently exist as well as the impact of MCCA on Medicaid eligibility and on the financial and estate planning strategies used to deal with the rules.

Current Medicaid Eligibility Requirements

Treatment of income. Subject to certain exclusions, an individual's income may not exceed a specified monthly level (currently $469) that is subject to periodic increases, and a couple's income may not exceed a slightly higher level. If the income of an individual or a couple exceeds these levels, they may still qualify to receive Medicaid benefits provided that, under certain circumstances, they personally incur a specified amount of medical expense. This so-called spend-down provision effectively requires applicants to spend the difference between their actual income and the permissible level on medical expenses. Although only one spouse may apply for Medicaid benefits (the DAT patient, for example), the respective individual incomes of both spouses (their separate pensions, for example) are considered initially in determining the eligibility of the individual applicant.

Treatment of assets, generally. Subject to certain exclusions, an individual is not permitted to own assets valued in excess of $2,000, and a couple, in excess of $3,000. For purposes of qualifying for medical assistance, Medicaid regulations divide all assets into two categories: those assets that are considered for eligibility (so-called countable assets) and those that are not (noncountable or "exempt" assets). The category of exempt assets principally includes, among others, a home used as a principal place of residence, household items (such as appliances, furniture, and furnishings), personal property (such as clothing, jewelry, and books), one automobile, life insurance with a face value of $1,500 or less, certain assets specifically designated for burial, and certain so-called inaccessible assets (such as term life insurance and *certain* types of irrevocable trusts). Virtually all other assets, real and personal, tangible or intangible, are considered in determining an applicant's eligibility.

The foregoing asset valuation levels are also subject to the so-called spend-down provisions applicable to excessive income. Accordingly, if the value of such "countable" assets exceeds the specified level, the applicant may expend the excessive amount on medical expenses in order to qualify for assistance.

Treatment of joint assets. Jointly held assets create their own set of issues for determining eligibility and therefore receive somewhat different treatment. Because under banking rules and regulations, either owner of a joint bank account may freely withdraw the entire amount standing on deposit, Medicaid regulations *presume* that the entire account belongs to the applicant. Accordingly, the entire account is considered in determining eligibility whether or not the spouses reside together and even though the applicant's spouse or other joint tenant—such as the applicant's child, for example—actually contributed a portion of the funds to the account from that cotenant's personal sources. On the other hand, because the action of all joint tenants is generally required for the sale or other disposition of virtually all other types of jointly held assets, such as securities and real estate, Medicaid regulations *presume* that merely an equal share of the particular asset, rather than the entire asset, belongs to the applicant. Accordingly, the proportionate share of such a joint interest is considered in determining eligibility, again whether or not the spouses reside together and even though the applicant's spouse or other joint tenant actually contributed a proportionately greater amount from his or her personal resources. Either of these two presumptions regarding the joint ownership of assets may be overcome by demonstrating a different proportion of contribution to the account or other asset, and only that portion actually belonging to the applicant will be considered. Although the burden is on the applicant to prove the actual contribution, this verification may usually be made by any documentation tending to verify a source other than the applicant, such as, for example, social security records indicating a source of income and probate records indicating an inheritance. In the absence of such documented proof, under certain circumstances a simple sworn affidavit may be acceptable.

The foregoing is intended to provide merely a general overview of the current Medicaid statutory and regulatory framework as it relates to the application for medical assistance. Within this framework, there exists a wide latitude for interpretation, as well as a broad diversity of approaches to these matters among the various states. Depending on a particular state's attitude toward welfare assistance generally, the public policy of the various jurisdictions spans the spectrum from the very liberal to the ultraconservative. The practical application of the various laws and regulations reflects this diversity. However much room there may be for interpretation, and whatever the individual state approach to these matters, liberal or conservative, one fact is unavoidably and undeniably clear: To qualify for public assistance, within the broad design of the Medicaid program as it was constituted prior to the passage of MCCA, one must be impoverished or become so.

Although "spending" a patient and a family into virtual poverty does achieve the objective of eligibility for public assistance, its impact—financial, psychological, and social—is far more extensive. With minimally available assets and income, the patient essentially becomes completely dependent on the services provided by the Medicaid program and, for all practical purposes, financially unable to provide for those personal necessities not covered by the program. Such dependence, however, may not be limited to the patient alone. Depending on the family's financial arrangements at the time the patient begins to incur extraordinary expenses, the spouse and perhaps the dependent children may become dependent on other welfare programs, such as SSI, and also financially unable to provide for personal necessities, much less such extensive commitments as a college education. The consequence of this application could well be the placement of an entire family, not just a patient, on welfare, and perhaps for a period of time far longer than the limited life expectancy of the patient. The financial impact notwithstanding, the psychological impact of such a consequence would be devastating to the family, and the resulting social impact could be extensive.

The conclusion evidently to be drawn from this analysis is that an individual must either have sufficient personal and family financial resources to support annual nursing-home expenses while still adequately providing for a spouse and other dependents or lose whatever financial resources are available for the family unit. One must either rely exclusively on personal resources or spend oneself and perhaps one's family into exclusive reliance on public resources. There would appear to be no middle ground. Because the vast majority of families could not sustain such a financial burden for any length of time, the family faces financial ruin—their accumulated lifetime savings wiped out. [It should be noted at this point that the enactment of the Medicare Catastrophic Coverage Act of 1988 (MCCA) in July was largely in response to the financial plight of spouses and other members of the dependent family unit facing impoverishment as a result of extraordinary uncovered health care expenses.]

The current alternatives are equally unattractive—one practically unattainable by most, the other manifestly undesirable by any. If they were the only alternatives, the prospects for most patients' families would be bleak indeed. Fortunately, however, they are not the only options currently available. Perhaps an obvious compromise would be to achieve Medicaid eligibility while still retaining some measure of continuing benefits from assets and income—all without the potential financial hardship and deprivation to other family members that sometimes appear unavoidable within the current application of the Medicaid laws. With foresight, an understanding of the available estate-planning opportunities, and timely action, these objectives may still be attainable.

Current Financial and Estate-Planning Strategies

Transfer of Assets

An applicant might well wish to consider the advisability of a transfer of both individually owned and jointly held assets to a spouse, a child, or other beneficiary. Such a transfer could assume the form of an outright transfer, a transfer with a retained interest, or a transfer in trust, depending on the overall objectives of the transfer. The legal nature of trusts and of transfers with or without a retained interest were previously considered in detail, together with their use as asset management devices for the patient; their use as postmortem estate-planning devices is considered in detail in the next section. An additional transfer option not previously considered is the private annuity. Inherently more an estate-planning device than an asset management device, the private annuity is also considered in detail in the next section.

Because so many legal issues and considerations are involved in the care of Alzheimer's disease patients and their property, there are a myriad of interdependent objectives in the creation of a comprehensive patient plan. All these objectives together should determine the form of the transfer. Whatever form is selected, however, the clear objective from the prospective of Medicaid assistance should be the removal of the patient's property from harm's way in order to qualify the patient for public assistance and to preserve the property for the patient's spouse and others economically dependent on the patient who need these assets for their very survival. Such transfers, however, are not without potential problems and issues that require consideration.

Disqualifying Transfers. Because applicants who possess "countable" assets valued in excess of the permissible levels could, as was just suggested, transfer assets to others in order to qualify for public assistance rather than spend them down in support of their own medical needs, a degree of closure was deemed necessary to thwart the most blatant of such circumventions. Accordingly, Medicaid regulations currently deny eligibility to applicants who transfer excessive assets within a 30-month period before application, but only if the transfer is fraudulently motivated, that is, if its intent and purpose is to qualify the applicant for medical assistance. These denial provisions do not apply to all transfers made within 30 months, however; there are certain exceptions. Moreover, these provisions serve only to encumber such contrivances; they do not completely prevent them because transfers made before the prescribed period, regardless of motive and intent, do not fall within the regulations.

Therefore, careful attention must be given to these regulations. Inasmuch as Medicaid regulations provide that medical assistance can, in certain circumstances, be granted retroactively for up to three months, wherever possible such transfers should be made more than 33 months before application.

Transfers in Trust. Careful attention must also be given to a 1986 change in the Medicaid laws regarding certain transfers in trust for the benefit of the patient (the applicant). For a number of years, a legal device specifically designed and successfully used in the effort to circumvent eligibility requirements was a trust popularly known as the *Medicaid trust.* Established by the patient or the patient's spouse for the benefit of the patient, in its most simple form this trust permitted assets and income to be used for the patient's benefit but limited this use to a mere supplement of Medicaid benefits. The trustees were, in essence, forbidden to use the assets and income to replace these benefits. Because the assets and income were held in a trust that could not be revoked or amended by the patient, they were "inaccessible" to the patient and were therefore exempt from considerations of applicant eligibility. This arrangement permitted patients to receive all the benefits of Medicaid, while still enjoying the benefits of their assets, a result that created a serious moral dilemma among both patients and planners and no small amount of consternation among policymakers. As might well have been anticipated, the law was changed in 1986 to provide that assets held in trusts created by the patient or by the patient's spouse, together with the income produced by them, would no longer be considered exempt and would thereafter be considered in determining eligibility. The new law, however, did leave unaffected trusts created by someone else for the benefit of the patient. Although that omission does little for the preservation of the patient's assets directly, there is now some speculation that a "straw" transfer of assets by the patient through another—a patient's child, for example—could circumvent these restrictions. Although such a maneuver has yet to be administratively or judicially tested, it is anticipated that such a transaction will be treated as an attempt to elevate form over substance and will accordingly be unsuccessful in achieving the desired results.

At first glance, then, this change in the law practically eliminates the use of the *inter vivos* trust as a device for preserving the patient's assets in the Medicaid context. On further reflection, it might well be discovered that the changes had more far-reaching consequences—in fact, that they seriously curtailed the use of the *inter vivos* trust to accomplish other planning objectives as well, such as *inter vivos* asset management for the patient. If, as an illustration, a patient were to transfer assets to a trustee to manage on his behalf for the rest of his life in anticipation of an impending loss of capacity, and if such an interest existed at the time of the patient's application for Medicaid benefits, the patient-applicant would clearly not qualify, and his assets would have to be expended. Moreover, if such an interest were created but were relinquished by the patient within 30 months of application, the relinquishment would doubtless be a disqualifying transfer within the interpretation of Medicaid regulations. However, timing, as they say, is everything. A prior relinquishment of such an interest would not disqualify the patient-applicant. If, then, assets were placed in a trust for the patient's benefit for asset management purposes, and if the trust contained provisions for a timely relinquishment of the patient's interests, the trust could accomplish both asset management and asset preservation. Additional trust provisions could thereafter accomplish a variety of postmortem planning objectives (see the next section).

Accordingly, if a decision is made now, for whatever planning reasons, to transfer the patient's assets into an *inter vivos* trust, care must be taken to limit the interest of the patient-applicant in both the assets and the income of the trust.

Spousal Transfers. Careful attention should also be given to problems presented by the transfer of assets to a spouse. Because of the immediacy and magnitude of the DAT patient's estate-planning problems, it is easy to become completely immersed in them and to overlook and neglect the corresponding estate-planning problems of the patient's spouse. A transfer of the patient's assets to the patient's spouse may be the appropriate solution to the asset preservation issue and other objectives, but in spite of all expectations to the contrary, it is conceivable that the patient's spouse may not survive the patient. Out of love and deep commitment, spouses have driven themselves to a state of exhaustion, a nervous breakdown, and worse—a premature death on more than one occasion. Only then is it discovered that the assets transferred to the spouse will unavoidably be returned to the patient, together with the spouse's own assets. Much to the consternation of the patient's children or other relatives, the patient will be the recipient of some or all of these assets from the estate of the predeceased spouse, either through the operation of the intestate statute because the spouse had no will, or pursuant to the provisions of a will drafted long before the onset of Alzheimer's. This rather embarrassing situation can be avoided simply by ensuring that the spouse-transferee also has an adequate estate plan that appropriately disposes of the transferred assets as well as the personal assets.

In all probability, however, the spouse will indeed survive the DAT patient, thereby avoiding such reversionary embarrassments. Nevertheless, the transferee-spouse may encounter his or her own management problems thereafter. There does exist the possibility, however remote, that the surviving spouse may contract DAT. Even if not, the surviving spouse will doubtless encounter some of the same management issues in advanced age as an Alzheimer's patient. The matters considered in this chapter are by no means the exclusive realm of victims of Alzheimer's disease. Most of them are equally valid considerations for the elderly population, generally. It would therefore seem prudent to plan for such matters on behalf of the patient's spouse at the same time, or at the very least to give them a measure of consideration.

It should be noted, however, that the issue of unintentional inheritance is not limited simply to the patient's spouse. Although, the spouse is the most likely source of an unintended inheritance, other individuals within, and even outside, the immediate family may be a potential source of inheritance to the patient. Accordingly, the estate-planning instruments of all family members should be carefully analyzed to ensure that assets will not be inadvertently conferred on the patient.

Competency to Transfer. Careful attention must be given to the legal competency of the patient to transfer assets. As was previously discussed, a specified degree of mental capacity is required for all *inter vivos* transfers, whether outright, in trust, or with a retained interest. If the required degree of capacity is absent at the time of the transfer, a patient will be deemed legally incompetent to effect a transfer, and any transfers made by such a patient, individually, will lack full legal force and effect.

Psychology of Transfer. Careful consideration should be given to the psychological impact of transfer on the patient. All of the transfers considered here involve the patient-transferor's relinquishing some degree of control over the assets transferred; outright transfer involves the complete loss of control. As might be anticipated, this aspect of transfer may produce no small amount of anxiety. Not unreasonably, patients may fear not only for the integrity of the assets themselves, but for their continued use on the patient's behalf. For example, could these assets be legally attached and taken to satisfy the personal debts and obligations of the transferee? Moreover, contrary to the intent and wishes of the patient, could the transferee intentionally use the assets for personal benefit and refuse to use them for the benefit of the patient-transferor? Depending on the form of transfer selected, legal remedies exist, in varying degrees of effectiveness, to ensure the proper use of the transferred assets. Nonetheless, these transfers obviously involve an act in which personal trust is a necessary prerequisite. The issue of asset integrity and security was also considered in detail in the section on asset management.

Transfer and Health-Care-Facility Accessibility. Careful consideration should finally be given to the impact of asset transfer on admission of the patient to a health-care facility when it becomes necessary. Once the decision is made, locating a "suitable" health-care facility and securing admission may prove to be a formidable task, not simply because of the availability of space, but because of financial considerations. Although Medicaid law prohibits discrimination against Medicaid recipients by participating health-care facilities, the existence of widespread *de facto* discrimination in certain locales is readily acknowledged and very difficult to combat. Although legal remedies are available, the immediate practical concern is obviously admission, and soon. Accordingly, however distasteful the thought, practical consideration might be given to the patient's retaining "sufficient" assets to effectively "buy" his or her admission to a facility.

Severance of Joint Assets

In the event that a complete transfer of a joint asset to the patient's spouse or other cotenant is not an appropriate planning solution (for whatever reason), severance of the asset between the patient and the other cotenant proportionate to their respective contribution may be an acceptable alternative. If no acceptable proof of contribution is available, an equal severance should be considered. This might be an acceptable solution where transfer is rendered impossible because of the patient's loss of mental capacity (joint bank accounts excepted) or where complete transfer of the entire asset would very likely be rendered a disqualifying transfer because of a need to apply for Medicaid benefits within the succeeding 30 months. In the event that a patient lacks the mental capacity to sever the account personally, the patient's guardian or conservator could be authorized to do so by the court.

Once the assets themselves are physically severed, it would seem advisable to sever the income thereafter as well, that is, to keep the income produced by these severed assets segregated, particularly in the husband–wife context. If they are segregated, there will be two sources of income, one produced by the patient's assets, the other by the assets of the patient's spouse. Thereafter, while the patient is able to live at home, ordinary household and patient care expenses can be satisfied initially from the patient's income and then, if necessary, from the spouse's income. So prioritized, the patient's income would not be permitted to augment the patients' assets unnecessarily, and the patient's spouse would, if possible, be permitted to save from unexpended income in anticipation of the day when the patient's excessive income will be diverted to health-care-facility expenses.

Although perhaps not the optimal solution to preservation, such severances would at least serve to reduce assets for the purpose of Medicaid eligibility and would in addition, at the very least, preserve that portion of the particular asset attributable to contribution by the patient's spouse, child, or other co-tenant from expenditure for the patient's medical expenses. The advisability of the use of severances as planning devices, however, should be subject to some of the considerations discussed above with respect to complete asset transfers, in particular: disqualifying and spousal transfers, competency, psychological factors, and accessibility to health-care facilities.

Segregation of Income

Assets, of course, are not the only source of income generally available to the patient and the patient's family. There may be, in addition, non-asset-based income, such as social security, veterans' benefits, and certain retirement benefits. When a patient is receiving income from such other sources, the principles of income segregation and priority of use considered above would also be applicable to these situations.

Conversion of Assets

As was previously mentioned, Medicaid regulations divide assets into two categories: assets that are considered in determining eligibility (so-called countable assets) and those that are not (so-called exempt assets). A patient's family may wish to consider the conversion of some of the patient's countable assets into exempt assets, such as the purchase or repair of a home, an automobile, furniture, furnishings, and other qualified personal property, or the discharge of outstanding debts. The family may, in addition, wish to consider advance funeral and burial arrangements. Finally, they may wish to consider the conversion of assets from one form of joint ownership to another. As was previously mentioned, Medicaid regulations *presume* that the entire contents of a joint bank account belong to the patient. If the patient has contributed most of the amount in the account, the family may wish to consider conversion of the bank account to some other form of jointly held asset—stock, for example—where the presumption is equal ownership among owners.

Although the conversion of assets may, in many cases, be an acceptable solution to the "excessive" asset problem, it is not without potential problems. As was previously mentioned, the patient's "home" used as "a principal place of residence" is considered an "exempt" asset for purposes of Medicaid eligibility. Nevertheless, under certain circumstances, the home may lose its exempt status when the patient moves to a nursing home or when the patient dies.

Under certain limited circumstances, states may seek reimbursement from the estates of Medicaid recipients following their death for benefits provided during their lifetime. Obviously, such recovery could be enforced only against previously "exempt" assets—such as a recipient's home—in as much as all others would have been expended so that the patient could receive benefits in the first place. This kind of recovery is permitted only with respect to benefits provided after the recipient reaches the age of sixty-five, and then only if the recipient is not survived by a spouse or certain dependent children. The regulations further provide that, under certain limited circumstances similar to those above, states may actually impose a lien against the real property of the recipient. Accordingly, unless a spouse, dependent children, and certain others reside in the home, the lien could be enforced on the recipient's estate. The spouse, however, may predecease the patient, as was previously mentioned. On the patient's death, then, the house may comprise part of the patient's estate, from which reimbursement may be sought. The spouse, on the other hand, not being financially able to maintain the house, may sell it, rendering the individual or joint proceeds "available." There are numerous other possibilities. Accordingly, notwithstanding the house's so-called exempt status, it would seem advisable that the patient not own the home individually or jointly with the spouse. At the very least, the patient should transfer the home to the spouse.

Again, although perhaps not the optimal solution, such conversions do have the effect of removing some of the patient's assets from consideration for Medicaid eligibility and of preserving them for use by the patient's spouse, children, and other dependents.

The Impact of the Medicare Catastrophic Coverage Act of 1988 (MCCA) on Medicaid Eligibility Requirements

MCCA contained several important expansions on *Medicare* coverage principally in regard to inpatient hospitalization, skilled nursing care, physician services, outpatient prescription drugs, and respite care for the chronically dependent and disabled. The new law did not, however, significantly expand Medicare coverage for the type of nursing home care typically required by the DAT patient—long term intermediate levels of nursing service—Level II and Level III placements. The "catastrophe" which MCCA sought to address is the need for long term acute-care hospitalization. Thus Medicaid remains as the primary public resource for patients who require such services.

MCCA did, however, contain several specific amendments to the Medicaid law regarding eligibility requirements. MCCA's major innovation is the treatment of the patient and the patient's spouse as a single economic unit rather than separately for purposes of eligibility. It has little effect, if any, on unmarried patients. The principal features of these amendments include: a limitation on the amount of assets (resources) that can be protected for the patient's spouse; an increase in the amount of income that can be protected for the patient's spouse; and an increase in the period of ineligibility for patients who transfer assets in order to qualify for Medicaid. These amendments specifically pertain to the treatment of income, the treatment of assets (resources), and the treatment of transfers. As was previously noted, some provisions of the law do not become effective until September 30, 1989, while other provisions arguably became effective on July 1, 1988. Moreover, some of the specifics of implementation are left to state discretion and therefore must await state legislative action.

Treatment of Income. Effective September 30, 1989, the patient's spouse is permitted to keep all of such spouse's own income, and in addition, an amount of the patient's income sufficient to raise the spouse's income to a "minimum monthly maintenance needs allowance." The specific amount of the allowance, which is subject to state discretion, must fall within a range (currently at least $786/month and not more than $1500/month) and which amount is subject to periodic indexing increases. The spouse may, in addition, be granted a shelter allowance. Moreover, the amount of the allowance may be increased by a court order of support or by a welfare department administrative finding that such an allowance would cause "significant financial distress." Finally, MCCA permits an amount of the patient's income to be applied as a "family allowance" for minor or dependent children, dependent parents, or dependent siblings living with the patient's spouse. Under existing Medicaid law, the spouse is permitted to keep all of such spouse's own income, but if most of the couple's income is in the name of the patient, the spouse is only entitled to keep an amount of the patient's income sufficient to raise the spouse's income to $469/month, and then only provided that the couple's assets do not exceed the asset limit of $2000. This is clearly a significant change in favor of the spouse and family of the patient.

Treatment of Assets (Resources). The new law does not change the basic categories of assets as between exempt and nonexempt. Nor does it change the resource limit, which remains at $2000. To qualify for Medicaid benefits, excess assets must still be spent down. However, effective September 30, 1989, *all* of the nonexempt assets of *both* the patient and the patient's spouse in excess of a spouse's asset allowance are considered to be available to the patient. Since all of the couple's assets are available however they are held (whether in the name of either spouse, individually, or in both names jointly), the issue of which spouse holds title becomes irrelevant, a significant departure from current law. The specific amount of the spouse's asset allowance ("the community spouse resource allowance"), which is subject to state discretion, must fall within a range (currently at least $12,000 or one-half the couple's total assets, whichever is greater, but not more than $60,000). The amount of the allowance may be increased either by a court order of support or by a welfare department administrative finding that such an asset allowance is insufficient to produce the spouse's "minimum monthly maintenance needs allowance," after taking into account the spouse's other sources of income. The new law permits the patient to transfer assets to the spouse sufficient to constitute the community spouse resource allowance, and these assets are thereafter protected for the benefit of the spouse. Under prior law, all of the spouse's individually owned assets, as well as the spouse's proportionate share of jointly held assets, were basically protected. While this new provision clearly assists couples of highly moderate means, it penalizes most other couples. Whereas before such couples could successfully shield a significant portion of their asset pool, now all of their assets in excess of the resource allowance will be at risk and must be spent down in order to qualify the patient for Medicaid benefits.

Treatment of Transfers. Effective July 1, 1988, the period of ineligibility for disqualifying transfers was extended from 24 to 30 months. Accordingly, subject to certain exceptions, Medicaid benefits will be denied for a period of time if the patient transfers excessive assets within 30 months of application with the intent of qualifying for Medicaid benefits. The period of ineligibility runs from the date of the transfer. In addition, the new law includes the family home within the disqualifying transfer provisions of the law, its exempt status notwithstanding. Under prior law, the family home was considered to be outside of the provisions of disqualifying transfers because of its status as an exempt asset.

The Impact of the Medicare Catastrophic Coverage Act of 1988 (MCCA) on Financial and Estate Planning Strategies

MCCA provides planners with many problems and challenges, not the least of which are the law's substantive provisions. MCCA is replete with material conflicts and ambiguities. Technical amendments are expected. Planners still await the issuance of regulations. Moreover, some of the federal changes provide states with discretion within certain limitations to conform. Much still awaits state legislation. Because it is difficult at this time to reach any precise conclusions with respect to the interpretation of the law, it is therefore difficult to develop specific strategies for estate and financial planning. Still, some general conclusions are possible this degree of uncertainty notwithstanding, but they await further refinement as the federal law and state conformity become more clear.

The issues that are of concern to the DAT family following the implementation of MCCA are basically the same as those which were of concern under prior law. Moreover, the objectives of financial and estate planning will remain the same: to remove assets and income from harm's way in order to qualify the patient for public assistance and to preserve it for the patient's spouse and others economically dependent upon the patient who need such assets for their very survival. The approach, however, will be different.

The principal difficulties will revolve around MCCA's treatment of the patient's spouse. Although the spouse will be able to retain assets up to $60,000 and at least a monthly income of $786 so as to prevent complete impoverishment, the new law's treatment of couples makes it more difficult to devise estate and financial plans. But it is only a matter of degree. There still are planning opportunities that can be effective to attain these objectives.

Transfer of Assets and Severance of Joint Assets and Income. While the new law restricts certain transfers by the patient within thirty months of application, it makes no such provisions for transfers by the patient's spouse. And while the new law now considers the couple's assets in excess of the spouse's allowance so that the issue of who holds title becomes irrelevant, the new provisions only consider such assets at the time of institutionalization and application for benefits. Accordingly, the strategies of asset transfer and severance and income segregation discussed earlier remain viable strategies following implementation of MCCA, subject of course to all of the previously enumerated caveats such as disqualifying transfers, the "Medicaid" trust, competency, and psychology. The major distinction, however, is that following the implementation of MCCA, patients' spouses must divest *themselves* of ownership prior to the patient's institutionalization. Such divestiture could take the form of outright transfers, transfers with a retained interest, or a transfer in trust depending upon the overall objectives, provided that once the assets were divested they were "inaccessible." Once the assets were divested, only the patient's remaining assets would be considered in determining eligibility and from those the spouse is entitled to both a resource allowance and a monthly income.

Conversion of Assets. The options available for reducing excess assets through conversion to exempt property, purchases, and debt reduction previously discussed remain the same under MCCA as they did before. The new law did, however, change the treatment of the family home by including it within the disqualifying transfer provisions of the law notwithstanding its exempt status. Certain transfers are specifically exempted from the disqualifying transfer provisions, including a transfer to the patient's spouse. Thus, the previously suggested strategy of a transfer to the patient's spouse remains viable. A transfer to anyone else, however, could potentially subject the patient to a period of disqualification and therefore the other specific transfer exemptions must be carefully observed.

Long-Term Care Insurance

In the development of financial and estate planning strategies, the availability of long-term care insurance should not be overlooked. Although long-term care insurance is relatively new, an increasing number of companies are beginning to offer policies. Perhaps due to their novelty, there appears to be little standardization among these policies at this time. Virtually every year finds the presentation of some new offering or variation on a theme. It is therefore difficult to treat them in a detailed manner. It may be said, however, that such policies should be carefully reviewed to ascertain the extent of coverage and, perhaps more importantly, the limitations on coverage, including: coverage of nursing home care and/or home care; extent of financial coverage commitment; limitations on pre-existing conditions; exclusions of mental disorders [DAT]; requirements of prior hospitalization; waiting period requirements; and the existence of options for renewal. Due to policy limitations, some long term care policies are not available to DAT patients, or if available, application for insurance coverage is made after the patient becomes uninsurable. If however, a policy is available, its benefits, though limited, may help to mitigate the financial burdens of the patient.

Reflections

This section has reviewed a few of the more important points about *inter vivos* financial and estate planning for the DAT patient and his or her family. It should be emphasized once again that financial decisions should optimally be made in the larger context of all other considerations of the patient.

POSTMORTEM ESTATE PLANNING

The Nature of the Problem

When a medical diagnosis is finally made, the patient's prognosis becomes clear, and the patient and/or the family begin to consider *inter vivos* estate and financial planning, consideration should optimally also begin to be given to postmortem estate planning, the traditional estate planning that focuses on asset transfer at death. As enumerated earlier, the traditional estate-planning objectives include asset transfer and management, the minimization of taxes, and probate delays and expenses.

General Considerations

The orderly transfer of patients' property to their intended beneficiaries is certainly an immediate and compelling issue for both the patient and the family, whatever the legal instruments used to effectuate the estate plan and therefore the transfer of assets (a will, for example).

There is more to this issue, however. As patients develop their intended plan of asset distribution, for instance, they must specifically consider the individuals and institutions that will be receiving and sharing their assets (e.g., a spouse, children, siblings, an elderly dependent, such as a parent, and perhaps, a charitable institution) and the beneficiaries' present and future needs, their ages, their financial capabilities, and their personal wishes and objectives with respect to the property.

One of the issues that must be considered is the management of assets for those beneficiaries who are either unable or unwilling to manage the assets received. For whatever reason, advanced age or lack of aptitude, some individuals will never develop management skills and therefore should not be given such responsibilities—ever. Moreover, not all individuals want the burden of asset management and should not be so encumbered. On the other hand, despite youth or lack of experience, other individuals may subsequently develop sufficient management capabilities and will then want to assume the responsibility. Such considerations require answers to these questions: What legal instruments or combination of them will be most effective to achieve these objectives? What forms should the transfers assume? Should the beneficiaries receive the property outright, or should the property be held in trust for some period of time for their benefit?

In addition to the form and the effectiveness of the asset transfer, there is the concern that such assets be transferred with a minimum of loss in value. A number of factors may contribute to the diminished value of estate assets; most commonly, they are the ordinary cost of the transfer, the absence of an orderly plan of property transition, and delays in estate administration. The transfer of virtually any asset involves some cost. This cost may be held to an acceptable level, however, by the selection of the least expensive mode of transfer for different assets—the use of a discount stock broker, for example.

Beyond ordinary asset transfer cost and expense, unanticipated difficulties and delays in accomplishing a particular transfer can prove to be expensive and therefore wasteful of estate assets. The characteristics of certain types of assets require a measure of foresight and advance planning. When, for example, an estate holds assets for which there is no active market, such as a "family" business or undeveloped real estate, careful advance estate planning is essential if the full value of the assets is to be preserved and realized by the beneficiaries. A forced or distressed sale to discharge estate debts, taxes, and other expenses of administration rarely realizes an asset's fair market value; rather, estates have frequently diminished in value significantly when such sales were rendered necessary by the owner's failure to plan adequately for the costs and expenses of death. Ensuring the availability of adequate liquid funds in the estate will prevent the untimely and unorganized disposition of assets for which there may be no active market.

The unanticipated difficulties and delays frequently encountered in the process of estate probate may also increase the expenses of administration and reduce the value of the estate assets available to the beneficiaries. Again, certain assets inherently require anticipatory planning for their administration within the estate context, such as an asset that may require "active" participatory management, like a family business. A dispute over a fiduciary authority often requires judicial resolution. Pending court action, estate-held businesses, formerly productive, have declined when such disputes paralyzed their daily operation and jeopardized their continued viability. Expressly conferring the powers necessary to manage such assets effectively should not only prevent costly disputes over authority but should create an economically productive administration.

Similarly, as one or more of the beneficiaries may not be

pleased with their treatment in the will, a skillfully prepared will, carefully executed in accordance with all of the requirements of the state statute and with a thoughtful consideration of the various grounds for the contest of wills, can prevent costly and time-consuming probate challenges to its validity and to the legitimacy of its provisions.

Finally, not least among the estate-planning objectives is a near universal concern with the protection of assets against the various taxes usually considered by estate planners: federal and state income taxes (both of individuals and of estates and trusts, that is, fiduciary income taxes), the federal estate and gift tax, the federal generation-skipping transfer tax, and state inheritance and estate taxes—all essentially transfer taxes imposed on the *inter vivos* or testamentary transfer of property. Avoidance of these taxes is one of the most important reasons for estate planning and, to many individuals, perhaps its principal motivating factor, and although the majority of estates are not subject to all of these taxes, a competent estate planner must consider their possible effect in any comprehensive estate plan.

Many individuals assume that their estates are too small to be significantly affected by taxes. This widely held view, unfortunately, reflects an inadequate understanding of the reach of the various taxes involved. As an illustration, a division of the ownership of income-producing property among various family members or trusts frequently produces a net increase in the overall spendable income of the family as a unit. Unfortunately, this aspect of estate planning is often overlooked.

It should also be pointed out, however, that the avoidance of taxation is frequently overemphasized by estate planners and is permitted to become the principal, if not the sole, motivating factor. This unbalanced emphasis can lead to a plan that fails to accomplish the other personal and financial objectives of the patient.

Estate-Planning Forms

A number of estate-planning devices are available to the Alzheimer's patient and family with which to accomplish the various lifetime and postmortem estate-planning objectives. For purposes of analysis, we may divide these planning devices into two principal categories, based upon the time they become effective in transferring property interests:

1. *Testamentary devices*—Instruments intended to take effect only upon the patient's death, which transfer no property interests to others until then.
2. *Inter vivos devices*—Instruments intended to take effect immediately, which transfer property interests at that time and/or on the patient's death.

Testamentary Forms

Technically, there is really only one truly testamentary device: the last will and testament. Simply defined, a will is a person's postmortem declaration of intention. Although traditionally regarded as expressing a plan for property disposition, wills may express wishes with respect to other matters as well, such as the nominations of an executor and a guardian for minor children. However simple or extensive the plan, the purpose of the will is to place an obligation on the executor to carry out the legitimate intentions of the testator under the supervision of the courts.

Although the creation of a will requires no court authority, it does require a specified degree of mental capacity, which in some states may be less than that required for the execution of a contract and other similar matters of personal property management. Whatever the level of capacity required, however, it is absolutely clear that, in order for the will to be valid, the testator must possess that degree of capacity at the time the will is executed.

Most individuals correctly perceive that a will must be in writing and properly witnessed in order to be effective. Indeed, most states unequivocally require such a witnessed writing. Several states, however, permit unwitnessed writings in the hand of the testator, and a few even permit oral wills in certain limited circumstances. Nevertheless, to ensure the will's validity, the best practice is to execute a written will in the presence of the requisite number of attesting witnesses, all in accordance with the particular state's statutory requirements. Such a procedure should be accomplished under the supervision of an attorney skilled in the preparation and execution of such instruments in order to ensure statutory compliance.

Once duly executed, the will remains completely revocable and amendable by the testator until death. It is only the testator's death and the subsequent "admission" of the will to probate that gives the will legal effect.

Although a close family member is often selected for the office of executor, there are few restrictions in this regard. Usually, anyone of full age and capacity who is capable of administering estate assets may be appointed as the executor, regardless of his or her relationship to the patient. As with the various management forms considered in the section on asset management, this may be a professional adviser, a close friend, or a corporate entity such as a bank or a trust company. When the assets are extensive or complex and the objectives of the will are sophisticated, a professional or corporate entity could, indeed, be a desirable choice, serving alone or together with a family member.

Unlike those asset management forms, however, the *simple* will is inherently a property transmittal device and not an asset management device. When compared to the duties of a trustee, for example, the duties of the executor are circumscribed to a considerable degree. In summary, the executor is charged with several specific duties: (1) to locate all of the decedent's property that will be subject to the operation of the will; (2) to reduce this property to his or her possession and control; (3) to take the necessary measures to preserve and protect the estate assets; (4) to manage them effectively during the relatively brief period of the estate's administration; (5) to discharge all estate obligations—debts of the decedent, taxes, and expenses of administration; and (6) to distribute the remaining assets to whoever is entitled to receive them pursuant to the terms of the will. Any asset-management activities undertaken by the executor are purely tangential to his or her duties in winding up the affairs of the decedent. Barring unanticipated disputes and delays, this process may require three to five years, depending on the extent and complexity of the estate assets and the relative sophistication of the testator's objectives. Administration could take far longer.

Not all wills, however, are *simple* wills designed exclusively to transfer property at death. Occasionally, the will itself may contain a trust, as a variation on the *inter vivos* trust form. Accordingly, as an alternative to outright distribution to beneficiaries, some or all of the property passing through the will may be subsequently held in trust for the accomplishment of the testator's objectives.

Aside from their effective commencement, a principal distinction between the *inter vivos* trust and the *testamentary* trusts lies in their independence or lack of it. The *inter vivos* trust is a separate and distinct legal entity that is created by the patient or donor during his or her lifetime, and that accordingly may stand on its own—independent of any other instrument. The testamentary trust, on the other hand, is an integral part of the will and becomes effective only when the will becomes effective. Otherwise, with the exception of a few technical distinctions, the testamentary trust is similar to the *inter vivos* trust in that it may accomplish the myriad of asset management objectives of the patient, subject, however, to one very important qualification: Because a will does not become effective until the decedent's death and, thereafter, until it has been given legal effect to operate on persons and property by its admission to probate, the management of the assets will not begin until at least the death of the decedent, and perhaps not even until the estate is fully or partially administered.

A consideration of the will as an estate-planning device would be incomplete without reference to its statutory counterparts, the intestacy laws. Ownership and use of property are universally subject to certain general rules. A number of these—statutes of descent and distribution—govern the distribution of property interests and control in the absence of a conscious distribution plan. Effectively, they act as an estate-planning device by default when a person fails to leave a valid will, and they confer the patient's property interests in certain proportions on those individuals specifically preferred by the law. Thus, a person's choice is not between a deliberate estate plan and no plan. As a practical matter, individuals do not really have such a choice. Rather, the choice is between an active plan and a passive plan—the intestacy statutes. Although the actual distributive plans vary in their preferences among the various states, the design, however comprised, applies uniformly to all family situations, regardless of differences in individual needs, deeds, and abilities. And although a particular statutory design may be based on that particular legislature's notions of an equitable distribution of property or its perceptions of commonly held dispositive preferences, rarely does such a uniform plan accord with the testamentary intent of any particular individual.

An individual might wish, for example, to confer an entire estate on a surviving spouse to the exclusion of the children. In smaller estates, this result might be based on a desire to provide primary support for the survivor and on the belief that the survivor will care for the children. Moreover, an individual may wish to give extraordinary recognition to one child's special needs and services, to the diminution of the other children's shares. Similarly, an individual may wish to remember a close or distant relative. Notwithstanding these personal motives and objectives, state laws frequently confer less than the entire estate on a surviving spouse, regardless of the size and composition of the estate, the number and ages of the children, and other factors usually relevant to such a consideration. Moreover, state statutes uniformly treat all children alike, without regard to their special needs. And personally preferred individuals, however dear and meritorious, may not fall within the technical definition of the class preferred by the intestacy law in any given situation and accordingly would not receive any part of the estate. Although these laws provide certainty of result, they are generally inflexible in their application to individual circumstances.

Accordingly, if a patient's preferred pattern of distribution does not conform with the particular jurisdiction's intestacy statute, some form of active planning is absolutely essential to ensure the accomplishment of that person's objectives, in the form of either a will or some other property transmittal device.

Inter Vivos Forms

In contrast to the limited number of testamentary forms—one active (the will) and one passive (the intestacy statute)—there are a number of *inter vivos* forms available to effect the patients' estate-planning objectives. Several of these have already been considered in some detail as asset management devices, inasmuch as they are effective forms for that purpose as well.

Inter Vivos **Trusts.** *Inter vivos* trusts are fiduciary agreements by which a patient may transfer assets to a trustee during his or her lifetime for management purposes. The legal nature of *inter vivos* trusts, together with their utility as a management form, was considered in detail in the section on asset management. As was suggested there, these fiduciary agreements may, in addition, be used as asset transfer devices and, accordingly, may be used to achieve a number of the patient's postmortem estate-planning objectives.

Where, for example, patients transfer assets to the trustees of an *inter vivos* trust during their lifetime for the accomplishment of a variety of lifetime management objectives, that trust instrument may, in addition, be specifically designed to control the disposition of those assets on the death of the patient. Accordingly, the terms of the trust instrument, rather than the terms of the patient's will, would control the disposition of the assets held in that trust. In this sense, the trust could be considered an alternative to the will. This result alone could significantly mitigate the problem of diminished asset value due to the delays encountered in their transfer as well as those encountered in the probate process.

When assets have been transferred to a trust during the lifetime of the patient, problems of asset transfer not encountered then may be anticipated and adequately provided for, such as the disposition of a difficult asset and provisions for estate liquidity. Moreover, as the assets held in the trust would not normally be subject to the terms and provisions of the will and therefore to the probate process, neither would they be subject to the variety of challenges and delays frequently encountered there—such as a challenge to the will's provisions or its validity.

Unlike conservatorships, guardianships, and powers of

attorney, however, the life of an *inter vivos* trust may be designed to extend beyond the death of the patient. And unlike the *simple* will (one without a *testamentary* trust), its life may be designed to extend beyond the relatively brief period of the estate's administration—in each instance to perform a variety of functions both after the death of the patient as well as after the administration of the patient's estate.

For instance, a patient may be reasonably concerned about beneficiaries' capacity to manage assets, fearing that an aggregation of assets could be dissipated through imprudent investments or improvident expenditures. Accordingly, it may be unwise to transfer the assets outright to the beneficiaries immediately on the death of the patient. Alternatively, the patient may prefer that the assets being transferred to beneficiaries be held in trust for their benefit until such time as they acquire the capability to assume management responsibilities. Assets held in the *inter vivos* trust at the time of the patient's death could, accordingly, be retained there until such time as is appropriate for the beneficiaries to assume the management burdens and responsibilities, if ever.

In this respect, the *inter vivos* trust may perform trust functions similar to those of the will that contains a testamentary trust. But unlike that arrangement, the *inter vivos* trust may provide opportunities for a continuity of management. In the *inter vivos* trust arrangement, the trustees who managed assets throughout the patient's lifetime may simply continue to manage them for a different group of beneficiaries following the patient's death. In addition to a variety of other benefits, this arrangement provides the patient with the clear opportunity to observe and judge the various management capabilities of the trustees before they assume that role for the beneficiaries. It further provides the patient the opportunity to act on those observations by, for example, replacing trustees. The testamentary trust obviously offers no such opportunities.

Finally, the complex nature of the *inter vivos* trust form permits the skilled estate planner to create a variety of property interests in the beneficiaries other than simple outright ownership. The interests thus created may be advantageous from an income-tax-planning perspective as well as from a transfer-tax perspective, while still accomplishing the personal and financial objectives of the patient. Income-producing assets, for example, could be allocated among members of a family group in such a manner as to lessen the overall tax burden among them and, accordingly, to increase the overall expendable income within the family unit.

As a legal form, the trust is one of the most highly flexible arrangements available to the planner and the patient alike. Alone, it is capable of immense sophistication. When used with other legal forms, it is capable of accomplishing an almost infinite array of objectives, limited only by a few important principles of law and the imagination of the creators.

Joint Tenancies. Joint tenancies are forms of joint ownership by which a patient may transfer assets to a joint account during his or her lifetime for management purposes. The legal nature of a joint tenancy, together with its utility as a management form, was also considered in some detail in the section on asset management. And it was also suggested there that these owner relationships may be used as asset transfer devices, as are *inter vivos* trusts, in addition to their management capabilities. But although they may be used to achieve some of the postmortem estate-planning objectives of the patient, joint tenancies possess neither the flexibility nor the potential sophistication of the *inter vivos* trust.

Although joint tenancies are inherently inflexible, the relationship may, nevertheless, serve to transfer ownership to the surviving joint tenant upon the patient's death, provided that the survivorship was intended when the relationship was established. Thus created, the joint tenancy, rather than the terms of the patient's will, controls the asset's disposition. In this sense, the joint tenancy could be considered yet another alternative to the will. This result could also significantly mitigate the problem of diminished asset value due to the delays encountered in asset transfer as well as those encountered in the probate process.

When assets have been transferred to a joint tenancy during the lifetime of the patient, problems of asset transfer not encountered then may be anticipated and adequately provided for—such as the disposition of a difficult asset and the provision for estate liquidity, although it is unlikely that assets other than fairly simple ones will be placed in a joint tenancy. Moreover, as the assets held in the joint tenancy would not normally be subject to the terms and provisions of the will and therefore to the probate process, neither would they be subject to the variety of challenges and delays frequently encountered there, such as a challenge to the will's provisions or its validity.

Unlike the *inter vivos* trust, the life of the joint tenancy may not be designed to extend beyond the patient's death. The death of the patient terminates the relationship. Thereafter, complete title resides in the survivors, unencumbered by any legal obligations to hold or use the property for any particular purpose. Although the joint tenancy is sometimes used as a trust substitute, this use is fraught with practical and legal difficulties. Realistically, this form should not be used to perform management or any other functions on behalf of the beneficiaries.

Finally, although the joint tenancy form may be useful as an estate-planning measure to reduce some of the asset transfer costs and expenses associated with death, it may not be as effective in reducing income and transfer taxes as certain other forms, in particular both the *inter vivos* and testamentary trusts. The skilled planner simply does not have the same degree of flexibility to create a variety of property interests in the beneficiaries. Although income-producing assets can be allocated among members of a family group in such a manner as to lessen the overall tax burden among them, the planner is, nevertheless, limited to the form of outright ownership, which reduces the ultimate effectiveness of the form in accomplishing the objective.

Deeds of Conveyance. Deeds of conveyance are transfers of assets, with or without retained interests (legal rights), by which a patient may transfer assets to another during his or her lifetime for management purposes. The legal nature of asset transfers with or without retained interests, together with their utility as a management form, was also considered in some detail in the section on asset management. These arrangements, however, are primarily asset transfer devices. As a practical matter, their capacity for asset management is an adjunct to this principal function. And although these transfers may achieve some of the postmortem estate-planning objectives of the patient outlined in the foregoing section, they do not possess the flexibility or the potential sophistication of the *inter vivos* trust.

The deed of conveyance serves to transfer ownership of the asset to the transferee immediately, subject to the interest retained, if any. The retained interest generally terminates on the death of the transferor or on his or her earlier relinquishment of the interest. Thus executed, the deed controls the disposition of a particular asset—a portion on the delivery of the deed, and the balance on the subsequent relinquishment of the retained interest rather than the terms of the will. In this sense, the deed of conveyance could be considered still another alternative to the will. Again, this result could serve to mitigate significantly the problem of diminished asset value due to the delays encountered in their transfer, as well as to those encountered in the probate process.

When assets have been transferred outright or with a

retained interest during the lifetime of the patient, problems of asset transfer at death will be virtually eliminated. Although estate liquidity may continue to be an issue, it, too, may be anticipated. Moreover, as the assets will not be subject to the terms and provisions of the will and therefore to the probate process, neither will they be subject to the variety of challenges and delays frequently encountered there—such as a challenge to the will's provisions or its validity.

The conveyance terminates the interest of the patient in the property transferred except for the interest retained, if any. At the latest, the death of the patient terminates the retained interest and thus the relationship. Thereafter, complete title to the particular asset resides in the transferees, unencumbered by any legal obligations to hold or use the property for any particular purpose. Accordingly, as this form may not be designed to survive the patient-transferor, it may not be used to perform management or any other functions on behalf of the transferees-beneficiaries.

Finally, although deeds of conveyance are certainly useful as an estate-planning measure to eliminate the significant expenses normally associated with death, they may also be instrumental in reducing both transfer taxes and income taxes that might otherwise be more burdensome at the patient's death. Where, for example, a patient transfers to a beneficiary outright an asset that has the potential for appreciation in value and retains no interest, legal or otherwise, the appreciation in value following the transfer may, under certain circumstances, escape taxation upon the death of the patient.

Still, notwithstanding such opportunities, the conveyance may not be as effective in minimizing taxes as certain other forms. Again, the skilled planner simply does not have the same degree of flexibility in creating the variety of property interests in the beneficiaries that might be more advantageous from an income- and transfer-tax-planning perspective. Although income-producing assets can be allocated among members of a family group so as to lessen the overall tax burden among them, the planner is, nevertheless, limited in the available forms of ownership, and the ultimate effectiveness of the arrangement to accomplish the objective is diminished.

Life Insurance Policies. Although frequently overlooked by many individuals as an estate-*planning* device, life insurance often is, in fact, the key element of an estate plan. In modest estates, proceeds of life insurance frequently comprise a significant portion of the estate, hence the term *estate builder*. In larger estates, proceeds are used to provide necessary estate liquidity to prevent the unnecessary liquidation of estate assets at a potential loss to the estate. So ubiquitous is life insurance that it is highly unusual not to find it present among estate assets, and it is potentially a useful element of an estate plan.

A life insurance policy is essentially a contractual agreement that provides that, in consideration for the payment of periodic premiums by the insured, the company agrees to pay a certain sum to a designated beneficiary upon the death of the patient. There are a myriad of insurance products on the market. Virtually every year brings the presentation of some new product or a new variation on a theme. So numerous are these products that any exhaustive treatment is simply beyond the scope of this summary. Nevertheless, there appear to be four principal forms of life insurance contract, which exist in a multitude of variants:

1. *Term insurance.* Premiums are paid for a specified period of years to provide for pure life insurance (risk) coverage for that period, with no investment or savings (cash value) feature.

2. *Whole life insurance* (of which the "Ordinary Life" policy remains the most common form). Premiums are paid during the life of the insured to provide life insurance coverage (the risk element) with an investment (a savings or cash value) feature that increases over time and may be withdrawn, borrowed against, or converted into paid up insurance. There are a myriad of variations on this "Whole Life" concept including "Modified Life," "Adjustable Life," and "Money Market Life," as well as a recently popular form known as "Split-Element" Life, in which the "risk" and "investment" elements of the policy are handled separately. Within this latter variant, there are several subvariations including "Universal Life-Phase I," and "Variable Life," which itself has several variations; the principal distinguishing characteristic among these is not only the way in which the "investment" element of the policy is handled, but also the way in which the premiums are treated.

3. *Endowment insurance.* Premiums are paid until the insured reaches a specified age, at which time the face amount of the policy becomes available or may be converted into an annuity, a form frequently used to provide for education and retirement.

4. *An annuity.* Although the variations on the simple annuity are infinite, in its elementary form a premium is paid, often in the form of a lump-sum, single-payment deposit, to provide a specified income on some periodic basis (monthly) for life.

Payment of the sum due on the death of the patient may be made by numerous methods, or so-called settlement options. Again, although the sheer volume of products and variations renders any definitive treatment here impractical, there appear to be approximately five fundamental settlement options:

1. *Outright payment of principal.* Known as the lump-sum settlement, and typical of the payment options, this involves the payment of the proceeds in their entirety outright to the beneficiary.
2. *Interest option.* This option involves the retention of the proceeds by the company at interest and the payment of that interest to the beneficiary on some regular periodic basis.
3. *Fixed payment.* This option involves the retention of the proceeds by the company at interest and the payment of a fixed amount to the beneficiary on some regular periodic basis until the proceeds (principal) and the interest are exhausted.
4. *Fixed period.* This option involves the retention of the proceeds by the company at interest and the payment of the entire proceeds, together with interest, over a fixed period of time, such as ten years.
5. *Annuity.* This option usually involves the retention of the proceeds by the company at interest and the payment over the future lifetime of the beneficiary as determined by actuarial tables; there are a number of variations on this method, commonly including (a) the life annuity, which terminates on the death of the beneficiary; (b) the number-of-years-certain annuity, which guarantees payment to the beneficiary for life, but with the added provision that if the beneficiary fails to survive for the "certain" period (ten years, for example), the balance remaining will be paid to a named beneficiary; and (c) the survivorship annuity, which terminates on the death of the survivor of two beneficiaries.

These options are usually exercised by the beneficiary after the insured's death, but they may be exercised by the insured on behalf of the beneficiary before death.

Because these contractual agreements effectively transfer property (the proceeds of the policy), there is no reason that they may not be affirmatively used as asset transfer devices and, accordingly, to achieve a number of the postmortem estate-planning objectives of the patient. Where, for example, the insurance company is obligated to pay the proceeds of the policy to the patient's named beneficiaries upon death, it is the contract (policy) that controls the disposition of the proceeds (assets) on the death of the patient, rather than the terms of the patients' will. In this sense, the insurance policy could be considered still another alternative to the will. Once again, this result could serve to significantly mitigate the problem of diminished asset value due to the delays encountered in their transfer as well as those encountered in the probate process.

Because of the contractual nature and the inherent simplicity of the relationship among the insured, the insurance company, and the beneficiaries, delays are uncommon, and attendant expenses are minimal. Barring an inquiry into the cause of death and a refusal to pay proceeds, delays in the processing of life insurance claims are unusual. Moreover, as the proceeds are not usually subject to the terms and provisions of the will and therefore to the probate process, neither will they be subject to the variety of challenges and delays frequently encountered there, such as a challenge to the will's provisions or its validity.

Unlike conservatorships, guardianships, powers of attorney, and joint tenancies, the insurance contract may be designed to extend beyond the death of the patient. And unlike the *simple* will (one without a *testamentary* trust), the provisions of the insurance policy may be designed to extend beyond the relatively brief period of the estate's administration—in each instance, to perform an asset management and protection function both after the death of the patient as well as after the administration of the patient's estate.

Once again, for example, a patient may reasonably be concerned about beneficiaries' capacity to manage assets, fearing that substantial funds could be dissipated through imprudent investments or improvident expenditures. Accordingly, it may be unwise to transfer the proceeds outright to the beneficiaries upon the patient's death. Alternatively, the patient may prefer that the proceeds be held for the beneficiaries pursuant to one of the settlement options outlined above. By electing one of these options before death, the patient can effectively guarantee the safety of the proceeds and ensure adequate support for the beneficiary over some appropriate period of time, a few years to life.

Where, however, the patient's concern is not that the beneficiaries will never acquire sufficient managerial capabilities, but that the beneficiaries simply need adequate time to develop them, the settlement options may not provide the necessary degree of flexibility desired. A decision merely to hold the proceeds until the beneficiaries acquire the capability to assume management responsibilities clearly requires the exercise of discretion by the holder of the fund. Once a settlement option is selected, however, payments pursuant to it are severely restricted. Traditionally, little or no discretion is conferred on the payer to exercise any judgment with respect to the propriety of the payments. Accordingly, the insurance company/payor's duty is simply to pay in accordance with the option selected.

Although these settlement options are frequently compared to testamentary or *inter vivos* trusts because they perform similar functions, they are not trusts. They are contracts, and in the performance of this function, they clearly lack a trust's discretionary flexibility.

The inherent limitations of the settlement options are

often circumvented as a practical matter through the use of a device popularly known as the *life insurance trust*. Seemingly a contradiction in concepts, this device combines the flexibilities of trusts with the estate-building capabilities of life insurance. The creation of the arrangement usually requires the delivery of insurance policies to a trustee pursuant to a trust agreement, or at the very least, designation of the trustee as the beneficiary of the proceeds. Accordingly, the trustee agrees to hold the policies (whether the trustee or the insured pays the premium), to collect the proceeds upon the death of the patient, and to apply the proceeds in accordance with the terms and provisions of the trust, whatever they may be. In modest estates, this arrangement is a simple device that provides assets to fund the trust. In larger estates, the trust may be funded from a variety of sources, including such insurance proceeds. Thereafter, the trustees act in accordance with the provisions of the trust, as is true of any other trust. This arrangement permits the management and protection of the insurance proceeds and the exercise of discretion in their ultimate distribution.

Finally, although insurance contracts may be useful as an estate-planning measure to reduce or effectively eliminate death expenses, standing alone they may not be as effective in reducing taxes as certain other forms. Once again, the skilled planner simply does not have the greatest degree of flexibility possible to create a variety of property interests in the beneficiaries. Through the skillful use of insurance, the planner may still allocate income-producing assets among members of a family group so as to lessen the overall tax burden among them. And although the planner does have a greater availability of beneficiary ownership alternatives through the use of the settlement options, those alternatives are, nevertheless, limited by the available policies, a circumstance that, to a lesser degree, diminishes the ultimate effectiveness of the form to accomplish the objective. When insurance is coupled with the *inter vivos* or testamentary trust form, however, the strength of insurance as an asset builder is once again united with the strengths and flexibilities of the trust form, and its capacity is enhanced to accomplish a variety of income- and transfer-tax objectives.

Retirement Plans. Retirement plans include pension plans, profit-sharing plans, corporate savings plans, individual retirement plans (IRAs), deferred-compensation plans, and self-employment retirement plans (Keoghs).

No survey of estate-planning devices would be complete without some reference, however brief, to retirement plans. Again, frequently overlooked and not generally considered as an estate planning device, the income received from a retirement plan together with some form of entitlement income, such as social security, often comprises the foundation of most retirement arrangements. Moreover, depending on the terms of the particular plan and individual circumstances, these plans may also be an element of a postmortem estate plan.

Although their basic objective is similar (providing for the security of the employee or the self-employed individual on retirement), these various retirement plans differ, sometimes significantly, in their approach to the objective. The diversity of their elements and characteristics, together with the infinite variation in the terms of individual plans themselves, is sufficient to discourage a detailed treatment here.

Generally, however, these various plans do possess some common characteristics. Fundamentally, a retirement plan is a contractual agreement by which the patient's employer and perhaps the patient as well contribute funds to a retirement plan during the patient's employment. The contributions are thereafter managed and subsequently paid to the patient on retirement pursuant to the terms of the plan, which may provide the employee with a variety of payout options. Self-employed individuals contribute to their own retirement plan. Normally, these plans further provide, that if the employee dies before complete payout, the balance may be paid to a designated beneficiary, likewise pursuant to a variety of options.

Because these contractual agreements effectively transfer property, just as life insurance policies do, there is no reason that they, too, may not be used as asset transfer devices and, accordingly, to achieve some of the postmortem estate-planning objectives of the patient. Where, for example, the funds standing in the patient's retirement plan must be paid to the patient's named beneficiaries upon death, it is the contractual agreement, rather than the terms of the will, that controls the disposition of the funds on the patient's death. In this sense, the retirement plan could be considered still another alternative to the will. And again, this result could serve to significantly mitigate, if not eliminate altogether, the problem of diminished asset value due to the delays encountered in asset transfer as well as those encountered in the probate process.

Because of the contractual nature of the relationship between the patient, the retirement plan administrator, and the beneficiaries, delays and the attendant expenses are virtually nonexistent with respect to these particular assets. Further, as the funds paid pursuant to the terms of the plan would not normally be subject to the terms and provisions of the will and therefore to the probate process, neither would they be subject to the variety of challenges and delays frequently encountered there—such as a challenge to the will's validity or the validity of some of its provisions.

Finally, these various retirement plans offer a variety of opportunities to shelter income and to defer the payment of income taxes during the lifetime of the patient and after her or his death. By reducing the diminution of estate assets attributable to income taxes, these plans serve to enhance the growth of an individual's estate.

Private Annuities. Like insurance policies and retirement plans, private annuities are frequently overlooked as an estate-planning device. Fundamentally, a private annuity is a contractual agreement, usually between two individuals. The agreement generally provides that, in consideration of the transfer of property by the patient, the transferee agrees to pay an annuity to the patient for some particular period of time, typically for life. Although the property is usually transferred to a close family member, there are no particular restrictions in that regard. Any one of full age and capacity may enter into this agreement, regardless of his or her relationship to the patient. Although there are numerous technical differences, this arrangement may, in many practical respects, be closely analogous to the transfer with a retained interest.

Estate-Planning Strategies and Recommendations

No two patient and family situations are alike. The specific strategy of any individual's estate plan will therefore depend to a large degree upon the unique needs and circumstances of each family situation and to some degree upon the specific provisions of state law. Nevertheless, a few general suggestions are appropriate:

1. The patient's will and any other estate-planning documents (such as a trust) should be reviewed with an eye toward accomplishing not only the patient's traditional estate planning objectives, but their *inter vivos* asset management and *inter vivos* estate and financial

planning objectives as well. Appropriate changes should be made to these instruments.

2. All of the patient's assets and sources of income, their nature and forms of ownership, should be similarly reviewed. Forms of ownership should be changed as appropriate.

3. Consideration should be given by the patient to the immediate transfer of assets to family members or to others outright, in trust, or with a retained interest and the assignment of income where permissible, in order to achieve the various patient and family objectives.

4. Consideration should also be given by the patient to the placement of assets into various legal forms designed to transfer the interest to family members or to others only upon the eventual death of the patient in order to achieve the various patient and family objectives.

5. The estate-planning instruments and the assets of the patient's spouse, parents, and other family members should be reviewed. Despite expectations, the patient's spouse and others may predecease the patient. Without appropriate planning, their deaths could result in assets being transferred or retransferred to the patient notwithstanding the patient's personal objectives to the contrary. If, however, the spouse or family desires to make such assets available to the patient, then consideration should be given to an alternate form of transfer and ownership such as for example the use of a trust. Moreover, if the patient has been designated as executor or trustee of any such estate-planning instruments, another person should be designated in his stead, as the patient's deteriorating mental condition will doubtlessly preclude his capacity to serve.

Reflections

This section has reviewed a few of the more important considerations of estate-planning for the DAT patient and family, as well as a few of the options available to them for addressing these issues. It should be emphasized once again that decisions made in this context should optimally be made in the larger context of the other considerations of the patient.

CONCLUSION

The financial plight of the Alzheimer's disease family has long been a source of significant alarm among citizen and professionally based associations that concern themselves with health-care cost containment, generally, and with Alzheimer's disease in particular. Though long overdue, the tireless efforts of the associations to bring this national tragedy to public attention are finally achieving a measure of success. At long last, they are beginning to receive the legislative attention that this acute matter deserves. The Medicare Catastrophic Coverage Act of 1988 is in large measure a response to this effort. State commissions have been formed to investigate the issues and to make recommendations. Other citizen-based organizations are placing pressure on insurance companies to provide nursing-home coverage at a reasonable cost. With an increased awareness of the nature and extent of the disease and its expanding population, there is hope that, in the long run, these custodial-care issues will be satisfactorily addressed. For the present, however, only those with significant financial resources can afford the type of care required. It is therefore imperative that everyone else engage in some form of financial and estate-planning.

This chapter has undertaken to discuss a few of the more important legal considerations confronting the DAT patient and family as they contend with patient care and property management. Additionally, it has endeavored to suggest a few strategies and options that may be considered in addressing these issues. And finally, it has sought to review the various legal forms generally available to implement such strategies.

It should be emphasized, however, that each of the strategies, options, and legal forms considered here have advantages as well as limitations. Not all are necessarily appropriate for every patient or family situation. Rather, each patient's particular financial and family circumstance and objectives require careful analysis, as well as a selection of the appropriate measures or combination of them by one skilled in their use. Moreover, although the various legal forms and options have been considered and analyzed separately, they are by no means mutually exclusive. They are, in fact, often used together, as circumstances require.

The day when a person's estate consisted solely of real and personal property managed individually and transferred by will has largely passed. The nature and types of property interests held by individuals have changed dramatically, as have the measures for their management and transfer. Nowadays, sophisticated asset management, as well as financial and estate-planning, uses a variety of legal devices, both testamentary and *inter vivos,* and an array of strategies to accomplish the various lifetime and postmortem objectives of the owner. When properly integrated, a combination of devices and strategies will often overcome the inherent limitations of any one of them and should result in a substantial saving of time, expenses, and taxes, as well as in the critical preservation of the assets themselves.

It should also be emphasized that state laws vary, sometimes significantly. Moreover, the maze of Medicaid laws, in particular, and the regulations promulgated under them are highly technical and complex, and they are subject to a broad range of interpretation among the various states. Furthermore, given the sensitivity of the area, it is anticipated that there will be periodic changes in the law, as there was, for example, in 1986 regarding the "Medicaid trust" and the Medicare Catastrophic Coverage Act of 1988. Accordingly, competent local counsel should be sought to refine the options and perhaps to expand on them according to the current laws and regulations of the particular jurisdiction and, in addition, to place them appropriately within the perspective of the other concerns of the DAT patient and family.

It is perhaps axiomatic to the process of estate planning that the earlier it is begun, the better. Such an admonition is certainly interwoven throughout this summary, implicitly if not explicitly. As perhaps in no other planning context imaginable, the problems and issues presented here dramatically emphasize the critical importance of timing to a comprehensive plan that will successfully accomplish the objectives of the family.

Because of the progressive degeneration in this disease, at some point the patient will become incompetent. Because some level of mental capacity is required for the use of nearly all of the management and planning options discussed, its loss will significantly reduce the available options. Moreover, because Medicaid regulations require timely action, failure or inability to comply likewise reduces the available options. As options decrease, so do the creative solutions to difficult asset management, preservation, and transfer problems.

A substantial benefit to be derived from an attorney skilled in management and planning lies not simply in the execution of estate-planning instruments, but in the formulation of a comprehensive design that will respond creatively to the unique requirements of particular family circumstances. Accordingly, legal counsel should be sought immediately.

The advice and the assistance of a capable attorney, however, are only part of the solution. The issues considered here are both complex and frustrating. Because of the diversity of the problems and objectives, as well as the diversity of local laws, regulations, and practices, families need information and assistance from a wide variety of sources, including support groups, medical personnel, social workers, and friends, as well as attorneys. The completion of a Medicaid application, for example, can be overwhelming. Although attorneys experienced in asset management and estate-planning can provide valuable insights into meeting the particular legal needs of a patient and determining an appropriate course of action—formal or informal—the other support groups can balance that advice within the perspective of the other concerns of the DAT patient and family. Even with such an array of assistance, assuming the responsibility for the care and management of the DAT patient is a monumental task.

ACKNOWLEDGMENTS. The author wishes to acknowledge the invaluable assistance of Julia O. Gregory, Esq., of Cambridge, Massachusetts in the research, preparation, and writing of this chapter. Attorney Gregory practices law in Cambridge, where she specializes in estate-planning and legal problems of the elderly.

Chapter 8

Alzheimer's Disease and Public Policy

Robert Mullan Cook-Deegan

Families that include a member with Alzheimer's disease face problems not shared by other families. Some issues stem from the disease itself and become apparent regardless of whether it is sporadic or familial (e.g., burdens of caregiving and fiscal and emotional costs). Other issues are specific to families in which more than a single member has Alzheimer's disease. This chapter focuses on the second category. There is great discouragement about what constitutes familial Alzheimer's disease (hereafter called FAD) because there is no specific genetic marker. Indeed, there is residual disagreement whether FAD is even a single-gene defect or hereditary. For the purposes of this chapter, *FAD* refers to Alzheimer's disease in at least three people in at least two generations (with autopsy or biopsy confirmation in at least two cases in two generations), with an inheritance pattern compatible with autosomal dominant transmission (see Chapter 4 on definitions).

The issues that face families with FAD center primarily on dilemmas stemming from diagnosis. They include difficulties in genetic counseling in the absence of a genetic marker, whether or not prenatal diagnosis should be attempted if a marker becomes available, who should know that such a diagnostic test has been done, what the results of the test are, how test results should be reported (and to whom), and how being part of an FAD family should influence employment, insurability, and privacy within the family.

The first issues discussed are those related to genetic testing, followed by a more detailed discussion of the issues related to employment and insurance.

ISSUES RELATED TO GENETIC TESTING

Some issues will not become acute until and unless a diagnostic test is developed. These issues include the degree of specificity and sensitivity that a test should attain before it is widely used, the degree to which laboratory testing should be linked to genetic and medical counseling, and the specific reporting requirements of test results. Early testing for Huntington's disease, for example, was not even noted in the medical record, because a prospective client must make medical records available for insurance company perusal when applying for life insurance. The researchers involved believed that the test was unlikely to help those who consented to it (as it was not even known if the test would work) and yet might possibly harm them by causing denial of life insurance. (A note in a patient's chart that a test for Huntington's disease was being administered would indicate to an astute insurance auditor that the subject was at risk.) Omitting notice that the test was being administered permitted the researchers to report results to the participant alone, to be used at his or her discretion. Results were reported only as over 95% probability of having the Huntington's disease gene, 95% probability of not having it, or inconclusive. The issues that relate specifically to genetic testing for Alzheimer's disease are quite similar to those faced by families with Huntington's disease. More detailed descriptions of these issues are available elsewhere. The uncertainty about the prevalence of a familial type of Alzheimer's disease further complicates the analysis. In Huntington's disease, it is clear that the disease is due to a single gene, and the mutation rate is low.

Alzheimer's disease, in contrast, is beset with controversies about how many people have the genetic versus the sporadic form. Different investigators estimate that of all cases of Alzheimer's disease, 25–78% are due to an autosomal dominant trait. The recent life-table projections of Folstein and Breitner provide the upper limits, and Heyman and co-workers reported the low figure. For many purposes, which of these figures is most accurate may not matter to a family member (although it *will* matter to some family members, and it matters greatly to those concerned with projecting costs or setting public policy—see below). This is because it is clear that *some* cases are genetic (at least predominantly) and others are not. The relative simplicity of the genetic testing situation for Huntington's disease is complicated by a further layer of uncertainty in Alzheimer's disease, regardless of the exact prevalence of the familial form. Whether the chances are one in four or three in four of having a genetic disease in one's family, the chances are still substantial and fall into the range of probability for which psychological adjustment is most difficult. The psychological trauma stems from not being able to seek solace when the probability of an adverse event is low, yet also being denied sufficient certainty to accept and adapt to an unpleasant event.

In those families in which it is clear that the trait is familial, this layer of uncertainty is removed, and the case becomes much like that of Huntington's disease. Such families do, however, differ from Huntington's families in some respects. Most notably, less is known about the genetic aspects of Alzheimer's disease, there is virtually no information about the causal relation (if any) between familial and sporadic Alzheimer's disease, and there has not been anywhere near the intensity of investigation on familial Alzheimer's disease that there has been on Huntington's disease (although this is changing as federal agencies devote greater resources to Alzheimer's disease research).

The restriction-fragment-length polymorphism test for Huntington's disease is one example of why this matters. The linkage of Huntington's disease to a DNA marker depended on a large base of previous work and the discovery of a large family with Huntington's disease in Venezuela. Finding the Huntington's gene itself will depend on a great deal more work, but the core of researchers has been assembled, and a method of coordinating and funding the work has been in place now for over a decade. Coordination and funding mechanisms for Alzheimer's disease research, particularly genetic research, are still largely inchoate if not in chaos. Finding a genetic marker for FAD is likely to be more logistically difficult than was the case for Huntington's disease, and it will be more scientifically difficult to the degree that finding a genetically homogeneous population to study is a problem not faced by those studying Huntington's disease. It will be easier scientifically in other ways, however, because the human genetic map is much more complete now than it was in 1982 and 1983, and the techniques of molecular genetic inquiry are both faster and more sophisticated than those available when Huntington's disease was first researched.

GENETIC COUNSELING

Uncertainty about familial versus sporadic Alzheimer's disease becomes especially unbearable in the counseling of individual families. In the majority of cases, a health professional is presented with a family containing a single well-characterized case of Alzheimer's disease. Often, one will hear that another relative has acted a bit "senile" or "crazy," or that the proband's parents died too early to show whether they would have developed Alzheimer's disease. It is thus usually impossible to determine with any certainty whether others in the family may also have been affected. This uncertainty stems from several sources. Some is due to vague clinical reports of distant relatives or those long dead. Some is due to incomplete communication among families; few medical details may be shared among cousins, or even siblings. Fear of discovering that an illness is indeed familial can also inhibit communication because of psychological denial defenses. The social expectation of "senility" among all older individuals has also obscured the true incidence of Alzheimer's disease until very recently (and continues to do so in many places). This means that many are uncertain whether those who died in the remote past had or did not have a dementing illness. Finally, it is only in the last few decades that substantial numbers of people in developed countries have lived long enough to reach the age of risk for Alzheimer's disease. Therefore, pedigree information about the risks of Alzheimer's disease (and other diseases that are most common in old age) is usually incomplete because the ancestors are not informative for the pedigree.

Because of the uncertainty, a genetic counselor is unable to give families the information they want in the vast majority of cases. A genetic counselor can be most helpful only in extreme cases: when a complete pedigree with full medical information shows that a case must be sporadic, or when the number of cases and the age of onset make clear the existence of FAD. When FAD is definitely established, there are still problems. Heston has put forward age-associated risks of developing Alzheimer's disease and has a formula for calculating relative risk, but these tables are based on incomplete information, particularly regarding the oldest age groups, where the prevalence is highest (the data most needed to resolve the uncertainty are those least available). Further, these tables are not directly applicable to all families, depending on whether there is one form of FAD or many, on whether the age of onset of FAD clusters within families, and on the degree to which environmental factors influence the age of onset. Even rudimentary data that can be used to assess these factors are lacking.

The multiple layers of uncertainty underscore the need to intensify the research effort on FAD, not only to further an understanding of Alzheimer's disease in general, but also to facilitate genetic counseling and diagnosis.

EMPLOYMENT DISCRIMINATION

Employment discrimination is a potential problem for those who develop Alzheimer's disease before retirement or who are at risk of doing so in an FAD family. Those with FAD may encounter difficulties in establishing eligibility for disability

benefits and medical benefit programs that require certification of disability (eligibility for Medicare before age sixty-five,
for example, requires certification of disability, followed by a
twenty-nine-month waiting period). This problem is not
unique to FAD, however, as it is also encountered by those
with sporadic Alzheimer's disease and other dementing
illnesses.

Employment discrimination against those who may have
a parent with Alzheimer's disease has not been reported as a
major issue to date (to this author's knowledge), perhaps
because of the general ignorance about Alzheimer's disease
in general and a lack of awareness that it can be familial in
particular. If lack of discrimination is due to ignorance, then
employers may be more likely to ask employees about their
family medical history of dementia in the future, if it becomes
more widely known that familial dementia may not be uncommon. Employers would have two reasons to do so. First,
the employee, particularly if seeking a new job after age fifty-
five, may be thought to be a risk for the company. Highly
paid positions with great responsibility are most often held
by those in this age group. It is precisely such positions for
which companies are least willing to take risks, and such
positions are notoriously difficult to monitor for poor performance. In this author's practice, it has been those working in
subordinate positions who have been identified early as having dementia. Doctors, lawyers, and corporate chiefs often go
for years before their dementia is sufficiently severe to insti-
gate medical evaluation, or before subordinates become wor-
ried enough to express concern and to risk retaliation from
the disabled person in a powerful position.

Second, companies may be concerned about the stresses
caused by caring for dependent elders, or by arranging for
others to provide care. Companies may well choose not to
hire a person they know will be saddled with the burden of

caring for a parent with Alzheimer's disease. Elder care has not yet emerged as a major public issue, but it very likely will. It may or may not arise first in connection with the workplace.

Public policy solutions to these issues are difficult. Barring discrimination based on genetic factors is quite logical (that is, putting genetic traits in the legally protected categories along with race, color, and religion), but it is also dangerous if carried to the extreme. Protection based on genetic endowment is different from race and color because the disabilities caused by genetic diseases can create problems for public safety. One does not want the pilot of an airliner to have FAD or Huntington's disease, nor those making important strategic decisions for one's company to have dementia. Protections against discrimination based on genetic factors must thus be balanced by provisos that will permit action when disability becomes manifest.

INSURANCE

Issues are different for the different types of insurance available. These can be divided into four categories for the purposes of this discussion: employment-based group health insurance, individual health insurance, life insurance, and long-term care insurance. Points made about long-term care insurance will also hold for arrangements that include an insurance component such as life-care communities and social and health maintenance organizations.

Two general types of problems arise in discussions of each of the four types of insurance. The first is called *moral hazard* and refers to the fact that having insurance makes one more inclined to overuse the services that it covers. A shady businessman may be more inclined to torch a building he owns, knowing that it is covered by fire insurance, for example (hence the term *moral hazard*). A more relevant example, associated with considerably less moral certainty, is greater use of medical services by those who are covered by health insurance. Moral hazard means to a company offering insurance that its projections of outlays may be underestimates if based on consumption patterns before insurance was available. Moral hazard encourages insurers to structure benefits so that they cannot be "gamed."

The second issue is called *adverse selection*. This refers to the phenomenon faced by a company offering insurance when the company has less information about the clients than the clients do. A person who knows she or he has Alzheimer's disease, for example, may wish very much to obtain coverage under long-term care insurance (knowing that she or he is likely to need it). If the company bases its projections of outlays on statistics for the general population, then it will dramatically underestimate the true costs because those who know they will need the covered services will be much more likely to buy insurance than those who do not know. Further, if the company anticipates that this is the case, then it will charge higher premiums, which will make the insurance less attractive to those who are not sure they want the insurance, but still attractive to those who know they need it. This process spirals until the possibility of risk sharing (combining the risks of many people so that each pays only a fraction of the overall cost)—the whole point of insurance—is lost, because the insurance is covering only those who know they will need coverage.

Group health insurance generally covers hospital care and ambulatory care and may also include psychotherapy, drugs, and other services. Group health insurance gets around the problem of adverse selection by marketing to large groups of individuals who are employed. Most group-health-insurance plans do not make deep inquiries into medical history. The fact that those covered are all employed acts to screen out many of those who are severely disabled and who would be likely to make higher-than-average use of health services. It also screens out most of the severely indigent, the homeless, the mentally ill, and other groups that are more likely to suffer ill health. Group health insurance, for those who have it, is therefore not likely to be a major problem for those with Alzheimer's disease in their family, because volunteering a family medical history is generally not made a condition of getting the insurance.

Loss of group health insurance becomes an issue, however, when a working person becomes disabled because of dementia. The loss of the job is attended by loss of the health insurance. In 1986, Congress passed a new law (P.L. 99-272) that made the tax subsidy to businesses that offer group health insurance dependent on extending health insurance coverage for variable periods after the termination of employment for most reasons (the length and extent of the coverage depend on several factors spelled out in the bill). This means that those who are fired or laid off because of disability will have the option of maintaining their health insurance, usually for eighteen months to three years. Whether or not this provision will appreciably improve the lot of those who become demented while working will remain to be seen in coming years as businesses adjust to the new law. The law does not apply to those employed by governments or religious organizations.

Individual health insurance generally covers the same services as group health insurance, but it is marketed to individuals rather than large employers. Thus, some of the protective screens are removed from the insurers' point of view, and the costs of marketing are also increased. Rates are therefore higher for individual health insurance covering the same services as comparable group plans. Eligibility for individual health insurance often does depend on answering questions about one's health, including a family medical history. Most companies to date have not based premiums on genetic predispositions (such as the risk of developing Huntington's disease, Alzheimer's disease, cancer, or heart disease, for example), but they may base premiums on smoking or drinking habits. Some companies have noted that they may in the future base eligibility or premium level on genetic predispositions. If genetic factors can determine rates, then FAD families may have to pay somewhat higher rates than other families for health insurance (and would definitely have to do so for programs that cover long-term care). Companies may even deny insurance to FAD families. This may not be a major problem for health insurance, however, because there is no evidence available now that those with Alzheimer's disease consume more acute-care resources than others (in contrast, they *do* use many more long-term care resources, as noted below). Long-term care, the set of services most used by those with dementia, is not generally covered in current health policies.

Life insurance does not cover services in the same way as health insurance. Rather, in its simplest form, it pays an amount to survivors when the insured person dies. Life insurance is partly marketed on an individual basis, partly on a group basis, and partly through employers. Eligibility for life insurance may or may not be contingent on answering questions about family medical history. When it is, FAD may become a reason for exclusion or higher premiums because dementia is associated with premature death, particularly for those families reporting early onset. Young members of FAD families who wish to buy life insurance with a long-term obligation on the part of the insurance company may be discriminated against. This discrimination should be less of a problem with yearly term life insurance, which is renewed each year (and for which the availability of insurance the next year is not guaranteed by the company).

The problems of health and life insurance may become more prominent in future years as awareness of the prevalence of dementia continues to rise, and as insurers become more aware of the possible genetic contributions to Alzheimer's disease. The issues relating to health and life insurance pale, however, in comparison to the severe problems faced by the experimental but growing movement to develop insurance for long-term care.

Long-term care insurance has been increasingly marketed in recent years. Congress and many state legislatures have introduced bills to encourage companies to offer long-term care insurance. Dozens of companies now offer insurance programs that are labeled long-term care insurance. Most are misleadingly named, as they are really short-term nursing-home insurance. Most do not include benefits other than nursing homes, focus on the medical aspects of nursing-home services (not the ones sought by those most needing truly protracted long-term care), or are good for only limited periods. Reluctance to broaden coverage results from uncertainties about how many people may live longer than anticipated (actuarial uncertainty), may use services they would not use if not insured (moral hazard), and would buy the insurance knowing they planned to use it (adverse selection). Information about nursing-home care is much less complete than that about hospital care, and that relating to home care, respite care, and other alternatives is even less complete. Insurers thus do not know what they are getting into.

In addition, many people do not know that long-term care is not covered by Medicare or most health insurance. Medicare pays for less than 2%, and private insurance for less than 1%, of nursing-home care in the United States. The percentage for other forms of long-term care is unknown, but it is also low.

Individuals and Medicaid are the primary sources of payment for nursing-home care. Individuals pay for roughly half and Medicaid for an estimated 43% (in 1984). Medicaid is a federal–state joint program of health care for the indigent. It is available only to those who are impoverished or who become impoverished in paying for their care. Potential insurers assert that the existence of Medicaid nonetheless reduces the incentive to buy long-term care insurance because all citizens know that they will eventually be taken care of. This is certainly true of those with low income and few financially valuable holdings, who have few assets to protect; for them, spending down to Medicaid eligibility may not be threatening. For those with large assets, however, this is certainly not the case because such individuals wish to protect their assets and to pass on a substantial inheritance to their heirs. Some quirks of Medicaid eligibility allow people to protect certain assets (e.g., homes) and yet remain eligible for Medicaid, but such protection is inconsistent and incomplete. Most people may well wish to avoid the risk of losing their assets, and many are ideologically opposed to using public monies for services they can obtain for themselves by prudently buying insurance. Thus, there is probably a group of people who would like to protect themselves and their families from the risks of catastrophic long-term care expenses, and to whom long-term care insurance theoretically could be marketed. More than 200,000 policies have been issued for "long-term care" insurance already.

The policies must, in most cases, be individually marketed. This necessity increases costs and exposure to adverse selection. Businesses have not shown a desire to add long-term insurance to employee benefits because of the increased costs, because of a general reluctance to add further benefits to employee contracts in the current international competitive environment (because such benefits are said to increase labor costs relative to those borne by employers in other countries), and because those most in need of long-term care insurance—those over seventy-five—are unlikely to be employed. Early efforts to do group marketing (e.g., a test marketing by Prudential Life in cooperation with the American Association for Retired Persons) have not been encouraging. Further, the benefits vary greatly. Some plans pay only a fixed amount per day, some pay only for a specified period, and others do not begin to pay until after three to six months of nursing-home care. These provisions are intended to protect the insurer from financial ruin by limiting moral hazard. For those with a dementing condition, the policies that pay a fixed amount per day or that do not pay for several months may well be acceptable, because they would greatly limit the damage of catastrophic expenses associated with nursing-home care that is required for years. Most policies, however, have an upper limit of coverage—usually two to four years. Those needing care for longer would again have to use their own funds. This plan may or may not be acceptable, depending on the degree to which the covered period substantially reduces the total risk of catastrophic expense. Policies that require previous hospital admission, or that cover only short periods or a certain period for the first couple of years, are clearly not true long-term care insurance and would be of only limited use to those with dementia.

Long-term care insurance is of special interest in connection with familial Alzheimer's disease. First, if FAD is as common as Folstein and Breitner project, then it is the single major cause of nursing-home placement in the United States (50%– 70% of residents of nursing homes have dementia, two thirds of those with dementia have Alzheimer's disease, and if three fourths of these have FAD, then 25%–30% of all nursing-home residents would have FAD). If the lower figures for FAD as a proportion of all cases of Alzheimer's disease are correct, then FAD is proportionately a much smaller problem for long-term care insurance (and would account for only 8%–10% of all cases). It is thus extremely important to determine the true prevalence of the familial form of Alzheimer's disease, particularly among nursing-home residents.

The prevalence of FAD matters also because it could make long-term care impossible to market. Members of a family with Alzheimer's disease have strong incentives to get long-term care insurance, because those who know they are at risk of dementia of the Alzheimer's type also know they are likely to need extended long-term care. If the higher FAD prevalence figures are correct, then a substantial fraction of the total pool of potential beneficiaries would have strong incentives to buy insurance. If companies failed to ask about Alzheimer's disease family history, they could face financial ruin because of strong pressures toward adverse selection. If they *did* ask, however, and denied insurance to those with a positive family history, then they would be denying insurance to the very group most likely to need it. If companies are allowed to charge higher rates for familial Alzheimer's disease, Huntington's disease, familial Pick's and Parkinson's diseases, and other familial dementias, then difficult decisions must be made about whether particular cases are familial or not. For the diseases other than Huntington's, this is an insurmountable problem in most individual cases (for reasons noted under "Genetic Counseling" above).

The problem of adverse selection is not necessarily restricted to familial forms of dementia, however; it exists for anyone with a debilitating condition that lasts for years. Someone first learning of a diagnosis of Alzheimer's disease could purchase insurance immediately, knowing that he or she may not need the nursing-home benefit for some years. This is an independent risk for insurers, who would therefore wish to exclude the coverage of such persons in order to limit fiscal risk. Insurers usually try to protect themselves by denying benefits for "preexisting conditions" that the patient knew existed before he or she obtained insurance. The preexisting-condition clauses, however, are often subject to legal challenge by both sides, and the legal battlefields may run red before a coherent set of guidelines emerges from case law.

The magnitude of the problem of adverse selection suggests that long-term care insurance may work only if it is made mandatory—by forcing all people or all those over a certain age to purchase insurance for long-term care. This approach would enforce risk pooling but would also obviously restrict freedom of choice. Mandatory long-term care insurance could be either government-sponsored (like social security or Medicare) or government-mandated (like automobile insurance). Whether there is sufficient consensus and public demand for long-term care insurance to result in a mandatory program is a political question that can be resolved only over time in state legislatures and in Congress.

Part IV

Personal Perspectives

Chapter 9

Family Reactions
Plight of Alzheimer's Victims and Caregivers

Compiled by Linda A. Winters-Miner

The following is a letter to the editor which appeared in and is reprinted from *The American Journal of Alzheimer's Care and Related Disorders*, Vol. 1, No. 3. This letter typifies the situation that Alzheimer's victims and their caregivers face:

> To the editor: My husband is in the advanced stage of Alzheimer's Disease. My doctor refuses to say it's Alzheimer's without an examination of the brain (on autopsy)! Most of the Alzheimer's material I've seen offers no information about caring for an individual who no longer walks, talks, feeds himself, or fully understands. My husband is such a case. He's in a nursing home, but because he cannot begin to get the personal care he needs or deserves, I spend hours every day, doing what the home aides fail to do. Furthermore, they aren't told what Alzheimer's patients need, and they don't understand his inability to respond to simple requests. (His lack of response isn't due to a "mood," as one of the nursing-home staff suggested.)
>
> My husband has been sick almost nine years, and spending eight to 10 hours a day with him has taken its toll on me.

(He is 88, I am 77, and we have been married for 55 years.) My doctor advised me to remedy this situation, so I've hired an aide eight hours a day, four days a week, at $7 per hour. Over the past three years, my husband's illness has cost $150,000. There's no help from Medicare or other insurance policies.

It's heartbreaking to see these advanced cases wasting away in the face of callous indifference. Can't victims of this disease be given more informed, practical care? Half of those afflicted with Alzheimer's Disease are half-fed. The food is removed in 15 minutes when they require 45 minutes to an hour to eat. Newspaper articles and television shows should explain why the victim isn't responding. Why his responses change from day-to-day. Why he'll indicate "no" when he means "yes." Why he doesn't follow seemingly simple instructions. Why he's forgotten how to swallow food and, instead, spits it out. Why? Why? Why? I'd like some answers.

The author of this letter prefers to remain anonymous. She fears that publication of her name could negatively impact her husband's care.

Editor's Note: No one knows the depth of pain of Alzheimer's disease except those who have experienced it. The very word *clinical* connotes judgments based on sterile measurements. We in the scientific community must never lose human touch in the name of objectivity. People become ill. Family members suffer. Loss is profound. It does hurt. It hurts to get close even as researchers. We would like to pull back and ignore the anguish. But we must embrace it as we hug the family members, for we really are connected one to another. The disease robs us of so much. It must not be allowed to rob us of empathy. The next three subchapters, written by caregivers, bring us closer to the pain, the reality, and also to the courage and the love.

Chapter 9A

A Spouse-Caregiver's Experience with Alzheimer's Disease

Anson P. Hobbs

Editor's note: Mr. Hobbs's wife, Mildred Hobbs, died of dementia of the Alzheimer type on January 6, 1986, after suffering for many years with the illness. Her disease appeared to fit the "sporadic" form of the illness, as there was no record of any of her siblings, parents, or grandparents having the illness. Her parents lived well into their nineties, with no signs of dementia. She did experience a severe blow to her head at one time in her life (head trauma is a putative "risk factor" for Alzheimer's disease). Because of the family history, there appears to be no genetic risk to this victim's children. Mr. Anson Hobbs is a retired industrial-research chemist who blends his scientific knowledge and insight with his personal experience. He has personally supported magnetic-resonance-imaging (MRI) studies on Alzheimer's patients at the City of Faith Medical and Research Center in Tulsa, Oklahoma, and continues to promote research on this illness.

I have a different story to tell of my experience with Alzheimer's disease from Bea Gorman's (see her story in Chapter

219

9C). She knew about the disease and what it did to individuals while she was a child. I knew nothing about Alzheimer's disease and its ravages on an individual until I was fifty-five, and then I learned the hard way.

My wife began to do peculiar things for which I had no explanation. At this point, I started to take her to a doctor for monthly checkups. The doctor didn't tell me just what was the trouble, but he continued to check her every month. I'd have a checkup at the same time, having her go in to see the doctor first so that the doctor could tell me what was going on. This continued for some time.

Then my children told me that I should have a brain scan run on her. When she wrote to them, the lines would run in all directions and the letter wouldn't make sense. When one would talk to her, she would appear at first to be all right, but as one listened, she would change subjects and not make any sense. I also noticed that when she wrote her name, she would put many arches in the letters *m*, and I'd have to tell her when to stop. I also started to cook for us because she'd forget what she was doing.

I had the doctor run a brain scan on her. When he gave me the results, he said that she didn't have a brain tumor, but that she had atrophy of the brain cells. I didn't connect this diagnosis with Alzheimer's disease because I'd had no experience with the term, nor did I know of anyone who had the disease. Soon after this, I retired and we moved to Tulsa and into the University Village. I had talked to the doctor about moving to Tulsa and about the "Village" and all its facilities. He told me that he was glad we were moving to a place that could take care of Mildred when I could no longer care for her. This statement didn't mean anything to me at the time because I didn't know what lay ahead of me.

After we had moved, Mildred wanted me to write down what was wrong with her so that she could tell people. She said that she couldn't remember what it was. Neither of us knew just what it meant. At that point, she had to be with me constantly because she did not know how to take care of herself. We were in a church choir but had to quit because she couldn't follow instructions. Sometimes, when someone else would get up to do something, she would get up and start to follow.

I continued to take her to a doctor for monthly exams. I told the doctors in Tulsa what the medical people in Pittsburgh had said about her. One doctor told me that I should take her to a neurologist. After the second or third visit, the neurologist advised me to obtain a "CAT scan" on her to show whether her trouble was caused by pressure on the brain, which could be released by a shunt, and she would be all right. Instead, the CAT scan report said that she had Alzheimer's disease. He saw her several times afterward, but he was not doing her any good as far as I could see, so I just stopped taking her.

I began to read everything that I could about Alzheimer's disease. As I was a research chemist, I read *Science* magazine, which printed some of the early research results on Alzheimer's disease. I read there that Canadian researchers had found aluminum in the neurons of the brain of an Alzheimer's victim. I also read about victims of Alzheimer's disease and began to see what was ahead of me in taking care of Mildred. I began to see the hopelessness and began to understand the desperation of the caregivers who grasped at the promises of unscrupulous people. They did not have enough knowledge or information to see that such people were fakes preying on unfortunate people who had no hope. About this time, it came out in the papers that Rita Hayworth had Alzheimer's disease, so more information about the disease was being published in the media, and it seemed to spark more research on the disease.

In the meantime, Mildred was deteriorating and was having to be helped more and more. She also knew that she had changed a lot. She couldn't read, and she wanted to do something rather than just sit around. Earlier in life she had knitted, and she decided she wanted to do it again. I tried to help her but she couldn't remember for long enough how to do it, and she had to give up. I would take her out, but when she had to go to the toilet, I'd have to go with her to pull her panties down, and when she was through, I would have to go to her to pull up her panties because she didn't know how to do it. It was embarrassing to have go to into the women's toilet to help her when I couldn't find any woman to help her. Finally, I was feeding her, bathing her, dressing and undressing her, helping her out of bed and back into bed, and taking care of her as if she were a little child. It was becoming a twenty-four-hour job, with no help, no one to take care of her so that I could get even an hour's rest.

The doctor and the nurses at the health center urged me to put Mildred in the health center because they were afraid that I would deteriorate physically under the burden of being her sole caregiver. Several times she became violent, and I was afraid that I would be unable to handle her. I had to have the doctor put on her chart that, whenever I called the health center and told them that she was becoming unmanageable, they had permission to come and give her a shot to calm her. Another complication was that her mother, who was in her nineties, was in the health center, and I was also having to attend to her welfare. Finally, I had to put Mildred in the health center because of her constant constipation, which was unmanageable at home.

Placing Mildred in the health center was hard to endure. We had been married for forty-four years. I could tell what she wanted before she even asked for it. I felt that I could take care of her better than anyone else, but I finally had to realize that I could not continue to take care of her twenty-four hours a day. I was working as a security guard at University Village to help a little in the cost of taking care of her and her mother, and I had to patrol the building, including the health center. As I was passing her room on the day I put her in the health center, I could hear her calling "Anson, Anson, Anson." That was one of the hardest times that I had.

It is heartbreaking to see a loved one gradually deteriorate to the point where she is just like a baby and doesn't recognize you when you go to see her. No recognition and no response. During the five years that she was in the health center, our children didn't want to come to see their mother because they wanted to remember her as she was the last time they saw her. This is hard to understand until you have to go through it yourself.

Following is a list of various behavior patterns my wife exhibited during her illness that haven't been mentioned above;

1. She'd remove toilet paper from a roll but didn't seem to know how to use it and would simply put it in the toilet.
2. She wanted to dry dishes but would never completely dry them. She wanted to rearrange silverware even though it was already in its proper place. For example, she might put spoons in with the knives or forks with the soup spoons.
3. If we went into stores where there were clothes, she would buy clothes but would never wear them.
4. She had no peripheral vision to the left, and I had to make sure that she didn't run into anything to her left.
5. Reading became difficult for her. She needed larger and larger print, until she couldn't read and couldn't understand what she was reading.
6. I'd make trips to the store and other places to keep

her occupied. It was easy at first to get her into the car, but as the disease progressed, it became difficult to get her in or out of the car. I would tell her to put her left foot in the car, and she would turn to the right and place her foot toward the open door. I would turn her around and tell her to sit on the seat and then put her feet in the car. Instead, she would turn back and start to sit on the ground.

7. Eventually, she couldn't feed herself. Sometimes it would appear that she had no coordination. Later on, when she was told to open her mouth, she would close it, but she would open her mouth if one touched her lips with something sweet.

8. She got so that when using a straw to drink, she would sometimes blow instead of sucking.

9. Whenever they placed her in a chair at the health center, they had to tie her in or she would slide out of the chair.

10. Ultimately, she could not talk, except to say, "No" when she did not like what was being done.

11. Finally, she did not recognize me. I would stroke her hair and massage the back of her neck. This seemed to calm her down, as if she recognized that someone was doing something that pleased her.

12. During the latter stages, when she was in bed she was usually in the fetal position, and even when she was in a chair, she had a tendency to be in that position.

13. It was difficult going in to see her and having her lie there without any response. It was very discouraging.

A faith in God and a determination to make some good come from the death of my wife have caused me to back the

Familial Alzheimer's Disease Research Foundation (FADRF). My hope is that the FADRF will bring about cooperation among the researchers on Alzheimer's disease so that they can easily exchange information and produce ideas that will speed the discovery of the cause and the cure of Alzheimer's disease. I am hoping that in the future any news releases that are given to the press will not make claims that cause false hopes for the families of Alzheimer's patients.

I have been told by many people that, because it has been reported that researchers have found aluminum in the brains of Alzheimer's victims, they've thrown out all of their aluminum pots and pans. Some unscrupulous persons have used this revelation to sucker people into having chelating treatment to remove aluminum from the brain. People are not told that the original research found the aluminum not in the whole brain, but concentrated in the neurons. Also, Alzheimer's disease was first described in 1906 before there was any commercial aluminum on the market for making utensils. Chelating has not been proved to remove aluminum, and it may remove other metals that are vital to the operation of the human body. Desperate people will try anything when there is no true information.

This is one reason I'm supporting the Familial Alzheimer's Disease Research Foundation: because of its goal of making sure that any news that comes from research will be reported in such a way that false hope is not generated, and that the news is really new and not a sensational repeat of former news used to sell newspapers. Also, when there is cooperation, more and better research can be done faster. Although Mildred is gone, I am resolved to help find the cause and prevention of Alzheimer's disease.

Chapter 9B

Interview with Ester May Reiswig

When my husband began to show signs of being a lazy farmer—and the Germans aren't—I took him to the doctor, and the doctor gave him a thyroid medicine to improve his physical activity. It was also supposed to help his memory. But it didn't appear to help his memory, and he appeared to be getting lazier. So by the time he was forty-two, I began to take him to other doctors to try to find out what was the matter. There were various things that they would say was happening, and they would try to do something but didn't have any success.

The strange thing was that, as we went from one doctor to another, my husband was asked the age of his youngest son, and this son would get progressively younger, while the two older children stayed the same age. He couldn't remember who the President of United States was or what his present activities were, but he could remember some activities of the past.

Eventually, each doctor would conclude that he didn't know what was wrong with my husband, so we'd go home and then start in to find another doctor. We went from doctor to doctor to doctor to doctor. Finally, we went to the Wichita VA Hospital. The doctor there was talking to my husband, and all of a sudden turned to me and asked, "What have you done to this man?" I replied, "Nothing, but keep him and love him!" He replied, "Well, you've done something, because he's lost his self-confidence!" I replied, "I know he has, but I don't know what has caused it." He replied, "Try to build his confidence up again," and that was all.

I wasn't satisfied with that, so I just continued going to other doctors. By the time my husband was forty-four, he couldn't work. I took a job as a teacher of retarded children where one was available, in another city. He did take a job driving a vehicle, but he was obsessed with the idea that he would run over someone, so he quit that job. I couldn't leave him at home, as he wasn't dependable, so I took him to the mental health center during the day, where he did some handicrafts. One day, the director of this center called me in and advised me to take him to another mental health center where they could check for an organic cause of his problem. I replied, "Oh, the brain is diseased?" The doctor said, "I'm afraid so." So I took him to this other center. After the examination, that doctor came out to the waiting room, shook his head, and told me, "It's a shame that this man is unable to use his intelligence." And I asked, "Well, what do you mean?" He replied, "Well, he has superior intelligence, but he can't use it, and you'll have to go back to your doctor and have him give you the answer, as I can't give it to you." He wanted to know if I was aware that my husband was very intelligent, and I replied that I believed so, as after he had been out of school for many years, he went back to college and made A's in Greek, the first course he took; you have to have some intelligence to do that!

I went back to our regular doctor for the diagnosis. He told me that it wasn't good news, that my husband had "Alzheimer's disease." I said, "What in the world is that!" He got out his book and found one paragraph about an inch long on Alzheimer's disease. The paragraph said that, as the mind deteriorated, there would be depression and possible suicide, and that eventually the person would become a vegetable if he lived long enough. And sure enough, my husband lived long enough to become a vegetable. He became just a "nothing." He "ungrew" and went back through the years in a reverse order. He was doing this at the time that our son was "getting a year younger." My husband was also getting younger in his own mind. He became quite childish and regressed beyond that into a crawling stage, and then he went below that and was just an infant. At this time, I finally had to put him into a VA hospital. From the infant stage he went backward into the prenatal stage, and then he even went beyond this stage and became "flat," became "nothing." Nothing, just skin and bones lying there in the bed, with no response.

But many years elapsed before he came to this "nothing" stage. He was sixty-three when he died and had suffered from DAT for at least twenty-three years. We had a very good marriage for ten years, and then we had ten years of "hell"— and I mean it was "hell"—when his personality changed, with accompanying anger; and then we had ten years of the hospital stage, although the "hell" stage and hospital stage overlapped somewhat.

When my husband got to the point where he could no longer handle the paperwork and the legal business associated with farming, we went to a lawyer and had the farm transferred to my name so that I could sign all papers and he could continue farming. He was doing a sloppy job of farming at this time, however. Earlier, he'd been a perfectionist in keeping all the farm machinery parked in an orderly row, but he got so he would just drive an implement into the yard and park it wherever he stopped, and would never move it.

Another example was a new fence and gate he built to keep in some cattle. He nailed the gate shut! Then he came to the house and told me that the cows couldn't get out of their corral. I asked, "Well, why can't they get through there?" and he replied, "The gate won't open!" I went down and found that the gate had been nailed shut; so I unnailed it and showed him how the latch he had made would slide over and hook the gate closed. But he said, "No, they'll get out!" I repeated that the latch would take care of it, but he wouldn't believe it. He was never satisfied that the gate would work, but he left it that way. The rest of the fence that he built looked like a zig-zag maze of boards nailed up any which way; I was happy it was behind the barn, where no one could see it from the road. That was not my husband. In 1947, he and his brothers had built a barn that was strong, and that is still standing on that farm in 1985; but the fence has long since fallen down.

ALZHEIMER'S DISEASE, AFFECT ON SOCIETY, AND THE FUTURE

When I was fully aware of what was wrong with my husband and that essentially nothing was known about this disease, I began praying for a research doctor to study the illness. I went to my husband's older brother (both of my husband's parents were dead, and in German families, the older brother usually becomes the "ruler" of the family) and said, "I think we need to get a research doctor where we can take my husband. He acts just like your dad did, and like your other brother, and something is going on here that is bigger than any of us ever imagined!" And sure enough, it was.

After the original diagnosis of Alzheimer's disease was made, we took my husband to a VA hospital. We stayed three days while neurologists, psychologists, and others checked him in every conceivable manner. One doctor said he had a friend we should see, but we'd have to wait until she got through lecturing. When she did arrive and came into the room with my husband, she let out a great big gasp and put her hand over her mouth. She started asking him questions, but he couldn't remember the things she asked him about.* I told the doctor that we had never talked about my husband's disease in front of him, that he didn't know what he had.

So she and I went into a separate room and talked for an hour or two. She understood about Alzheimer's disease, but she said she never expected to meet a patient in her lifetime. From what she told us, my husband was the first *living* person in the United States to be officially diagnosed clinically with Alzheimer's disease and was Number 11 recorded in the medical literature. She followed the family for three years, until she relocated elsewhere in the VA system.

My husband made a profound statement in his early forties, at the time when the early clinical signs of the disease were apparent. He said, "My sister is forgetful, my brother is forgetful, and my dad is forgetful—and we're all going to be forgetful in this family!"

As far as the future is concerned, the answer is there. It is just waiting to be discovered. And when our Maker gets someone in the right place at the right time, He will reveal the answer. I believe I'm going to live long enough to see the answer.

---

*Editor's note: Apparently the doctor was questioning in a manner similar to the minimental exam.

Chapter 9C

Living with Familial Alzheimer's Disease

Bea Gorman

Editor's Note: Mrs. Bea Gorman is a member of a family group presenting Alzheimer's disease in more than one generation, and in many members of her generation. The age of onset is quite predictably in the late forties and fits a dominant-gene model of inheritance. The story presented below is a remarkable demonstration of how one person can make a tremendous impact on our world. This story was adapted from a talk Bea Gorman gave to a Tulsa, Oklahoma, Support Group meeting on July 2, 1986. Her story is a remarkable account of not only "coping" with difficulty, but endeavoring to make things different for others. Bea Gorman has been the recipient of several awards during the past few years, including the Jefferson Award, received in April 1986 from Channel 13, Sacramento, for outstanding public service. The Gormans have been influential in the state assembly and have worked with the governor's task force on Alzheimer's disease. Additionally, both Bea and her husband, John, serve on the advisory board for the University of California, Davis State Alzheimer's Disease Center. Mrs. Gorman is living proof that *one* individual can make a mark in her or his environment. Mrs. Gorman was also featured on the February 19, 1987, CBS Evening News (with Dan Rather) along with Dr. James Gusella (Harvard) and Dr. Michael Conneally (University of Indiana Medical Center) at the first public announcement of the discoveries of what are called the *FAD gene* and the *amyloid gene*, genes that may eventually prove to be important in the development of Alzheimer's disease.

My experience with Alzheimer's disease began in about 1945, when I was ten years old. Mama (as I referred to my mother) went into the University of Kansas Medical Center to determine what was wrong with her. She knew something was wrong, and the last words she said were, "I sure hope they can find out what's wrong with me." She was in her late forties.

While she was in the hospital, a spinal tap was performed on her and something went wrong. She came home in an ambulance, a complete invalid. We had to take care of her. Well, I thought that was the worst thing that could happen to my mother, but now that I've seen my other brothers and sisters go through the stages of Alzheimer's disease, I think it was a blessing in disguise. But we didn't know that at the time. Doctors at that time said it was unusual for more than one person in a family to have Alzheimer's disease. However, my mother and, later, two sisters and two brothers were afflicted with it. Death has claimed all but one sister, who is in the later stages of the illness.

Mama was a very special person, and I'm sure that it's because of her influence that I'm here today. Mama was a Pentecostal, and her life was the Bible, her church, and the Lord. When we children were growing up we always went to Sunday school, so we did know the Lord as children. I believe that this influence was a resource I fell back on when I needed it in my forties, and that allowed me to cope and even to turn a problem into an opportunity for helping.

Mama passed away at age fifty-one, when I was thirteen years old. The thing I remember the most about my mother and Alzheimer's disease was the dignity it took away from her. From the time she came home from the hospital, after the "spinal," I never saw her in a dress again, but always in hospital-like gowns that my older sister made for her. Earlier in life, she had worn her hair down to her waist and had braided it, like the old Pentecostals used to do, with the braids wrapped around the head; but at the hospital, they cut her hair off so it looked like a man's, to make it easier for the caregivers to wash. There were nine children, and we were poor, so we never thought about a nursing home. The nine of us took turns doing whatever we could do to take care of Mama. My older sister was married and away from home, but she took care of sewing gowns and whatever else she could do. We kids fed her and Daddy bathed her. I know it was my job, as the youngest child, about eleven years old then, to feed her one meal. I don't remember which meal.

When your mother lies there, every day, and she is a total vegetable, and the only thing she can do is follow you with her eyes, to a young kid this gets old real quick. Every day I went in that room I knew that this was the day she was going to say something to me: "I love you," "Hello"—anything. This was going to be the day. But it never was. She never did speak another word, but her eyes did follow us around the room as we took care of her. One day I didn't finish feeding her. My friends were outside the house, calling for me to come out and play with them, so that day I left early to play. For all these years, until recently, I've lived with this guilt: at the funeral, I heard some people talking about Mama probably dying of malnutrition. So I thought, "Well that's the reason"—all those times when she would eat so very very slowly, and my friends were out there, calling for me; and you know when you are thirteen years old, your friends are the most important thing in the world, and I wanted to get outside with my friends. So I carried that guilt from age thirteen until about two years ago, when I was back for my sister's funeral and one girl came up to me and said, "You don't remember me, do you?" She told me who she was and said, "I used to come over to your house when you fed your mother!" Of all the things in the world we could have talked about, the one thing that had been on my heart and mind was that I had probably starved my mother to death, so I said to her, "Did I feed her the whole thing?" She replied, "You certainly did!" So the Lord lifted that guilt from me after all those years. Later, when I got involved in Alzheimer's disease work and founded the Alzheimer's Aid Society of Northern California, I became very much aware that the lack of nutrition can be a problem with Alzheimer's disease because Alzheimer's disease victims eat so slowly in the advanced stages of the illness.

I don't remember my mother being normal, ever, like my friend's mothers. Even before the spinal and the bedridden stage, there were times when my father would come home from work and Mama had completely forgotten about fixing dinner. No one in the family realized, at first, just how ill Mama was. Daddy would often get angry with her for her forgetfulness. My older sisters talk about the "normal" things she did, but as the youngest child, I don't remember any of this normal behavior, so she must have been sick from the time I can remember. I remember her as being sweet, slow, passive, sitting around the house; she was more like a grandmother than a mother. So I don't remember her as do my older brothers and sisters.

I'm sure it left a great impact on me, losing my mother so

young, and I do remember going to my friends' houses, where their mothers were making formals for dances or were busy in the kitchen; I was very envious, I do remember that. But somehow, I survived.

Twenty-seven years later, one of my brothers who was an interior decorator, paper-hanger, and so on, who could do anything that needed to be done to a house with his eyes closed, started forgetting his tools, losing his tools, and even forgetting that he had appointments for decorating jobs. People started calling his house, and his wife would receive queries: "Where is he? Your husband was supposed to work on my house this afternoon!"

His wife finally took him to a VA hospital, where the usual questions were asked, including "What did your father die of?" and "What did your mother die of?" My brother was not very coherent at this time, so his wife had to answer most of the questions. In response she said, "Well, his mother had something, but I just don't know exactly what it was." The VA sent back to the University of Kansas Medical Center for my mother's records; the official report came back "presenile dementia." So my brother was diagnosed as having "presenile dementia." This same brother had a brain biopsy before death, at the VA hospital, but if we had it to do over again, we'd never have the biopsy done. It was painful and hard on him, and he went downhill very fast afterward (I don't think the medical doctors do this very often anymore). But in any case, because of this biopsy this brother had a definite diagnosis, prior to death, of Alzheimer's disease.

I have never been a full-time caregiver, except for those times in my youthful years when I provided partial care for my mother. One thing I have grown to appreciate as I go around the country speaking about Alzheimer's disease is that caregivers have a tremendous burden. The brother mentioned above came to visit us during his illness to give his wife some respite. My brother looked in excellent physical shape, and so I thought I'd have him help with some of our work—we were managing some condominiums at the time. I took him with me to help clean one of our units. He carried the vacuum cleaner, but when we got there, he didn't know what to do with it. He didn't know one end of the vacuum cleaner from the other. So, right then I became aware of how bad things were for my sister-in-law. At night, he would wander around the house, go out into the garage, and rummage through the drawers, looking for something. Then he would go into the kids' bedrooms and look over the kids, trying to find out, I guess, who they were and where he was. But this scared the kids: they hadn't been in the habit of seeing this person very often in their lives, and here was this strange uncle waking them up in the middle of the night. They would wake up crying and ask, "What is the matter with Uncle? Why is he doing this?" Well, the whole week was like this. One day he was walking around the house and I knew there was something he wanted but I couldn't figure it out; I was running some water in the sink, and he wanted a drink of water, but he couldn't tell me. One day he went in to take a shower; soon he yelled for my husband to come in. He had his T-shirt on his legs and his shorts on his arms. The whole week was like that, and he kept saying, "When is she going to come after me!" But he didn't even know his own wife's name.

This brother stayed home with his wife as caregiver for quite a while, but eventually she tried to place him in the VA hospital. He was put on the VA waiting list to get a bed, but in the meantime she was able to get him into the state mental hospital, where he spent his last days, until his death from pneumonia.

In the meantime, while this brother was dying, I learned that my sister back East was showing symptoms similar to

Mama and brother. I don't think we called it Alzheimer's then, but it was the "same thing." Because this sister and I lived several states apart, I didn't see her through all the stages of Alzheimer's. About this time, I was really getting scared! One day, I was in the house, and the kids and everyone were away, and I just jumped in the car and thought I'd drive to the nearest cliff and go off it—everything seemed to be going wrong, and I feared I was the next to get this dread disease. But I ended up in the church that we were members of. I remember getting out of the car and walking up to the church door, and thinking that it probably wouldn't be open, as churches usually keep their doors locked nowadays during the week, but it was open, and I walked in. The church was dark, but there was daylight, and some candles burning, and I sat down in the back. I don't know how long I sat there, but eventually I became aware that I was freezing to death. Now that I look back, I know that I was not praying, but I was listening—I was really listening. I walked out of that church and, as if someone was leading me, drove to the nearest public library, walked in just as if I knew what I was doing and what I was going to pick up, walked over to a shelf, and picked up the first book I came to, Norman Vincent Peale's book *The Power of Positive Thinking.* I turned around, walked out that door, went home, and started reading. I could not put the book down. I read it through. In the back of this book was another book suggestion. I went and got that, read it, and continued with further suggestions. All were inspirational books. It was as if these books were glued to my hands, I couldn't put them down; day and night I was reading books. As I read the books, they would tell about Scripture. I had memorized some Scriptures as a kid, but I really didn't know the Bible. I got the Bible and started looking up these Scriptures. Something started happening, something started coming alive to me! One day, later on, a friend of mine came over, and I was just so excited about this new thing that had happened to me. I wanted to go outside and scream it from the rooftops! She just patted me on the hand and said, "I know, I know," and I started crying; in retrospect I believe that was the time I accepted Jesus Christ as my personal savior and verbally told someone else about it. From that day on, my life has been totally changed.

I then told my husband that I had to go back East to visit my sister before she died—in my own mind I think I felt that I could go back to this sister and pray for her, and she'd be healed (I was on that sort of "high" in this new life in Christ). My relatives back East didn't want me to come. They said, "Your sister won't recognize you, and you'll just feel bad seeing her and feel it was a wasted trip," and "You know how emotional you are, Bea; we'll just end up putting you in the hospital also." But inside, I felt that I *had* to go back, and so I did. But it wasn't easy. I went to the nursing home where my sister was kept; she was tied in a wheelchair and just hanging there like a limp dishrag. I lifted her face up to me to see if she knew me, and she started calling me "Mama." We children looked quite a bit alike, so I thought either she recognized me or more likely thought I was Mama, or that Mama was all she knew how to say. But that split second of recognition was well worth the trip: she smiled, then she cried, and then it was all over. I've never been sorry I went back to see her; it has helped change my whole life.

When I arrived back in Reno and got off the plane, I told my husband, "We've got to do something about this disease; it is going to wipe us all out." I didn't know where to go, what to do, how to start. (Shortly after that, my sister back East died.)

We decided to go to Reno to a neurologist to see what he could tell us about Alzheimer's disease. At our appointment, the doctor pulled a medical book off the shelf and read me one sentence. That was all he knew! We walked out, and the nurse said, "That will be thirty-five dollars"; but I was still in a daze. I walked out of that office and said to my husband, "I know more about that disease than he does!" He replied, "Yes, I'm afraid you do."

During the next period of time, I worked at several odd jobs in South Lake Tahoe. One day, a woman came into the dress shop where I was working and somehow we started talking about this disease that was running in my family. She had been a nurse at the Mayo Clinic in Rochester, Minnesota, and suggested that I write there to see what they knew about it. I just laughed; "Me, with a ninth-grade education, writing to medical authorities?" She gave me the address, but I put it aside, as I was certain they wouldn't respond to me. But one day when I didn't have much to do and was bored, I got that address out and wrote. Well, sure enough, I received an answer! The first thing it said was, "I probably didn't know what I was talking about, it doesn't run in families, and it is a very rare disease. Was I sure of the diagnosis of the brothers and sisters?" But at least I got an answer.

So, I got out a reference book listing the addresses of most of the university hospitals in the United States and started writing, to see if anyone knew anything about Alzheimer's disease that ran in families. Almost all of them answered me, and almost all of them said the same thing as the Mayo Clinic (this was 1972–1974). So there wasn't very much known about this disease at that time.

For some reason, I had not written to the University of Colorado Medical School in Denver, where we had once lived, but on the encouragement of a friend visiting from Denver, I finally inquired there. I received an answer from Dr. James Austin, a neurologist. The letter said, "Not only are we doing work on Alzheimer's disease, but we are doing research on familial Alzheimer's disease." I took that letter and ran around the house like a nut, screaming, "Someone out there cares! Somebody wants to do something." Dr. Austin wanted to know how soon I could come to Denver and be tested. I couldn't pack my bags quick enough to go back to Denver. I took every bit of information I could get my hands on, every scrap of information that anyone had given me, that I'd collected. I even tried to compile a family tree. It was a bunch of junk as far as I was concerned, but the neurologists at Denver copied every piece of it and handed the original back to me, calling it my "manuscript." I spent three days in Denver undergoing every type of test they could think of at that time. At the end of the three days, I had the CAT scan, but at that time, the University of Colorado Medical Center did not have the CAT scanner, so I had to go across town to the Swedish Hospital. I was forty years old at this time; the CAT scan indicated no problem, but I was told that they could give no guarantees. They said it was like tossing a coin whether or not I was going to be a victim of Alzheimer's disease. While I was in Denver, I found out that Dr. Austin was studying three families, and that, as far as he knew, these were the only families that had ever been studied with this type of familial Alzheimer's disease.

While I was there, I met this young intern, Bob Cook; he looked like a fifteen-year-old kid at the time! Dr. Bob Cook* did most of the testing, but very important to me, he told about another family like ours. At that time, I would have traveled to the ends of the earth to find someone else who could understand our unique situation. I found out the name of this family. I tried and tried to get a hold of the lady who was the "spokesperson" for this family, but I could never get in touch with her. I had a brother-in-law who lived close to her, so I called him. He said, "Don't worry, I'll call the sher-

---

*Editor's note: Now Dr. Robert Cook-Deegan who wrote Chapters 4 and 8.

iff, and we'll track her down." So, call the sheriff he did, and this lady called me back within minutes! Since then, this person and I have had many long talks over the telephone, usually after 11:00 P.M. when the rates are low; this person is also a Christian, so besides the familial Alzheimer's disease, we have this common bond; our ability to share in this has helped immensely to keep me going. We have become good friends, and she has traveled out to California to speak at our support group meetings. Later, I received a telephone call from her saying that I should really come to Denver and hear this "lady" talk on Alzheimer's disease. Her name was Bobby Glaze, and she had started the National Alzheimer's Disease and Related Diseases Association. I did go to Denver to hear her, and this was my first "support group." I can't tell you what it meant to me, having all these people in the same room, at the same time, who knew what I was going through. They were all in the same boat. It was wonderful, but it was sad, and they all wanted to do something. There were about seventy-five people there. Bobby Glaze gave me a copy of her newspaper story "The Funeral That Never Ends," and I took it back to Lake Tahoe. Again, when I got off the plane, I told my husband, "We've got to do something about this." I wasn't sure yet what to do or where to go, but as it turned out, the Lord had a plan for me.

I took the Bobby Glaze story to the *Lake Tahoe News* (a weekly newspaper). They said, "It's a great story, but we need something local." So I said, "OK, you want something local, I'll give you something local," and I brought this great mass of stuff (my "manuscript") to the *News*. They copied it all, and the reporter made the most beautiful story out of it, a sad story, but my story. He put it in the *Lake Tahoe News* in August 1980. I got absolutely no response whatsoever from it! I was just floored! (The reporter hadn't put in the article how to contact me, so I don't know if this was a factor or not.)

One day at the *Lake Tahoe News*, where I now worked, this young woman came in, forty years old, and she asked emphatically, "Where is Bea Gorman!" I told her, "I am Bea Gorman." She had just come from the University of California, Davis, where they had diagnosed her husband as having Alzheimer's disease. She said, "He is forty-eight years old, I have a three year old son, and they told me to 'go home and live with it.' I don't know anything about it." She hadn't read my story but had been in her lawyer's office, and he had seen the story and referred her to me. I realized that I could help this lady. I could tell her what to expect in the future (as I had watched several members of my family go through the stages of the illness).

So we started getting together for coffee regularly, and I shared all the information that I had with her and advised her on how to handle her affairs at various stages of the disease. We tried to get something going in terms of a support group, to meet what we felt was a real need, but there didn't seem to be enough interest in Lake Tahoe. In the story that had been printed in the *Lake Tahoe News*, it stated that I'd like to start a support group in either Sacramento or Reno; I didn't care where, as long as people would come.

In the meantime, the reporter sold my story to the *Sacramento Bee*. When it was printed, I received hundreds of letters from all over northern California wanting to know when I was going to start the support group. (I didn't know what I was getting myself into!) In March 1981, we had our first support-group meeting; seventy-five people attended. They came from as far away as the Oregon–California border, the San Francisco Bay area, Fresno, and all the way from Reno. So we knew that there was a need. Just before we had our first meeting down in Sacramento, I was called by one of the men who had read the story, to see if I would be on a radio talk show in Sacramento with the head of neurology from the University of California, Davis. We announced our first support-group meeting on the talk show, which probably helped publicize it.

Another of my brothers who was suffering with Alzheimer's disease at that time lived in Sacramento. I guess it was meant for me to live in Lake Tahoe at that time, as we could travel the hundred miles down the mountain to Sacramento once a month for the support group meeting; at the same time, I could also visit my brother. When I returned to Tahoe, I was left completely drained of energy. But for 2½ years, we drove over that mountain, and we never missed a support group meeting. Even when the road went out (because of a landslide) and we had to drive to Reno via the Donner Pass, we never missed a meeting. But it got to the point where we were having to make two or three trips each month down to Sacramento because the demand for support and help was so great. So at that time, we decided it was necessary to live closer to Sacramento.

But let me tell you a little more about my brother, dying of Alzheimer's disease, in the Sacramento nursing home during this time. One time I went into the nursing home and saw him lying there naked. I don't think I had ever seen my brother naked before. I think the dignity that this disease takes away from people is more upsetting than anything else. The nursing staff said they were drying out his bed sores. Today I know that there are other ways of handling this, other things that could have been done, but the nursing personnel at that time were not trained in how to handle these cases. Another time when I visited, he had a wool robe on and was sitting in a wheelchair in 110 degrees of heat out in the yard of the home. It was little things like that, that I saw, that were heartbreaking; there didn't seem to be anyplace to take these Alzheimer's disease victims that was equipped to take care of them properly, and with dignity. My brother was fifty-four when he died in 1982. (At age forty-five he looked handsome, vigorous, and virile, like a Clark Gable, but by age fifty he was wrinkled and emaciated and looked like a ninety-five-year-old concentration-camp victim.)

My first sister to become a victim died at fifty-three (in 1972). Another sister now has Alzheimer's disease and is in the last stages. This sister recently visited me; I hadn't seen her for seven months, and she's got a lot worse. She can hardly do anything for herself. She needs help with walking. She could feed herself, but she makes a mess like a three-year-old. During this most recent visit, she threw a tantrum that lasted for about an hour. It was very hard on me and my husband, but it was good for him to see it. He had never seen an Alzheimer's victim throw a tantrum; I had seen it but had forgotten what it was like.

In the last 5½ years we have helped other support groups get started. Some of them have stuck with us, others haven't. We let them do whatever they want to do, in whatever manner they like. As of 1985 in August, we had sent out over one-half million pieces of literature. We now have an office in a town south of Sacramento, in addition to the Sacramento address. Over forty different support groups in middle to northern California have been started as a result of our initial effort—the need is great. They all have their own schedule of meetings, but they receive information from our central office listing all the individual meeting dates, contact persons, and so on. Each November we do a major workshop for continuing medical-education credits, usually in cooperation with one of the University of California medical centers. Additionally, my husband and I are constantly asked to do in-service nursing-home workshops to train the nursing staffs in the care of Alzheimer's victims; we have had to limit our schedule to a maximum of one workshop per week, as the demand is so great. I'm now fifty-one and don't know what the future holds (most in our family who develop Alzheimer's disease have onset in the late forties, but there appears to be variability in age of onset in some family groups). Throughout all this, my despair and feelings of hopelessness have been turned into opportunities to help others cope with this tragedy, and hopefully to advance research and bring us closer to the knowledge that will lead to treatment, perhaps prevention, and maybe even a cure.

Appendixes

Appendix

Appendix A

Selected Readings

Chermak, J. *Activities for Patients with Alzheimer's Disease and Related Disorders.* available from: The Hillhaven Corporation, Regional Office, 1835 Union Avenue, Suite 100, Memphis, TN 38104-3994.

Fall Creek, S., and Mettler, M., Eds. *A Healthy Old Age: A Sourcebook for Health Promotion with Older Adults.* New York: Haworth Press, 1984.

Heston, Leonard, L., and White, June A. *Dementia: A Practical Guide to Alzheimer's Disease and Related Illnesses.* New York: W. H. Freeman, 1983.

Karr, K. L., and Karr, J. D. *What Do I Do: How to Care for, Comfort, and Commune with Your Nursing Home Elder.* New York: Haworth Press, 1985.

Killeffer, E. H. P., Bennett, R. C., and Gruen, G., Eds. *Handbook of Innovative Programs for the Impaired Elderly.* New York: Haworth Press, 1984.

Mace, Nancy L., and Rabins, Peter V. *The 36-Hour Day: A Family*

Guide to Caring for Persons with Alzheimer's Disease, Related De-menting Illnesses, and Memory Loss in Later Life. Baltimore: Johns Hopkins University Press, 1981.

Miner, G. D., Blass, J. P., Richter, R. W., *et al.*, Eds. *Familial Alz-heimer's Disease: Molecular Genetics and Clinical Perspectives.* New York: Marcel Dekker, Inc. 1989.

Natow, A. B., and Heslin, J. *Geriatric Nutrition.* New York: Van Nostrand Reinhold, 1984.

Olson, D. H., McCubbin, H. I., *et al. Families: What Makes Them Work.* Beverly Hills, CA: Sage, 1985.

Weiss, J. C. *Expressive Therapy with Elders and the Disabled.* New York: Haworth Press, 1984.

Appendix B

Glossary of Terms

Acetylcholine   A chemical that acts as a messenger to transmit signals in the brain from one neuron to another; this chemical is decreased in AD brain tissue.

AD   Alzheimer's disease.

Age-dependent penetrance   A type of "penetrance" (see **Penetrance**) that depends on age; that is, the trait or disease shows itself at a more-or-less defined age.

Age of onset   The chronological age at which a disease is first noticed because of symptoms.

Agnosia   Loss of the ability to perceive normal stimuli of the senses, for example, hearing, smell, sight, taste, and touch.

Agraphia   Difficulty in writing (e.g., poor penmanship or legibility in writing).

Alexia   Difficulty in reading.

Alzheimer's disease   A disease characterized by dementia and

253

confirmed on autopsy by **neurofibrillary tangles** and **neuritic plaques** found in the brain, especially the cerebral cortex.

Aphasia   Loss of the ability to express oneself by speech.

Apraxia   Loss of the ability to use external objects correctly.

At risk   In medical or epidemiological terms, this term means that an individual has a greater chance than normal (or the average) of developing a disease, disorder, or effect (when a disease is due to an **autosomal dominant gene,** the exact risk of children of an affected parent can be calculated; it is 50% prior to the age-of-onset for the disease).

Autosomal gene   A gene found on any of the chromosomes except the X and Y **(sex chromosomes).**

CAT scans   Computerized axial tomography, a technique that uses X rays and computers to make a detailed scan of the brain; *CT* is also used to represent this technology (*CT* stands for computerized tomography).

CBF   Cerebral blood flow.

Concordance, or concordance rate   A term that refers to the percentage of both members of twin pairs developing the same disease, disorder, or trait.

Dementia   Loss of mental and higher level cognitive abilities; can be due to AD or other problems, including vitamin B_6 deficiency or arteriosclerotic problems.

DAT   Dementia of the Alzheimer's type

Dizygotic twin   A member of a twin pair in which each member developed from a separate fertilized egg; dizygotic twins genes are 50% identical, as compared to the 100% of **monozygotic twins.**

Dominant gene   When a gene is dominant, only one copy of the gene is necessary to produce a disease or effect when it is an **autosomal gene.**

Down's syndrome   A disease with symptoms of mental retardation and other physical effects caused by trisomy-21 (i.e., an extra, or third Chromosome 21, or at least the important part of Chromosome 21 being represented three times in the **genome**).

DSM-III   The American Psychiatric Association's *Diagnostic and Statistical Manual of Mental Disorders,* copyright 1980, which is a sourcebook for the diagnosis of mental disorders, and which provides the most widely used criteria for dementia.

Dysphasia   Impairment of speech; failure to arrange words in a proper order.

Dyspraxia   Loss of the ability to perform coordinated movements.

Epidemiological (population) studies   A research framework in which a disease or trait is studied in a fairly large sample of a population; such studies often give clues to what is going on, leading to a specific research hypothesis that can be tested on a much smaller segment of the population.

Etiology   The "cause" of a disease, disorder, or trait.

FAD   Familial Alzheimer's disease.

Familial Alzheimer's disease   AD that appears in more than one generation and involves at least three affected family members, with autopsy or biopsy confirmation in at least two cases from at least two generations, and an overall family pedigree compatible with autosomal dominant inheritance.

Family pedigree   See **Pedigree.**

Family risk   A figure *not* based on a clear genetic model, but determined from a sufficiently large population sample; such a figure will give a very rough estimate of the probability of an individual's developing AD based on whether there are any family members with AD, and if so, how many and at what age of onset.

Family Studies   A type of **epidemiological study** that assesses the possibility of genetic **etiology** by noting the percentage of cases (i.e., affected individuals) with a family history of the disease and by comparing this figure with a percentage of controls (i.e., nonaffected individuals) with a family history of the disease (this type of study is also referred to as a *case-control method*).

Genome   The complete complement of genetic information contained in the cells of an organism.

Hypertonia Increased muscle tension.

Incontinence Inability to control urine and fecal discharges.

Met-enkephalin A small peptide (chain of amino acids) that is believed to be a nerve transmitter, and that is possibly reduced in concentration in AD.

MID Multi-infarct dementia (caused by numerous small strokes).

Monozygotic twin A member of a twin pair in which both members developed from one fertilized egg and are therefore genetically identical.

MRI Magnetic resonance imaging, a brain scanning technique that makes use of magnetic fields and does not use X rays. For certain aspects it is superior to CAT scanning, and for other aspects, it is inferior; therefore, often both CAT and MRI scans are used in helping to make a diagnosis of AD.

Neuritic plaques Clusters of degenerating nerve endings associated with amyloid deposits.

Neurofibrillary tangles Neurofibrils of the nerve cell which have become abnormal in structure, appearing as a tangle and giving the entire nerve cell an abnormal appearance.

Norepinephrine A chemical that acts as a transmitter of signals the brain; this chemical is decreased in AD brain tissue.

Pedigree A chart showing several generations, marriage connections, and children; such a family pedigree is useful in studying the genetics or heredity of a disease or characteristic.

Pedigree studies Such studies trace a given family tree and look for relatives with the same disease or trait.

Penetrance A term in genetics that refers to whether a gene is expressed; a gene is "penetrant" if it is expressed.

Physostigmine A drug that blocks the breakdown of acetylcholine in the body; the use of this drug has shown modest improvement in memory tests but has been of little value in AD.

Probable FAD At least two cases of AD in at least two generations with autopsy verification in at least one case, and an inher-

itance pattern compatible with autosomal dominant transmission.

Recombinant DNA technology   A technology that involves the
cleavage of DNA strands into subunits, "probes" that can identify specific segments, cloning, and other molecular biology procedures, all of which allow the identification of genes.

SDAT   Senile dementia of the Alzheimer's type.

Serotonin   A chemical transmitter in the brain; this chemical appears to be decreased in AD brain tissue.

Sex chromosome   The X and Y chromosomes.

Short-term memory   A term reserved for memory of those
events that occurred in the recent past (i.e., usually within minutes or hours).

Sporadic Alzheimer's disease   A term given to those cases seen
in only one generation of a family, where no brothers or sisters
of the victim develop AD; this term was prevalent during the
late 1970s and most of the 1980s. For a case to be properly
labeled *sporadic*, there must be complete information about dementia available for all primary relatives who should have developed AD if the patient were at risk.

Twin studies   Studies that look at the **concordance rates** for
monozygotic and dizygotic twins in an attempt to determine the
genetic basis of a disease, disorder, or trait.

Appendix C

Bibliography for Selected Chapters

CHAPTER 3

Alzheimer, A. Über eine eigenartige Erkrankung der Hirnrinde. *Allg. Zeit. Psychiatrisch-Gerichtliche Med. 64*, 146–148 (1907), Trans. by R. H. Wilkins and I. A. Brody. *Arch. Neurol. 21*, 109–110 (1969).

Amaducci, L. A., Fratiglioni, L., Rocca, W. A., *et al*. Risk factors for clinically diagnosed Alzheimer's disease: A case-control study of an Italian population. *Neurology 36*, (1986).

Berg, L. Does Alzheimer's represent an exaggeration of normal aging? *Arch. Neurol. 42*, 737–739 (1985).

Breitner, J. C. S. Dementia of the Alzheimer type: Methodological comments. *Psychiatr. Res. 16*, 263–264 (1985).

Breitner, J. C. S., and Folstein, M. F. Familial Alzheimer dementia: A prevalent disorder with specific clinical features. *Psychol. Med. 14*, 63–80 (1984).

Breitner, J. C. S., Folstein, M. F., and Murphy, E. A. Familial aggregation in Alzheimer dementia: 1. A model for the age-dependent expression of an autosomal dominant gene. *J. Psychiatr. Res. 20*, 31–43 (1986).

Breitner, J. C. S., Murphy, E. A., and Folstein, M. F. Familial aggregation in

Alzheimer dementia: 2. Clinical genetic implications of age-dependent onset. *J. Psychiatr. Res. 20*, 45–55 (1986).

Brody, J. A. Prospects for an aging population. *Nature 315*, 463–466 (1985).

Burger, P. C., and Vogel, F. S. The development of the pathologic changes of Alzheimer's disease and senile dementia in patients with Down's syndrome, *Am. J. Pathol. 73*, 457–476 (1973).

Chandra, V., Philapose, V., Bell, P. A., Lazaroff, A., and Schoenberg, B. S. Case-control study of late onset "probable Alzheimer's disease." *Neurology 37*, 1295–1300 (1987).

Chui, H. C., Teng, E. L., Henderson, V. W., and Moy, A. C. Clinical subtypes of dementia of the Alzheimer type. *Neurology 35*, 1544–1550 (1985).

Cohen, D., Eisdorfer, C., and Leverenz, J. Alzheimer's disease and maternal age. *J. Am. Geriatr. Soc. 30*, 656–659 (1982).

Cook, R. H., Schneck, S. A., and Clark, D. B. Twins with Alzheimer's disease. *Arch. Neurol. 38*, 300–301 (1981).

Cook, R. H., Ward, B. E., and Austin, J. H. Studies in aging of the brain: IV. Familial Alzheimer disease: Relation to transmissible dementia, aneuploidy, and microtubular defects. *Neurology 29*, 1402–1412 (1979).

Corkin, S., Growdon, J. H., and Rasmussen, S. L. Parental age as a risk factor in Alzheimer's disease. *Ann. Neurol. 13*, 674–676 (1983).

Davidson, E. A., and Robertson, E. E. Alzheimer's disease with acne rosacea in one of identical twins. *J. Neurol. Neurosurg. Psychiatr. 18*, 72–77 (1955).

Ellis, W. G., McCulloch, J. R., and Orley, C. L. Presenile dementia in Down's syndrome. *Neurology 24*, 101–106 (1974).

English, D., and Cohen, D. A case-control study of maternal age in Alzheimer's disease. *J. Am. Geriatr. Soc. 33*, 167–169 (1985).

Feldman, R. G., Chandler, K. A., Levy, L. L., and Glaser, G. H. Familial Alzheimer's disease. *Neurology 13*, 811–824 (1963).

Folstein, M. F., and Breitner, J. C. S. Language disorder predicts familial Alzheimer's disease. *Johns Hopkins Med. J. 149*, 145–147 (1981).

Folstein, M. F., and Powell, D. Is Alzheimer's disease inherited?: A methodologic review. *Integ. Psychiatr. 2*, 163–170 (1984).

Glenner, G. G., and Wong, C. W. Alzheimer's disease and Down's syndrome: Sharing of a unique cerebrovascular amyloid protein. *Biochem. Biophys. Res. Commun. 122*, 1131–1135 (1984).

Goudsmit, J., White, B. J., Weitkamp, L. R., Keats, B. J. B., Morrow, C. H., and Gajdusek D. C. Familial Alzheimer's disease in two kindreds of the same geographic and ethnic origin. *J. Neurol. Sci. 49*, 79–89 (1981).

Hagnell, O., Lanke, J., Rorsman, B., Ohman, R., and Ojesjol, L. Current trends in the incidence of senile and multi-infarct dementia. *Arch. Psychiatr. Nervenkr. 233*, 423–438 (1983).

Heston, L. L. Ask the doctor: Genetics and dementia of the Alzheimer type. *ADRDA Newsletter 5*(2), 4 (1985).

Heston, L. L., and Mastri, A. R. The genetics of Alzheimer's disease. *Arch. Gen. Psychiatr. 34*, 976–981 (1977).

Heston, L. L., Mastri, A. R., Anderson, V. E., and White, J. Dementia of the Alzheimer type: Clinical genetics, natural history, and associated conditions. *Arch. Gen. Psychiatr. 38*, 1085–1090 (1981).

Heston, L. L., and White, J. Pedigrees of 30 families with Alzheimer disease: Associations with defective organizations of microfilaments and microtubules. *Behav. Genet.*, *8*, 315–331 (1978).

Heyman, A., Wilkinson, W. E., Hurwitz, B. J., Schmechel, D., Sigmon, A. H., Weinberg, T., Helms, M. J., and Swift, M. Alzheimer's disease: Genetic aspects and associated clinical disorders. *Ann. Neurol. 14*, 507–515 (1983).

Hunter, R., Dayan, A. D., and Wilson, J. Alzheimer's disease in one monzygotic twin. *J. Neurol. Neurosurg. Psychiatr. 35*, 707–710 (1972).

Jarvik, L. F., Ruth, V., and Matsuyama, S. S. Organic brain syndrome and aging: A six-year follow-up of surviving twins. *Arch. Gen. Psychiatr. 37*, 280–286 (1980).

Kallmann, F. J. Genetic aspects of mental disorders in later life. In *Mental disorders in later life* (2nd ed.) O. J. Kaplan, Ed. Stanford, CA: Stanford University Press, 1956, pp. 26ff.

Katzman, R. Alzheimer's disease. *N. Engl. J. Med. 314*, 964–973 (1986).

Kay, D. W. K. The genetics of Alzheimer's disease. *Br. Med. Bull. 42*, 19–23 (1986).

Knesevich, J. W. The author replies. *J. Psychiatr. Res. 16*, 265–266 (1985).

Knesevich, J. W., Toro, F. R., Morris, J. C., and LaBarge, E. Aphasia, family history, and the longitudinal course of senile dementia of the Alzheimer type. *Psychiatr. Res. 14*, 255–263 (1985).

Kolata, G. Down syndrome-Alzheimer's linked. *Science 230*, 1152–153 (1985).

Kolata, G. Researchers hunt for Alzheimer's disease gene. *Science 232*, 448–450 (1986).

Larsson, T., Sjogren, T., and Jacobson, G. Senile dementia. A clinical, sociomedical and genetic study. *Acta Psychiatr. Scand. 39*(suppl. 167), 1–259 (1963).

Lauter, H. Genealogische Erhebungen in einer Familie mit Alzheimerscher Krankheit. *Arch. Psychiatr. Nervenkr. 202*, 126 (1961).

Lowenberg, K., and Waggoner, R. W. Familial organic psychosis (Alzheimer's type). *Arch. Neurol. Psychiatr. 31*, 737–754 (1934).

McKhann, G., Drachman, D., Folstein, M., Katzman, R., Price, D., and Stadlan, E. M. Clinical diagnosis of Alzheimer's disease: Report of the NINCDS-ADRDA Work Group under the auspices of Department of Health and Human Services Task Force on Alzheimer's Disease. *Neurology 34*, 939–944 (1984).

McMenemy, W. H., Worster-Draught, C., Flind, J., and Williams, H. G. Familial presenile dementia. *J. Neurol. Psychiatr. 2*, 293–302 (1934).

Meggendorfer, F. Uber die hereditare Disposition zur Dementia senilis. *Z. Neurol. Psychiatr.* *101*, 387–405 (1926).

Moreau-Dubois, M-C., Brown, P., Dougsmit, J., Cathala, F., and Gajdusek, D. C. Biologic distinction between sporadic and familial Alzheimer disease by an in vitro cell fusion test. *Neurology 31*, 323–325 (1981).

Mortimer, J. A., Schuman, L. M., and French, L. R. Epidemiology of dementing illness. In *The Epidemiology of Dementia*, J. A. Mortimer and L. M. Schuman, Eds. New York: Oxford University Press, 1981, pp. 3–23.

Nee, L. E., Polinsky, R. J., Eldridge, R., Weingartner, H., Smallberg, S., and Ebert, M. A family with histologically confirmed Alzheimer's disease. *Arch. Neurol. 40*, 203–208 (1983).

Perry, R. H. Recent advances in neuropathology. *Br. Med. Bull. 42*, 34–41 (1986).

Powell, D., and Folstein, M. F. Pedigree study of familial Alzheimer disease. *J. Neurogenet. 1*, 189–197 (1984).

Prichard, J. C. *A Treatise on Insanity and Other Disorders Affecting the Mind.* Philadelphia: Haswell Barrington & Haswell, 1837.

Rocca, W. A., Amaducci, L. A., and Schoenberg, B. S. Epidemiology of clinically diagnosed Alzheimer's disease. *Ann. Neurol. 19*, 415–424 (1986).

Ron, M. A., Toone, B. K., Garralda, M. E., and Lishman, W. A. Diagnostic accuracy in presenile dementia. *Br. J. Psychiatr. 134*, 161–168 (1979).

Sayetta, R. B. Rates of senile dementia—Alzheimer's type in the Baltimore longitudinal study. *J. Chronic Dis. 39*, 271–286 (1986).

Sjogren, T., Sjogren, H., and Lindgren, A. G. H. Morbus Alzheimer and morbus Pick. *Acta Psychiatr. Neurol. Scand.* (suppl. 82), 1–152 (1952).

Sluss, T. K., Gruenberg, E. M., and Kramer, M. The use of longitudinal studies in the investigation of risk factors for senile dementia-Alzheimer type. In *The Epidemiology of Dementia*, J. A. Mortimer and L. M. Schuman, Eds. Oxford: Oxford University Press, 1981, pp. 132–154.

Terry, R., and Katzman, R. Senile dementia of the Alzheimer type: Defining a disease. In *The Neurology of Aging*, R. Katzman and R. Terry, Eds. Philadelphia: F. A. Davis Company, 1983, pp. 51–84.

Tomlinson, B. E., Blessed, G., and Roth, M. Observations on the brains of demented old people. *J. Neurol. Sci. 11*, 205–242 (1970).

Torack, R. M. Historical overview of dementia. In *The Pathologic Physiology of Dementia*, R. M. Torack, Ed. New York: Springer-Verlag, 1978, pp. 1–15.

Von Bogaert, L., Maere, M., and Desmedt, E. Sur les formes familiales precoces de la maladie d'Alzheimer. *Monatsschr. Psychiatr. Neurol. 102*, 294 (1940).

Weinreb, H. J. Fingerprint patterns in Alzheimer's disease, *Arch. Neurol. 42*, 50–54 (1985).

Weinreb, H. J. Dermatoglyphic patterns in Alzheimer's disease, *J. Neurogenet.* 3, 233–246 (1986).

Weitkamp, L. R., Nee, L., Keats, B., Polinsky, R. J., and Guttormsen, S. Alzheimer disease: Evidence for susceptibility loci on chromosomes 6 and 14. *Am. J. Hum. Genet.* 35, 443–453 (1983).

Whalley, L. J. Carothers, A. D., Collyer, S., De May, R., and Frackiewicz, A. A study of familial factors in Alzheimer's disease. *Br. J. Psychiatr.* 140, 249–256 (1982).

White, J. A., Mcgue, M., and Heston, L. L. Fertility and parental age in Alzheimer disease. *J. Gerontol.* 41, 40–43 (1986).

Wolozin, B. L., Pruchnicki, A., Dickson, D. W., and Davies, P. A neuronal antigen in the brains of Alzheimer patients. *Science* 232, 648–650 (1986).

CHAPTER 5

Alzheimer, A. A unique illness involving the cerebral cortex, trans. by C. N. Hochberg and F. H. Hochberg. In *Neurological Classics in Modern Translation*, D. A. Rottenberg and F. H. Hochberg, Eds. New York: Hafner Press, 1977, pp. 41–43. (Originally published 1907.)

Appell, J., Kertesz, A., and Fisman, M. A study of language functioning in Alzheimer patients. *Brain Lang.* 17, 73–91 (1982).

Bayles, K. A., and Tomoeda, C K. Confrontation naming impairment in dementia. *Brain Lang.* 19, 98–114 (1983).

Benson, D. F. *Aphasia, Alexia, and Agraphia.* New York: Churchill Livingston, 1979.

Benson, D. F., Kuhl, D. E., Hawkins, R. A., Phelps, M. E., Cummings, J. L., and Tsai, S. Y. The florodexoyglucose 18F scan in Alzheimer's disease and multiinfarct dementia. *Arch. Neurol.* 40, 711–714 (1983).

Besson, J. A. O., Corrigan, F. M., Foreman, E. I., Eastwood, L. M. Smith, F. W., and Ashcroft, G. W. Nuclear magnetic resonance (NMR): 2. Imaging in dementia. *Br. J. Psychiatr.* 146, 31–35 (1985).

Bird, T. D., Stranahan, S., Sumi, S. M., and Raskind, M. Alzheimer's disease: Choline acetyltransferase activity in brain tissue from clinical and pathological subgroups. *Ann. Neurol.* 14, 284–293 (1983).

Brant-Zawadzski, M., Fein, G., Van Dyke, C., Kiernan, R., Davenport, L., and de Groot, J. MR imaging of the aging brain: Patchy white-matter lesions and dementia. *Am. J. Neuroradiol.* 6, 675–682 (1985).

Brinkman, S. D., and Lorgen, J. W., Jr. Changes in brain ventricular size with repeated CAT scans in suspected Alzheimer's disease. *Am. J. Psychiatr.* 141, 81–83 (1984).

Brouwers, P., Cox, C., Martin, A., Chase, T., and Fedio, P. Differential perceptuo-spatial impairment in Huntington's and Alzheimer's dementias. *Arch. Neurol. 41*, 1073–1076, 1984.

Brun, A. and Englund, E. Regional pattern of degeneration in Alzheimer's disease: Neuronal loss and histopathological grading. *Histopathology 5*, 549–564 (1981).

Brun, A., and Englund, E. A white matter disorder in dementia of the Alzheimer type: A pathoanatomical study. *Ann. Neurol. 19*, 253–262 (1986).

Brun, A., and Gustafson, L. Distribution of cerebral degeneration in Alzheimer's disease. *Arch. Psychiatr. Nervenkr. 223*, 15–33 (1976).

Brun, A., and Gustafson, L. Limbic lobe involvement in presenile dementia. *Arch. Psychiatr. Nervenkr. 226*, 79–93 (1978).

Bucht, G., Adolfsson, R., and Winblad, B. Dementia of the Alzheimer type and multi-infarct dementia: A clinical description and diagnostic problems. *J. Am. Geriatr. Soc. 32*, 491–498 (1984).

Chase, T. N., Fedio, P., Foster, N. L., Brooks, R., DiChiro, G., and Mansi, L. Wechsler adult intelligence scale performance. *Arch. Neurol. 41*, 1244–1247 (1984).

Chui, H. C., Teng, E. L., Henderson, V. W., and Moy, A. C. Clinical subtypes of dementia of the Alzheimer type. *Neurology 35*, 1544–1550 (1985).

Coben, L. A., Danziger, W. L., and Berg, L. Frequency analysis of the resting awake EEG in mild senile dementia of the Alzheimer type. *Electroencephalogr. Clin. Neurophysiol. 55*, 372–380 (1983).

Cummings, J. L., and Benson, D. F. *Dementia: A Clinical Approach*. Boston: Butterworths, 1983.

Cummings, J. L., and Benson, D. F. Dementia of the Alzheimer type: An inventory of diagnostic clinical features. *J. Am. Geriatr. Soc. 34*, 12–19 (1986).

Cummings, J. L., Benson, D. F., Hill, M. A., and Read, S. Aphasia in dementia of the Alzheimer type. *Neurology 35*, 394–397 (1985).

Cummings, J. L., Benson, D. F., and LoVeune, S., Jr. Reversible dementia. *J. Amer. Med. Assoc. 243*, 2434–2439 (1980).

Cummings, J. L., and Houlihan, J. Reading impairment in dementia of the Alzheimer type: Observations and implications. *Brain Lang. 29*, 315–323 (1986).

Cutler, N. R., Haxby, J. V., Duara, R., Grady, C. L., Kay, A. D., Kessler, R. M., Magesh, S., and Rapoport, S. I. Clinical history, brain metabolism and neuropsychological function in Alzheimer's disease. *Ann. Neurol. 18*, 298–309 (1985).

Davies, P. Studies on the neurochemistry of the central cholinergic systems in Alzheimer's disease. In *Alzheimer's Disease: Senile Dementia and Related Disorders*, R. Katzman, R. D. Terry, and K. L. Bick, Eds. New York: Raven Press, 1978, pp. 453–459.

Davis, P. E., and Mumford, S. J. Cued recall and the nature of the memory disorder in dementia. *Br. J. Psychiatr. 144*,383–386 (1984).

Diagnostic and statistical manual of mental disorders (3rd ed.). Washington, DC: American Psychiatric Association, 1980.

Duffy, F. H., Albert, M. S., and McAnulty, G. Brain electrical activity in patients with presenile and senile dementia of the Alzheimer type. *Ann. Neurol. 16*, 439–448 (1984).

Erkinjuntti, T., Sipponen, J. T., Iivanainen, M., Ketonen, L., Sulkava, R., and Sepponen, R. E. Cerebral NMR and CT imaging in dementia. *J. Comput. Assist. Tomog. 8*, 614–618 (1984).

Faden, A. I., and Townsend, J. J. Myoclonus in Alzheimer disease. *Arch. Neurol. 33*, 278–280 (1976).

Foster, N. L., Chase, T. N., Fedio, P., Patronas, N. J., Brooks, R. A., and DiChiro, G. Alzheimer's disease: Focal cortical changes shown by positron emission tomography. *Neurology 33*, 961–965 (1983).

Foster, N. L., Chase, T. N., Mansi, L., Brooks, R., Fedio, P., Patronas, N. J., and DiChiro, G. Cortical abnormalities in Alzheimer's disease. *Ann. Neurol. 16*, 649–654 (1984).

Freedman, M., and Oscar-Bennan, M. Selective delayed response deficits in Parkinson's and Alzheimer's disease. *Arch. Neurol. 43*, 886–890 (1983).

Friedland, R. P., Budinger, T. F., Brant-Zawadzki, M., and Jagust, W. J. The diagnosis of Alzheimer-type dementia. *J. Amer. Med. Assoc. 252*, 2750–2752 (1984).

Friedland, R. P., Budinger, T. F., Ganz, E., Yano, Y., Mathis, C. A., Koss, B., Ober, B. A., Huesman, R. H., and Derenzo, S. E. Regional cerebral metabolic alterations in dementia of the Alzheimer type: Positron emission tomography with 18F-fluorodeoxyglucose. *J. Comput. Assist. Tomog. 7*, 590–598 (1983).

Goodin, D. S., Squires, K. C., and Starr, A. Long latency event-related components of the auditory evoked potential in dementia. *Brain 101*, 635–648 (1978).

Goodman, L. Alzheimer's disease. A clinicopathologic analysis of twenty-three cases with a theory of pathogenesis. *J. Nerv. Ment. Dis. 117*, 97–130 (1953).

Gordon, E., Kraiuhin, C., Harris, A., Meares, R., and Howson, A. The differential diagnosis of dementia using P300 latency. *Biol. Psychiatr. 21*, 1123–1132 (1986).

Gordon, E. B. Serial EEG studies in presenile dementia. *Br. J. Psychiatr. 114*, 779–780 (1965).

Grady, C. L., Haxby, J. V., Schlageter, N. L., Berg, G., and Rapoport, S. I. Stability of metabolic and neuropsychological asymmetries in dementia of the Alzheimer type. *Neurology 36*, 1390–1392 (1986).

Gustafson, L., and Nilsson, L. Differential diagnosis of presenile dementia on clinical grounds. *Acta Psychiatr. Scand. 65*, 194–209 (1982).

Hagberg, B., and Ingvar, D. H. Cognitive reduction in presenile dementia related to regional abnormalities of the cerebral blood flow. *Br. J. Psychiatr. 128*, 209–222 (1976).

Hauser, W. A., Morris, M. L., Heston, L. L., and Anderson, V. E. Seizures and myoclonus in patients with Alzheimer's disease. *Neurology 36*, 1226–1230 (1986).

Huber, S. J., Shuttleworth, E. C., and Paulson, G. W. Dementia in Parkinson's disease. *Arch. Neurol. 43*, 987–990 (1986).

Huckman, M. S., Fox, J., and Topel, J. The validity of criteria for the evaluation of cerebral atrophy by computed tomography. *Radiology 116*, 85–92 (1975).

Knesevich, J. W., Martin, R. L., Berg, L., and Danziger, W. Preliminary report on affective symptoms in the early stages of senile dementia of the Alzheimer type. *Am. J. Psychiatr. 140*, 233–235 (1983).

Koller, W. C., Wilson, R. S., Glatt, S. L., and Fox, J. H. Motor signs are infrequent in dementia of the Alzheimer type. *Ann. Neurol. 16*, 514–516 (1984).

Koss, E., Friedland, R. P., Ober, B. A., and Jagust, W. J. Differences in lateral hemispheric asymmetries of glucose utilization between early- and late-onset Alzheimer-type dementia. *Am. J. Psychiatr. 142*, 638–640 (1985).

Larsson, T., Sjogren, T., and Jacobson, G. Senile dementia: A clinical, sociomedical, and genetic study. *Acta Psychiatr. Scand. Suppl. 167*, 1–259 (1963).

Letemendia, F., Pampiglione, G. Clinical and electroencephalographic observations in Alzheimer's disease. *J. Neurol. Neurosurg. Psychiatr. 21*, 167–172 (1958).

Lishman, W. A. *Organic Psychiatry*. London: Blackwell Scientific Publications, 1978.

Mann, D. M. A., Yates, P. O., and Marcyniak, B. Alzheimer's presenile dementia, senile dementia of the Alzheimer type and Down's syndrome in middle age form an age related continuum of pathological changes. *Neuropathol. Appl. Neurobiol. 10*, 185–207 (1984).

Martin, A., and Fedio, P. Word production and comprehension in Alzheimer's disease: The breakdown of semantic knowledge. *Brain Lang. 19*, 124–141 (1983).

Mayeux, R., Hunter, S., and Fahn, S. More on myoclonus in Alzheimer's disease. *Ann. Neurol. 9*, 200 (1981).

Mayeux, R., Stern, Y., and Spanton, S. Heterogeneity in dementia of the Alzheimer type: Evidence of subgroups. *Neurology 35*, 453–461 (1985).

McKhann, G., Drachman, D., Folstein, M., Katzman, R., Price, D., and Stadlan, E. M. Clinical diagnosis of Alzheimer's disease: Report of the NINCDS-ADRDA work group under the auspices of Department of Health and Human Services Task Force on Alzheimer's disease. *Neurology 34*, 939–944 (1984).

Miller, E. On the nature of the memory disorder of presenile dementia. *Neuropsychology 9*, 75–81 (1971).

Molsa, P. K., Marttila, R. J., and Rinne, U. K. Extrapyramidal signs in Alzheimer's disease. *Neurology 34*, 1114–1116 (1984).

Moss, M. B., Albert, M. S., Butters, N., and Payne, M. Differential patterns of memory loss among patients with Alzheimer's disease, Huntington's disease, and alcoholic Korsakoff's syndrome. *Arch. Neurol. 43*, 239–246 (1986).

Muramoto, O., Sugishita, M., and Ando, K. Cholinergic system and constructional praxis: A further study of physostigmine in Alzheimer's disease. *J. Neurol. Neurosurg. Psychiatr. 47*, 485–491 (1984).

Nott, P. N., and Fleminger, J. J. Presenile dementia: The difficulties of early diagnosis. *Acta Psychiatr. Scand. 51*, 210–212 (1975).

Pearce, J. The extrapyramidal disorder of Alzheimer's disease. *Eur. Neurol. 12*, 94–103 (1974).

Pomara, N., Reisberg, B., Albers, S., Ferris, S., and Gershon, S. Extrapyramidal symptoms in patients with primary degenerative dementia. *J. Clin. Psychopharm. 1*, 398–400 (1981).

Reding, M., Haycox, J., and Blass, J. Depression in patients referred to a dementia clinic. *Arch. Neurol. 42*, 894–896 (1985).

Ron, M. A., Toone, B. K., Garralda, M. E., and Lishman, W. A. Diagnostic accuracy in presenile dementia. *Br. J. Psychiatr. 134*, 161–168 (1979).

Rosen, W. G. Verbal fluency in aging and dementia. *J. Clin. Neuropsychol. 2*, 135–146 (1980).

Rossor, M. N., Iversen, L. L., Reynolds, G. P., Mountjoy, C. Q., and Roth, M. Neurochemical characteristics of early and late onset types of Alzheimer's disease. *Br. Med. J. 288*, 261–271 (1984).

St. Clair, D. M., Blackwood, D. H. R., and Christie, J. E. P3 and other long latency auditory evoked potentials in presenile dementia Alzheimer-type and alcoholic Korsakoff syndrome. *Br. J. Psychiatr. 147*, 702–706 (1985).

Seltzer, B., and Sherwin, I. A comparison of clinical features in early- and late-onset primary degenerative dementia. *Arch. Neurol. 40*, 143–146 (1983).

Sim, M. Alzheimer's disease: a forgotten entity. *Geriatrics 20*, 668–674 (1965).

Sim, M., and Sussman, I. Alzheimer's disease: Its natural history and differential diagnosis. *J. Nerv. Ment. Dis. 135*, 489–499 (1962).

Soininen, H., Partanen, J. V., Puranen, M., and Riekkinen, P. J. EEG and computed tomography in the investigation of patients with senile dementia. *J. Neurol. Neurosurg. Psychiatr. 45*, 711–714 (1982).

Stefoski, D., Bergen, D., Fox, J., Morrell, F., Huckman, M., and Ramsey, R. Correlation between diffuse EEG abnormalities and cerebral atrophy in senile dementia. *J. Neurol. Neurosurg. Psychiatr. 39*, 751–755 (1976).

Sugar, H. J., Cohen, N. J., Corkin, S., and Growden, J. H. Dissociations among processes in remote memory. *Ann. N.Y. Acad. Sci. 444*, 533–535 (1985).

Sulkava, R. Alzheimer's disease and senile dementia of the Alzheimer type. *Acta Neurol. Scand. 65*, 636–650 (1982).

Sulkava, R., Haltia, M., Paetau, A., Wikstrom, J., and Palo, J. Accuracy of clinical diagnosis in primary degenerative dementia: Correlation with neuropathological findings. *J. Neurol. Neurosurg. Psychiatr. 46*, 9–13 (1983).

Tachibana, H., Meyer, T. S., Okayasu, H., Shaw, T. G., Kondula, P., and Rogers, R. L. Xenon contrast CT-CBF scanning of the brain differentiates normal age-related changes from multi-infarct dementia and senile dementia of the Alzheimer type. *J. Gerontol. 39*, 415–423 (1984).

Weingartner, H., Kaye, W., Smallberg, S. A., Ebert, M. H., Gillin, J. C., and Sitaram, N. Memory failures in progressive idiopathic dementia. *J. Abnorm. Psychol. 3*, 187–196 (1981).

Wilson, R. S., Kaszniak, A. W., and Fox, J. H. Remote memory in senile dementia. *Cortex 17*, 41–48 (1981).

Wu, S., Schenkenberg, T., Wing, S. D., and Osborn, A. G. Cognitive correlates of diffuse cerebral atrophy determined by computed tomography. *Neurology 31*, 1180–1184 (1981).

Yamaguchi, F., Meyer, T. S., Yamamoto, M., Sakai, F., and Shaw, T. Noninvasive regional cerebral blood flow measurements in dementia. *Arch. Neurol. 37*, 410–418 (1980).

Yerby, M. S., Sundsten, J. W., Larson, E. B., Wu, S. A., Sumi, S. M. A new method of measuring brain atrophy: The effect of aging in the application for diagnosing dementia. *Neurology 35*, 1316–1320 (1985).

CHAPTER 8

Bird, S. J. Presymptomatic testing for Huntington's disease, *J. Am. Med. Assoc. 253*, 3286–3291 (1985).

Breitner, J. C. S. Familial aggregation in Alzheimer dementia: 1. A model for the age-dependent expression of an autosomal dominant gene. *J. Psychiatr. Res. 20*, 31–43 (1986).

Breitner, J. C. S. Familial aggregation in Alzheimer dementia: 2. Clinical genetic implications of an age-dependent onset, *J. Psychiatr. Res. 20*, 45–45–55 (1986).

Breitner, J. C. S., and Folstein, M. F. Familial Alzheimer dementia: A prevalent disorder with specific clinical features. *Psychol. Med. 14*, 63–80 (1984).

Cantor, C. A. Huntington's disease: Charting the path to the gene. *Nature 308*, 404–405 (1984).

Folstein, M. F., and Breitner, J. C. S. Language Disorder Predicts Familial Alzheimer's Disease, *Johns Hopkins Med. J. 149*, 145–147 (1981).

Gusella, J. F., Wexler, N. S., Conneally, P. M., *et al.* A polymorphic DNA marker genetically linked to Huntington's disease. *Nature 306*, 234–238 (1983).

Heston, L. L. Ask the doctor: Genetics and dementia of the Alzheimer type. *ADRDA Newsletter 5*(4), (1985).

Heston, L. L., Mastri, A. R., Anderson, V. E., *et al.* Dementia of the Alzheimer type: Clinical genetics, natural history and associated conditions. *Arch. Gen. Psychiatr. 38*, 1085–1090 (1981).

Heston, L. L., and White, J. A. *Dementia: A Practical Guide to Alzheimer's Disease and Related Illnesses.* New York: W. H. Freeman, 1983.

Heyman, A., Wilkinson, W. E., Hurwitz, B. J., *et al.* Alzheimer's disease: Genetic aspects and associated clinical disorders. *Ann. Neurol. 14*, 507–515 (1983).

Heyman, A., Wilkinson, W. E., Stafford, J. A., *et al.* Alzheimer's disease: A study of epidemiological aspects. *Ann. Neurol. 15*, 335–341 (1984).

Koller, W. C., and Davenport, J. Genetic testing in Huntington disease. *Ann. Neurol. 16*, 511–512 (1984).

Martin, J. B. Editorial comment: Genetic testing in Huntington disease. *Ann. Neurol. 16*, 512–513 (1984).

Wexler, N. S. From a talk given at the Mary Jennifer Selznick Mini-Workshop, Hereditary Disease Foundation, Bethesda, MD, Nov. 30–Dec. 1, 1983.

Wexler, N. S., Conneally, P. M., and Gusella, J. F. *Huntington Disease "Discovery" Fact Sheet.* Santa Monica, CA: Hereditary Disease Foundation, May 1, 1984.

Appendix D

Alzheimer's Disease Resources

The following list provides the reader with resources that provide information, support groups, public awareness, specialized AD hospitals, caregiver support, and referrals to agencies that can help the victim and the family members who are caring for the Alzheimer's disease patient. These resources welcome your telephone call or letter of inquiry.

1. (Familial) Alzheimer's Disease Research Foundation (FADRF)— Serving Oklahoma, USA–Central Region, USA, and the world

    Mailing address: 8177 South Harvard, Tulsa, Oklahoma 74137

    Telephone: (918) 631–3665 (office)

    FAX: 918/495–3760

    Purpose: Raising funds and providing funding for research in AD with emphasis on FAD. Facilitation of "cooperation in research" among the major AD research laboratories of the world, and stimulation of periodic research symposia.

Official Affiliate laboratories

1. Neurobiology of Aging Laboratory of Harvard University and Massachusetts General Hospital, Fruit Street, Boston, Massachusetts 02114.
2. University of Southern California–Alzheimer Disease Research Center, Ethel Percy Andrus Gerontology Center, University Park, Los Angeles, California 90089.

2. Alzheimer Disease Community Resource Center (ADCRC)

Location: 209 Chapman Hall (College of Nursing Bldg.), at the University of Tulsa, 600 South College Avenue, Tulsa, Oklahoma 74104

Telephone: (918) 631–3665

Purpose: The ADCRC disseminates information concerning Alzheimer's disease research and treatments as they become available. Additionally, the ADCRC has books, videotapes, articles, and research papers that may be reviewed at the center. This resource is available to the community of Tulsa, Oklahoma, and also to anyone anywhere in the world who either writes or visits Tulsa.

3. Alzheimer's Disease and Related Disorders Association

Mailing address: 70 East Lake Street, Chicago, Illinois 60601

Telephone: (312) 853–3060

Purpose: Public awareness and facilitation of support groups in all states of the USA; publication of a newsletter and other materials of help to the caregiver; pilot research grants for new investigators; and tracking of U.S. congressional bills that propose aid for the AD problem.

4. The John Douglas French Foundation for Alzheimer's Disease

Mailing address: 11620 Wilshire Boulevard, Los Angeles, California 90025

Telephone: (213) 470–5462

Purpose: Development of "Alzheimer Center Hospitals" that provide models for the nation of the type of care needed by AD patients. The first such model hospital, a 150-bed facility, opened in November 1987 in Los Alamitos, California. Plans are under way for the development of more hospitals of this nature in the USA. The French Foundation also stimulates interest in the AD problem via periodic conferences, some for research scientists, and some for caregivers and helping professionals.

5. Alzheimer's Aid Society of Northern California

Mailing address: P.O. Box 1824, Sacramento, California 95812

Telephone: (916) 448–7001 or
(209) 333–2649

Purpose: To promote public awareness of Alzheimer's disease, and to facilitate the development of support groups. Over thirty support groups have been started in the northern California area since 1980. Additionally, this organization has been very influential in promoting the passage of many bills through the California legislature, aiding research, patient care, and caregiver support. Members of this group are in weekly demand to give "in-service training" at nursing homes and other care facilities for AD.

Appendix E

A Model Bus– Wheelchair Service for Alzheimer's and Geriatric Patients

Sharon Henning

Editors' Note: The following report describes a model "wheelchair ministry" for Alzheimer's disease (AD) and other geriatric patients. This project was developed in Phoenix, Arizona. The providers of this service do not have AD patients in their families, whom they have to care for themselves, but their dedication has spread out to six wheelchair buses plus walk-on transportation, such as motor homes, vans, and cars. This ministry helps to keep AD victims more active.

Although the service currently gets these individuals out one to three times a week, it could easily be extended to include doctor visits, shopping-center tours, and so on.

This model service is provided as an outreach program of a church in Phoenix. The editors of this book believe that many more voluntary services like this are necessary to serve the needs of the AD population and their caregivers.

Phoenix First Assembly is one of the growing number of "mega-churches" in the United States. It has grown rapidly over the past few years, with over ten thousand members, and meets the needs of all kinds of people. In fact, the meeting of people's needs is why this church has grown; it is a model of how the church can provide needed community service, to help the AD population.

* * *

Our elderly and wheelchair people at Phoenix First Assembly are very special people in our fellowship. They know the difference when love is phony; they receive much of that indifferent love daily at all levels of care. Many (about a third) are mentally and/or physically incapable of communicating, and yet they respond incredibly to real love, the kind of love that comes directly from the heart. We call our program the "Phoenix First Assembly Prime-Time Wheelchair" Ministry. In the following paragraphs I will describe how this program came about, the great need it serves, and our plans for the future.

In early spring of 1985, a new church building opened next to a mountain. My husband and I were intrigued by its architecture, a majestic circle, and went to check it out. Its massiveness was overwhelming, and it was much too large for us: it seats six-thousand-five-hundred and has two balconies. But we were drawn back time after time because it was different from any other church we had attended. The people were so warm and caring, and there were so many types, rich and poor, young and old, and in between. Love permeated the place and was on the faces of the people and the pastors. Every time we attended, we knew we were where we were supposed to be. And that's just the beginning!

This church had buses everywhere, filled with kids, adults, the elderly, a few wheelchairs. We wondered what was going on. We found out that the church had a bus ministry to bring in those who wanted to participate but who didn't have transportation: children whose parents didn't come, elderly people who couldn't drive anymore or didn't have a car, adults living in the streets, and handicapped homebound people without transportation. Out of curiosity, we rode a bus one night. What an experience! Our eyes were opened to a world we didn't even know existed. We picked people up on street corners, at outdoor city shelters, in open parks, in the projects, all over.

We started working with the bus ministry. One day we got a call asking if we would pick up some elderly people and said, "Sure, why not?" They were precious, and we fell in love with them. Almost before we knew it, we were driving a van, and then a bus. We came up against all kinds of problems and situations, but we continued to persevere and to love and be loved. A few times (big days), when the buses were filled, we transferred those in wheelchairs onto regular bus seats and used trucks to transport their wheelchairs.

In early 1987, I was asked to take over the entire Prime-Time Wheelchair Ministry, temporarily until a staff person was found. But I knew how these things worked. Temporary? No such thing! As I continued working with this project, I saw that the elderly and wheelchair ministry could meet needs all over the country. Churches and community organizations could start with whatever they had available: cars, vans, motor homes, whatever.

We visit the nursing homes and invite the people living there; we encourage families to reach out and adopt them; we bring the elderly from private homes and care homes; we find the shut-ins and bring them. They are rich with wisdom and have so much to offer. In our ministry an eighty-year-old makes wheelchair-arm book-holders, another has made twenty-five afghans, another cooks, another sends cards, and another makes phone calls. Creativeness is important for their quality of life.

The elderly need to feel some kind of control over their lives, especially when more and more people are trying to make decisions for them. We can be a support system for them. They are lonely and get depressed, and depression leads to apathy and early death. We don't treat them as old, but as special. Fear causes argumentativeness in them and pain causes interference, but love never fails. We use pleasant words: health is in the bones, and noncritical people are healthier. A merry heart is a good medicine. We encourage them to take their eyes off themselves and to reach out to others. We can touch these elderly people with gentleness and kindness. Some of the specific things we do are to offer to write letters for those who can't, to bring books for them to read or to read to them, to pick up things at the store, to take them grocery shopping, or to fix a meal. The idea is to be creative. These are genuine deeds of kindness that don't require much and that have lasting results—perhaps even changing a life.

Our program in Phoenix is running six wheelchair buses as well as vans, motor homes, cars, and regular buses. We are currently working with about two hundred elderly. We use a large map, mounted on cardboard, of the entire area of the Phoenix valley. Pins color-coded for particular bus routes indicate which homes we pick up at and how many people at each home. All the routes are on a computer with driver and helpers and phone numbers, as well as all the riders, their addresses, phone numbers, birthdays, special needs, and so on. Each week, for every route, I receive a report on how many were transported, who was missing, any problems that need solving, repairs to be made, special needs of individuals, and so on. During the week, a group of young people in our church ministers to the nursing homes. Any special problems or concerns we have are directed to these young people, so they can check and report back. Many of our bus pastors also stop and check on the individuals. We have found a need to help some with legal problems; a lawyer in the church provides advice.

Our church also has a food ministry; when someone is in need it delivers food to them and helps in any way it can.

I am currently involved in learning more about the placement of the elderly in residential-care homes, nursing homes, and so on. There is much negligence in this area and careful screening is of the utmost importance. We also work with the county long-term health-care program. This county program places in private homes those who are not financially able to care for themselves through private means, such as insurance, pensions, or personal funds, and/or who have no family to take the responsibility for their care. These people have been made wards of the state and no longer have much control over their lives. The county program appears (so far) to be caring and open to us, and to be responsive to the needs and changes we have presented. Several times we have requested that people be moved to other facilities. Recently, one facility was closed and some of our wheelchair people were placed too far away for us to provide transportation. We requested moves; the county staff are very receptive and are working toward that goal. They see the love we have for our special people and see that we are the only family that many of them have.

The response from some of the homes and caregivers is not always good, however. It takes extra effort on their part to have those in their care ready, fed, and treated in time for us to pick them up. Additionally, in many cases, lunches have to be held up for their return. We have to be rather firm about the time our people must be ready and about the need to keep their lunches until their arrival back at the home. We call ahead to most homes and caregivers, either the night before or in the early morning. We have found that the people to be picked up can make a big difference in this area: they call their nurse or orderly so that they can get up on time and be ready. The ambulatory ones are always at the door waiting for us with great anticipation.

The majority of our people live from Sunday to Sunday or, in some cases, from service to service, as we bring some to the two services held on Sunday and Wednesday evenings. It is the only time they go out and can see and talk to others. We encourage everyone to speak and fuss over these special people as well as to bring the babies and toddlers to them. These elderly people are ecstatic with the little ones and love to hold them.

Our special people are as much a part of our church family as everyone else. Our pastor makes reference to them all the time, which gives them a great sense of belonging and security. We have quite a few who moved away but then came back *because* they missed and needed this church family.

This ministry is always open to new ways of reaching these people and giving them reasons to go on. We challenge them with memorizing Bible verses by giving out a printed verse each week and then asking who knows it the following week. Some, of course, cannot read or speak but they love to have us read to them. We also play music tapes in the buses; they love music and love to sing. We use children's songs that are repetitive, simple, easy to follow, and short with catchy tunes. The music also keeps them occupied while riding, and it keeps complaining and idle chatting down, putting them in a mood of joy and happiness, and preparing them for the church service.

The Prime-Time Wheelchair Ministry also holds what we call "Big Days" specifically geared to these people. Our Fourth of July celebration draws twenty thousand people onto our grounds, with great music, fireworks, clowns, balloons, and sky divers, and the elderly go wild over it all. One of them had not seen fireworks for many years. We have a special area just for them and serve hotdogs, popcorn, watermelon, and ice cream—all the stuff that kids like. They are a mess when it's over, just like kids, and that makes it even better. They love picnics with lots of old-fashioned fried chicken and music and singing. Other "Big Days" include potlucks and dinners; we have foods that they love and don't get in most homes.

The entire atmosphere created for these special people is important. We are in the process of fixing up the interiors of the buses that are used just for them. We use paint with cheerful colors. Carpeting is used to keep the noise level down. Posters and pictures that are happy and full of life are put around the inside of the bus. This decoration provides another point of security and a caring atmosphere.

We are aware of each individual's condition, and each bus pastor and helper tunes in to changes in people, like moods or depression. In these circumstances, we try to take extra precautions by having someone sit next to the person and provide extra loving care. At the church, we put the wanderers in the centers of pews with people on both sides, so that it is harder for them to get out. We also have workers seated in strategic locations to keep watch over each one. Anyone who does get up is followed by a worker. They do not even go to the bathroom without one of us. (Before we had learned of this wandering problem, we lost one man. He got up and left the church and continued walking; he was found two days later several miles away, thankfully just fine.)

We have medical doctors in our congregation, and I know approximately where they usually sit, so if an emergency should arise I can get to them immediately. The ushers are also very aware and will always come and get us if we are needed. Everyone helps.

Our workers are motivated and committed by their love for the elderly. We have drivers and helpers who are nurses, aides, and paramedics, as well as mechanics, computer and electrical engineers, schoolteachers, and cabinet builders. They all have a special caring way about them.

We receive calls from all over the country asking how to initiate a ministry like this one. The interest must indicate that it is needed. We get calls from caregivers, placement services, individuals, families looking for good homes, members of the church that want to open their homes, and elderly that need a home, as well as from other churches that are small and whose elderly have needs. Many of the small nursing homes and other caregivers have no mode of transportation for wheelchairs. On weekdays, there are a few vans with lifts available to be donated for rides. On weekends, one is available, but at a very high cost, and it can transport only a very few. In our program at Phoenix First Assembly we can carry as many as eleven wheelchairs on one bus, and we can carry five on our smallest. The smallest bus can also carry eighteen walk-ons. We needed more wheelchair spaces, so we removed a lot of seats from buses that were being used for other purposes.

We have taken some of our special people on field trips, but we find it difficult to get a driver from our church on weekdays. Our insurance coverage is for people in the church who have gone through training, have a chauffeur's license, are twenty-five to sixty-five years old, and have clean driving records.

With some changes, weekday trips can be arranged. We plan to take trips to the zoo, to football games, and shopping. We are also planning a once-a-month lunch with arts and crafts, plays, and whatever else will make a good program; this will be started on the completion of our new building, which will give us a cafeteria and kitchen with room to hold everyone.

Familiar voices and faces remove doubts and fears for these people, so we keep the same workers on the same routes as much as possible.

We are so blessed and grateful that we have a congregation that cares enough about our special people to support them with their finances and to give of themselves spiritually, physically, and emotionally. We are most thankful to a staff and pastors who have shepherds' hearts to reach out and touch our "special people" with genuine love.

Contributors

Paul A. Bell, Ph.D.   Department of Psychology, Colorado State University, Fort Collins, Colorado 80523

John P. Blass, M.D., Ph.D.   Dementia Research Service, Burke Rehabilitation Center, Cornell University Medical Center, White Plains, New York 10605

Robert Mullan Cook-Deegan, M.D.   Office of Technology Assessment and Biomedical Ethics Board, United States Congress, Washington, DC 20510; and Research Fellow, Kennedy Institute of Ethics, Georgetown University, Washington, DC 20057

Jeffrey L. Cummings, M.D.   Neurobehavior Unit, West Los Angeles VAMC (Brentwood Division), Departments of Neurology and Psychiatry and Biobehavioral Science, UCLA School of Medicine, Los Angeles, California 90073

283

Bea Gorman   Alzheimer's disease family member, caregiver, and support group organizer, Lodi, California 95240

Sharon Henning   Wheelchair Ministry of the Phoenix First Assembly Church, Phoenix, Arizona 85022

Anson P. Hobbs   Alzheimer's disease family member, caregiver, and promoter of Alzheimer's disease research, Tulsa, Oklahoma 74137

Gary D. Miner, Ph.D.   Familial Alzheimer's Disease Research Foundation, Tulsa, Oklahoma 74137 and Oklahoma Medical Research Foundation, Oklahoma Health Sciences Center, Oklahoma City, Oklahoma 73104

Linda A. Winters-Miner, Ph.D.   Familial Alzheimer's Disease Research Foundation; and Alzheimer's Research Unit, St. John's Medical Center, Tulsa, Oklahoma 74137

Ester May Reiswig   Familial Alzheimer disease family member, caregiver, and promoter of Alzheimer's disease research, Oklahoma

Ralph W. Richter, M.D.   The University of Oklahoma, Tulsa Medical College, and Alzheimer's Disease Research Unit, St. John's Medical Center, Tulsa, Oklahoma 73104

Anthony B. Sandoe   Suffolk University Law School, Boston, Massachusetts 02114

Carrie R. Valentine, Ph.D.   Department of Microbiology/Immunology, Oral Roberts University School of Medicine, Tulsa, Oklahoma 74137

Jimmie L. Valentine, Ph.D.   Department of Pharmacology, Oral Roberts University School of Medicine, Tulsa, Oklahoma 74137

Index